PETE
SPENCER
093

MW00616301

The meditation techniques included in this book are to be practiced only after personal instructions by an ordained teacher of Life Bliss Foundation (LBF). If some one tries these techniques without prior participation in the meditation programs of LBF, they shall be doing so entirely at their own risk; neither the author nor LBF shall be responsible for the consequences of their actions.

Copyright © 2009 - 'Living Enlightenment year'

First Edition: Dec 2005 as *Guaranteed solutions for Sex, Fear, Worry, Attention-need, Jealousy, Ego, Discontent*

Second Edition: May 2006 as *Guaranteed solutions for Sex, Fear, Worry, Attention-need, Jealousy, Ego, Discontent*

Third Edition: Aug 2006 as *Guaranteed Solutions for Sex, Worry, Fear etc.*

Fourth Edition: Aug 2008 as *Guaranteed Solutions for Lust, Fear, Worry...*

Fifth Edition: June 2009 as *Guaranteed Solutions for Lust, Fear, Worry...*

ISBN 10: 1-60607-031-2   ISBN 13: 978-1-60607-031-4

All rights reserved. No part of this publication may be reproduced, or stored in a retrieval system, or transmitted by any form or by any means, electronic, mechanical, photocopying, recording or otherwise, without written permission of the publisher. In the event that you use any of the information in this book for yourself, the author and the publisher assume no responsibility for your actions.

All proceeds from the sale of this book go towards supporting charitable activities.

Printed in India by W.Q. Judge Press, Bangalore.
Tele: +80 22211168

Guaranteed Solutions
for Lust, Fear, Worry...

Nithyananda

[Taken from talks in
chakra meditation programs such as the
Ananda Spurana Program (ASP)
and the Life Bliss Program (LBP)]

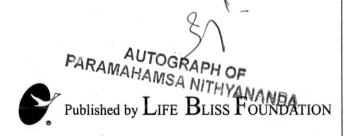

Published by LIFE BLISS FOUNDATION

TABLE OF CONTENTS

Chapter 1

Interaction

I welcome you all with my love and respect.

You have all come here with some expectation, some hope, to enhance your knowledge; to get a new perspective of life; to see if you can live your life in a better way.

I want to tell you a few things before we get into the subject so that you can get the maximum benefit from your stay here.

Become Empty First!

You might have gone to many other places, listened to many other lectures, practiced many other techniques before coming here. All that is alright. Just one thing: when you are here, just be totally here, that's all.

Leave behind all the knowledge that you have gathered in other places and then come in here. You would have seen a board outside that said, 'Leave your shoes and mind outside'. You might have wondered what it meant. It means: when you leave your shoes outside, just decide and leave your mind also! Leave all your gathered knowledge next to your shoes and come in. You can take it back when you go out. Don't worry, no one will take it away. It will be perfectly safe. At least your shoes, people might take, but your mind, people will not touch; I will guarantee you that!

People are unable to handle their own minds; they will surely not touch yours!

When you come in with an empty mind, with no prejudice, you can absorb what I am saying in its totality. If you come in with your knowledge, you will be constantly comparing every word of mine with what you know about it, with what you have heard about it from someone else earlier, and you will simply miss what I am trying to tell. You can absorb me only if there is some space in you. If you are already full, you cannot take me in.

A small story:

> A learned professor from the West went to meet a Zen master in the East, in Japan.
>
> The professor had done a lot of research in many areas of study.
>
> He went to meet the master to get some spiritual knowledge, to understand spirituality in a better fashion.
>
> He arrived at the master's place and found the master brewing tea.
>
> The master saw him and gestured to sit, and continued to brew tea.
>
> The professor sat down and after a while, started talking of his background, of all his studies, his discoveries, his travels around the world, his experiences with different people, his conclusions on various subjects and what not.
>
> The master finished brewing the tea and placed two cups between them.
>
> He began pouring tea into the professor's cup.

He poured and poured and slowly the cup started overflowing.

The tea spilt over the saucer and flowed onto the table.

The professor was watching what was happening.

He could not contain himself any more.

He screamed out, 'Master, what are you doing? Stop pouring! The cup is overflowing!'

The master stopped and calmly said, 'So are you.'

The professor was shocked but understood what the master was trying to tell him.

The professor was so full like the teacup! Anything that the master might tell him would only overflow outside, not into him. The professor understood from that one word of the master, what he meant, what he was trying to tell him.

So understand: if you really want to gain something, just be like an empty cup here. Be totally open and receptive. Be like a child, innocent and curious; like a sponge, ready to absorb; that is enough.

Three Types of Knowledge

You see: there are three types of knowledge. The first is intellectual knowledge – the knowledge of the mind. For this, you need only your mind, nothing else. If you are attentive and have a good memory, it is enough. If you can apply logic well, if you have a little common sense to connect things and understand, it is enough. This is the kind of knowledge that you gain in school, with your books. To learn mathematics and science, your mind is enough. You can become a great mathematician or a great scientist.

The second type of knowledge is knowledge of the heart. Here, you need to use your heart also, not just your mind. Art, music, poetry, dance – all these come under this category. If you use only your mind, nothing will happen. You have to use your heart also. To paint, to write poems, to sing, you need to emote. All these are creations. They are expressions from your heart. Can you write a poem with no feelings at all? Can an artist draw and paint with just his mind? No! He needs to connect with his heart, then he will simply flow.

With only the mind, you can pick up certain points, certain techniques about writing poems or about painting, but ultimately the stuff will come from only your heart.

The third type of knowledge is spiritual knowledge – knowledge that is neither of the mind nor of the heart, but of your being! Actually, we can't even call it knowledge; it is just a deep understanding beyond your logic. It can neither be taught nor picked up. It can happen simply out of a deep communion - at the being level.

I always tell people: I cannot teach you spirituality, but you can learn! You can learn by just absorbing these words at the being level – like energy. The energy behind the master's words is so powerful that if you allow it, it can penetrate you and touch you at the being level. It can bring about a transformation that cannot happen with just words of the mind and feelings of the heart.

When I talk, I talk from my experience of the ultimate truth; from my being. So when you listen, listen totally, from your being. Only then can you get a glimpse of the experience behind these words. I am not here to give you just words. I am here to take you beyond words. If you are here with acute awareness and silence, you can go beyond words and get a glimpse of your own being.

Trust and Be Open

Alright, let us alter the seating arrangement a little. When you sit, don't sit with your relatives or friends or people known to you. Sit at random, next to anyone whom you don't know much, with whom you are not very familiar. When you sit with familiar people, you will be compelled to exchange glances, exchange words while I am talking. If you sit with strangers, you can absorb me better, by yourself.

One more thing: When the session is happening, there will be a beautiful flow, there will be an energy that is created and vibrating in the room, a deep communion between you and me. Don't interrupt it by coming in late. The flow will be broken. It is just like encountering a speed breaker when you are going smoothly on the highway. The speed breaker is only a small interruption, but to cross it, you have to slow down, go over it and pick up speed again. The smooth flow will be broken.

And please switch off your mobile phones. They are another very common speed breaker today! In fact they can cause the journey to be totally bumpy, one speed breaker after another! I am sure each of you has a cell phone here!

Next, when you are here, don't be serious and heavy. Be sincere in listening and listen with an open mind. Don't expect that in the very first session, you will experience God! Just be with a light and easy mood, without expectations, you will be able to receive much more.

The next thing: decide and leave your social ego outside and try to be an ordinary person while you are here. The ashram and the presence of the master is the best laboratory for you to experiment with yourself, to let go of your ego, to shed your illusions, and understand that you are just a beautiful part of Existence. So even if you are somebody in society, try to be ordinary here and mix with everyone from your heart. Not only my words, but every moment of interaction, every moment of just being here, can cause a transformation in you. You just need to be aware, that's all.

A small story:

> There was a great Zen Buddhist monk, an enlightened master.
> One day, the Governor of Japan came to visit him.
> The Governor sent in his visiting card to the master.
> It had the words, 'Zak-San - Governor of Japan'.
> The master took one look at the card and said, 'I have no business with this idiot!
> Ask him to leave this very minute!'
> Zen masters can be very harsh when they want to break somebody's mind, somebody's ego. They will never hesitate to use harsh words. The energy behind their words can simply pierce and transform a person.

The disciple came back to the governor, gave back his card and repeated what the master had told him.

The Governor saw the card and understood. He was an intelligent man...not just intellectual, but intelligent also!

He quietly struck out the words, 'Governor of Japan', and gave back the card to the disciple, who took it inside again. The master took one look and said, 'Show him in!'

All our titles, our designations, are mere labels pasted on us by society. And we go about thinking that we are these labels. We forget that we are not the labels but the stuff inside! We feel great about the labels. But you can never approach a master with these labels. You can never know Existence with your labels! A master is Existence in human form.

What the Governor did cannot be called wrong. It might have been the right way to approach society, to be in accordance with the social protocols, but with a master, awareness must step in and you must leave your ego behind!

Something transpires between the master and the seeker. They share something of the inner world. When this happens, labels of the outer world will stand in the way. Forgetting your personality is spirituality, because personality is societal. We are here to find our individuality – our inherent nature, our aloneness that we enjoyed in our mother's womb, our connection with Existence – the only connection we need to find and celebrate!

Decide to Experiment!

When you listen to whatever I say, there are two ways in which your mind will work. One is with doubt and the other is with belief.

Doubt is the way of the intellectual mind. With doubt, too much logic and reason will come in the way of receiving. When this happens, you will miss the whole thing.

With belief also, if you straightaway believe, you will miss. Understand: you don't need to believe in anybody, let alone in me. The so-called believers are the weakest people, because it takes great courage to live without beliefs. When you don't have a belief, you don't have a fall-back system to support your actions. You don't have a readymade idea to tell you what to think and how to act. To be without a belief requires great courage, because then you have to depend on your own intelligence for everything and this makes you feel unsure and insecure.

Both doubt and faith are two sides of the same coin – that is your mind. At a very deep level, your greatest doubt will carry some faith and your greatest faith will have some doubt in it. I can assure you that!

Then what should you do? How should you listen?

Just listen with an open mind, with a readiness to experiment, that's all. When you are ready to experiment, you are ready to translate teachings into practical life. When I tell you, 'The sun rises in the east', you neither need to believe nor doubt; just get up the next morning and see for yourself – as an experiment!

That is the right way. Just take in everything with an open mind and experience what I am saying every moment. There is no need to have faith. Just the willingness to experiment is enough. Take what I say as a hypothesis, integrate it into your life and see for yourself whether it works or not. To know that an apple is tasty, you don't have to believe or doubt. Just take a bite and you will know!

Stop Seeking, you are already bliss!

Time and again, ancient *rishis* and masters have said that man's true nature is bliss. Over the years, so many masters have happened on planet earth. Whether it was Buddha or Christ or Krishna or Mahavir, the core of their message was the same. They all said that man's true nature is bliss and they all gave techniques to connect to that bliss.

Their expressions might have been different, but their message was the same. Of course, again and again people miss the message because they cling on to the master instead of the message. This is the reason for fanaticism, religious wars and other such things that are happening on planet Earth.

Anyhow, all these masters had the same message, that man's core is bliss, and that all of man's effort is in seeking this inner space, this space of bliss within him. But due to social conditioning and distractions, man forgets his purpose and starts seeking this bliss in outer world things - in material things, in names, in forms, in labels given to him by society, in relationships, in careers and what not.

A small story:

> An old man went with his family to watch a movie in a theatre.
>
> The movie had just started when the man suddenly started groping about in the darkness on the floor.
>
> His grand-daughter who was sitting next to him got annoyed and asked him what he was doing on the floor.
>
> He said, 'Dear, I have lost my chewing gum. It has fallen out.'
>
> The child got irritated and said, 'Grandpa, it's alright, leave it. We will buy some more chewing gum. Now watch the movie.'
>
> The old man said, 'I want only that chewing gum.'
>
> The child said, 'Grandpa, don't behave like a baby. We will get more chewing gum.'
>
> The old man said, 'But dear, my teeth are in it.'

You see: what we are really seeking is something, but we are seeking it in the name of something else! We seek in the name of so many things. And at the end of it, even after achieving all those things, we feel that something is missing. There is a certain yearning in us. Understand: this yearning is because we are actually searching for bliss, but we search for it in the name of other things. That is why we never feel fulfilled. Our being calls out but we never listen. We ignore our being completely because we are so immersed in the outer world.

Unless we are centered upon our being, we will not experience a totality; we will not experience fulfillment. In our outer world achievements, we might be filled, but not fulfilled. And because we are not fulfilled, the yearning will remain. And we start searching again in the outer world. When we are centered within, we will have fulfillment every minute whatever we may be doing in the outer world, because the fulfillment does not come from what we are doing; it comes from the being, within.

So we need to look deep into what the masters have been saying time and again. There is no use simply seeking without stopping to get one glimpse of the truth in the master's words. Then you will remain a traveler, that's all.

This concept of traveling is like 'trying to pick up a book but not picking it up!' Can there be anything such as *trying to pick up a book*? You either pick it or not. How can you *try* to pick it? When you say that you are trying to pick it up, you are cheating yourself! You can't cheat others because they know it is not possible.

It is something like this: people who don't have the capacity to make money, claim that because they are very honest, they are unable to make money. Actually, they don't have the capacity, that is the truth; but they justify it with reasons.

In the same way, when we are unable to take a leap into real spirituality, and at the same time we are not ready to confess that we don't know anything about it, we create our own philosophies and go around saying, 'Short of enlightenment, I know everything about spirituality!' We just keep our ego alive. We use the 'seeker ego' as a buffer between the truth and us.

In the same way as the car has shock absorbers to keep us from getting hurt on the road, the seeker ego keeps us away from reality. It serves as the buffer between the truth and us. In the comfort of this buffer, we happily conclude that we were seekers all our lives!

Whatever I may be telling you these few days, just listen with complete awareness and try to catch the central chord, the composite thread that runs in the whole thing. Then, you will create a space in you for the transformation to happen. Otherwise, you will simply be collecting words and seeking all the time. Unless a transformation happens in you, all words are useless. You have to look with deep awareness, only then transformation is possible.

And be very clear: even if you are thousand people in this hall, I am talking to *you*. When I say *you*, I mean Y O U. There is a thread running with each of you; so don't ever apply what I am saying to others; you will simply miss the whole thing yourself.

Generally, when we hear anything about health, we will immediately apply it to ourselves and see where we stand; we will see whether we have any of the symptoms being discussed. If I talk about the skin, you will feel your skin and see; if I talk about the heart, you will feel your heart beat and see. But when we hear anything about spirituality, somehow, we always apply it to others! Our family, our friends, our neighbours, but never to ourselves! The problem is, whatever I say, you think, 'Ah! I know myself well. This message is for my husband. Master is saying this so that my husband can change his ways. I hope he has got the message.'

When I talk about worries, you will immediately think of how much your mother worries. You forget how much *you* worry! I am telling you because you also worry. Probably your mother worries more than you, but that is not the point.

Understand that every word is for you. It will come like an arrow bringing with it the energy of transformation. Don't dodge it. Just allow it to go in and transform you. Don't keep looking at other people to see if they are showing signs of understanding.

If you have really understood everything, then you should not have any worries or discontentment or pain or fear or lust or jealousy or ego, am I right? But you have all of this in you. That itself shows that you have not internalized completely. First of all, know that you don't know. Then at least you know that you don't know! If you don't even know that you don't know, then you don't even know that you don't know!

Q: But, we are traveling towards knowing ourselves, so at this point we may know partly...

Let me tell you one thing: in a deep spiritual experience, there will be no traveling. It is a moment's experience, that's all. All our so-called knowing is only creating a space inside us towards fully knowing. But ultimately, in the deeper sense, either we *know* or we *don't know*. But when we know more and more, we become clear that we don't know! That is enough. That will motivate us to really knowing.

In the first chapter of the Bhagavad Gita, *Arjuna Vishaada Yoga*, which is the Yoga of Arjuna's grief, Arjuna talks throughout and Krishna remains silent. It is only when Arjuna finally surrenders saying, 'I know nothing!' that he is at last ready to receive Krishna's message.

Although Krishna and Arjuna were friends, though there might have been hundreds of other more relaxed situations, the Bhagavad Gita was not delivered to Arjuna anytime earlier.

Why?

Because until then, Arjuna was not ripe enough to receive the Gita! It is only when he utters the words, 'I don't know' that he becomes qualified to know. The basic condition for spiritual progress is *to know very clearly that you don't know*. This is the first step towards really knowing.

So ask questions and make things clear for yourself and for others. Only if you ask questions, things can be worked out in a more practical way, in a way more adaptable to your life.

Some of you may think that you may look like a fool if you ask some of your questions. I tell you: if you ask questions, you will only look like a fool; if you don't ask questions, you will remain a fool! So if there is any concept that you don't agree with, please raise your hand and clarify.

Q: We are looking to destroy all our negativities and be reborn as a new person in these few days...

Understand: there can be no destruction on planet earth. There is always only transformation. All your so-called negative emotions like anger, jealousy and lust can be transformed into positive emotions like pure love, gratitude and compassion.

Society always teaches you to divide and destroy yourself. It never teaches you to become integrated. It places a wedge inside you between you and you, so that it can take control of you. It always talks to you in the language of lower and higher. It makes you think that you are inferior and makes you fight with yourself.

Society can rule you only if you are made to feel chaotic inside yourself. So it first makes you feel that you are no good and then comes up with remedies for it. That is why you start talking in this kind of inferior language.

A small story:

> A man was suffering from a common cold.
> He visited the doctor and asked for medicine.
> It was just an ordinary cold. The doctor looked at him for awhile and said, 'Do one thing. Just go out for some time in the night and get the chill wind to touch you. Then come back.'
> The patient was shocked. He said, 'But Doctor! I will catch pneumonia if I do that.'
> The doctor said, 'Yes. I can cure pneumonia in no time.'

Society makes you become something and then teaches you ways to come out of it. Understand: there is no higher or lower; there is no good or bad. There is only transformation. When you learn to look in with awareness, automatically you will be transformed. This is always the master's approach. He never divides you; he always integrates you. He teaches you to look in and integrate.

The master never tells you that you are negative. There is no negative. What you call negative and positive are just two extremes of the same spectrum. Negative is not any physical entity for you to destroy. If you transform, you move in the spectrum towards higher positive energies, that's all.

As I said earlier, this transformation is possible if you are just open and receptive to what is happening here.

Q: We have read in many books that our mind is nothing but maya or illusion and that all our questions are only an illusion. Please can you tell us something about this?

The famous question about *maya* is asked one more time! First thing: don't confuse yourself with complicated reading. Second thing: understand very clearly that there is nothing to be understood with the mind. The mystery of life cannot be solved with your mind. You cannot know the purpose of your life with your mind. That is why they say that your mind is an illusion.

The first step to solving the mystery of our life is 'dropping your mind'. If you allow your mind to play, you will continue to play, that's all. Life after life, you will play. Your deep inner thirst will

19

remain unquenched. Probably your seeker ego will get fulfilled, but that is of no use. You become only more confused inside you.

Try to move your centre of operation from your mind to your heart or being. If you operate with your mind as the centre, questions and more questions will follow. With questions, you cannot know. Only with awareness you can know.

If you operate with your heart, awareness and understanding will happen in you and then automatically your questions will start dissolving; like when the sun rises, the darkness simply disappears. When awareness happens in you, understanding will happen and your questions will dissolve.

You will start understanding things even before you come to the question! In this way, the questions will dissolve. It is difficult to understand this, but once you get an experience of it, you will know exactly what I mean by awareness. Questions will disappear and understanding will continuously engulf you.

If you understand this much, you need not worry about *maya* or illusion. In addition to intellectual understanding from my words, meditation can help you switch to the mode of awareness easily. We can talk for hours about *maya* and illusion, but you will only get more confused.

Instead, it is worthwhile learning the solutions that will help us to live intelligently; that is enough. One thing I want to tell you: *maya* or illusion is everything that your mind projects, so that is why I say, don't bother about knowing *maya*. Instead start living with more awareness, more consciously. Then the question of *maya* itself will not be relevant.

As I said earlier, bliss is continuously happening in us. This is the actual truth. But we continuously stop the flow of bliss, and as a result we suffer. Bliss is not something that you can get from outside and keep inside yourself. No. It is your inherent nature. When you arrive in this world, you are in a state of bliss. As society conditions you, you move far away from it. Then you start searching for ways outside of yourself to get it back.

We will see how to stop the stopping of bliss. When I say bliss, I don't mean the ordinary happiness that we feel in our everyday lives. Ordinary happiness is a result of something that happens outside: some happy occasion, some material benefit, some happy news, some relationship that worked out, something to do with a person or thing in the outside world. This kind of happiness is purely dependent on the people and circumstances outside of us. And this kind of happiness is what leads us to sadness also, because people and circumstances keep changing. They are not the same. Their behaviour is different at different times. And when their behaviour changes, our happiness too changes!

The bliss that we are talking about is different. It is purely a state inside yourself, which is in no way connected to outer world incidents. It is your core, your permanent state. When you find this, you will become a blissful watcher of the outer world. You will participate in it fully but without losing your bliss.

A small story:

> There was an old man in a family who could not be pleased at any cost.
>
> He remained stubborn and grumpy, no matter how much his family tried to keep him in good spirits.
>
> His children and grandchildren would come and visit him and try to cheer him up, but he would remain grumpy.
>
> Suddenly one day, he became very gentle and cheerful.
>
> His family was surprised at the sudden transformation.
>
> His grand daughter asked him, 'Grandpa, how come you have changed so suddenly?'
>
> The old man replied, 'All my life, I tried my best to get a contented mind, but never succeeded. So I have decided to be contented with it now.'

Everything is a projection of our mind! We can decide how we want to be. It is all in the mind. With the help of our mind, we have stopped the flow of bliss from within. That is the truth.

Understand: there is a universal consciousness that fills the entire cosmos and there is an individual consciousness that fills us. Man's whole purpose is to establish a connection between these two. When this connection happens, man is said to be enlightened or in eternal bliss or in *nithyananda*. *Nithyananda* means eternal bliss.

Through listening to all the great masters' words and practicing all the meditation techniques, we become more and more aware of this connection and try to experience it. Because once the connection happens, everything becomes easy in the inner and outer world!

There are two types of people: those who fight with others and win and those who fight with themselves and win. It is easy to fight with others. It is not a big deal. But it is difficult to fight with yourself. When you are courageous, you will fight with yourself and win. You will destroy what you are *not* and emerge as a blissful being; you will flower.

The greatest challenge for man is to realize his entire potentiality. This can be done only when he moves inwards and keeps purifying himself again and again until he becomes intelligent enough not to gather more.

Actually, the word *swami* means one who has realized his full potential. All our difficulties on planet earth are because we are not able to realize our potentiality. There is a saying that goes: the lion that is not allowed to be a lion will become a fox. If we are not allowed to realize our true potential energy, we will start expressing it in a wrong way – either self-destructive or destroying others.

So the creative energy, the potential energy, should be allowed to express itself in a free-flowing way. Society should allow us, that is one thing, and we should also know the technique to express it. *Swami* means a man who has realized his potential power, who is expressing himself as he is; who is completely in tune with his being; who is blissful!

You have tremendous potential in you. Time and again psychologists and mystics have said that man is not living up to his full potential. Where are we missing it? Where are we stuck? Why are we not able to realize our full potentiality?

We need the courage to let go and explore, that's all. We will then know the answers to all these questions. When you start exploring sincerely, you will experience a shift in consciousness and this shift will open a space in you where you flower.

When you flower, you become a king. You will live like a lord on this planet. People may have all the possible comforts, money, knowledge and what not. But they will remain beggars if they have not found their inner space. To find your being is to become rich. Inner richness is real richness.

We have become so engaged with what goes on outside that we remain completely ignorant of our inner space. We are so caught up in the outer world adventure that we miss the wonderful adventures of the inner world. We miss what the great *rishis* and masters experienced in their lives. This experience is what I want to share with all of you.

Q: How would you define spirituality in a nutshell?

Spirituality is nothing but the flowering of four things in you: physical health, mental health, smooth inter-personal relationships and the ability to respond spontaneously (what I call responsibility).

Physical health is being free from disease. When you visit a doctor, he should give you a report saying that you are clinically alright.

The second – mental health, is being free from all subconscious and deeply engraved negative thought patterns and being free from worries, pain, jealousy, discontentment, ego, lust etc.

The third – interpersonal relationships, is having a smooth relationship with everyone around you. It is not enough if you are just cordial with everyone. You should be able to go through any amount of interaction with any kind of person, without feeling pressure or pain! The moment you feel pressure or pain, it means that there is some block inside you, some block in your mental health.

The fourth – The ability to respond spontaneously, what I call responsibility. When you are able to take on responsibility, when you are able to say 'yes' to anything spontaneously, you will expand that very moment and energy will flow through you to accomplish it! Of course, it is up to you to use that energy to accomplish that task. When you keep doing this, you keep expanding.

So if these four things flower in you, then you are spiritual. And when this happens, it does not matter which profession you are in or whether you are married or unmarried or whether you are young or old.

Q: What would you say about eating vegetarian food and eating non-vegetarian food?

First, don't go around telling others not to eat non-vegetarian food. In departments unknown, it is better not to involve yourself and get into trouble! Certain issues cannot be resolved by logical reasoning. If we tell people not to eat non-vegetarian food, they will ask you that like animals, plants also have life and why are we eating plants? What will you tell them? There is no end to this subject.

This much I can tell you: The human body right from the teeth is designed for chewing and digesting only vegetarian food. I am a pure vegetarian. I eat vegetarian food because it is conducive to my body. There have been many masters who ate non-vegetarian food. Of course, when enlightened masters do certain things, we cannot pass judgment on them because their actions cannot be interpreted by our common dictionary. We will be misconstruing and missing the whole thing.

Just one thing: don't categorize people based on their eating habits and don't force people to give up eating non-vegetarian food.

A small story:

> At the time the television was introduced in India, a new television was bought in a certain house of mendicants.
> All except one person used to watch the programs on the television.
> The who never watched the television used to go to the president of the house and complain about how the others were watching television for so many hours.
> After he complained a few times, the president told him, 'You too should watch television from tomorrow.'
> The man was shocked and asked why.
> The president replied, 'You are not happy not watching and so you are grumbling about them. You have the desire to

watch but you don't watch it because you want to feel solid inside yourself. But this suppression is causing you to complain!'

You see: if you are not completely happy abstaining from eating non-vegetarian food, you will land up compelling others to become vegetarians. Only when you are into something totally, you will never force another person to do it. When you are doing it with a doubt or half-heartedly, you will pull other people also into it. This is the scale to see if you are in something totally or not. When you are total, you are enough unto yourself with no regrets. So you will not trouble anyone else. You will allow them to have their freedom.

In fact, I would go on to say that those who eat non-vegetarian food for one hour a day and forget about it, are better off than those who eat vegetarian food and think about non-vegetarian food 24 hours a day!

A small story:

> A Zen master was walking with his disciple towards his city.
> On the way, there was a river and a beautiful woman was standing near it.
> When she saw them, she requested the master to help her cross the river.
> The master promptly carried her to the other side of the river, left her there and returned.

The disciple was totally disturbed by what he saw. He was burning inside.

As they walked along towards the city, he couldn't resist asking, 'Master, how can you as a master touch and carry a young girl?'

The master replied, 'I left her there long back, why are you still carrying her?'

Masters always answer the questioner who is asking the question, never the question itself. In this story, the master could have as well explained to the disciple that to an enlightened person is beyond gender. But he did not do that. He made the disciple understand that the block was in the disciple's mind, not the master's act!

If you feel you cannot give up non-vegetarian food without craving for it, eat until it drops on its own. Please understard, this does not mean that I am advocating non-vegetarian food. For my own life, body and mind, vegetarian food is conducive and so I eat it. If you wish to adopt my way of life, become vegetarian, that's all!

But don't give it up and crave for it, and torture other people also to give it up. We all take up small issues like vegetarianism and contemplate on it for hours together; that is the problem.

There are three categories under which you can fall:

First would be, not to eat non-vegetarian food and not to think about it. The second category would be, to eat it and forget about it. The third category would be, not to eat it yourself, but feel deprived and hence torture people around not to eat it as well! Please don't fall in the third category!

Q: When I want to do good, for example, when traveling on a bus, I see an old man and I want to offer my seat to him, but I decide against it when I think that I have to stand for the rest of the journey. Whereas, when I want to smoke a cigarette, I get a total concurrence from inside me to go ahead, saying that one cigarette will not ruin my life. Why am I not able to control myself and do what is really correct?

You see, when you take in something with your mind, something that has been told to you from outside, you don't see its benefits clearly and deeply, although you understand it at the intellectual level. But when you experience something deeply yourself, it becomes your own understanding and so you stand by it without any problem.

The cigarette has merged with your being. You have experienced it yourself. It is not through someone else's preaching; it is your own experience. So your heart accepts it.

But the happiness that you get by offering your seat to someone on the bus is something that you have not experienced deeply. You have been told by people that it is good to offer your seat to an elderly person in the bus, that's all. At the most, you will feel a certain satisfaction at having followed social etiquette, that's all. In the case of the cigarette, you have become the experience itself!

What you have not experienced for yourself will not attract or pull you to it. If you had really experienced the joy of helping others, you would have offered the seat to the old man.

For true experience to happen, meditation is the way. When we meditate, our heart, which is as hard as a stone, will flower and become as soft and sensitive as cotton, and we will feel the compassion towards others.

At present, we either read in some magazine or we are told by elders that it is good to give our seat to older people in the bus, that's all. Instead, what should happen is, that feeling of helping should flower within us and we should offer help.

Sensitivity will become a way of life only if meditation has happened in you, or else it will remain just skin deep. Meditation is like a drill that pushes the teachings received through the head to the heart. Then, justice, honesty and similar virtues will become a way of life. Otherwise, all these virtues will remain as intellectual knowledge without turning into experiential knowledge.

Thank you.

Chapter 2

Indroduction

lright, let us now get into the subject.

First, let us see how the human mind works. The mind is the only thing that stands between you and You. If you can drop your mind, You become enlightened!

Reprogram your hardware and software

Before we get into how the mind works, let me explain something about the mind and how the presence of a master can change the entire mental setup of a person:

There are two things in you: hardware and software. Your mind is the software, your brain is the hardware. In the mind itself, that is in the software itself, there are two parts – the conscious zone and the unconscious zone. The conscious zone is the actual software; the unconscious zone is the virus! The conscious zone can be cleansed by teachings. The unconscious zone can be cleansed by meditation. Now the hardware, that is the brain itself needs to be then tuned to hold the changes in the software, that is the new experience that is created through the changed software. This can happen by the blessings of the master, by initiation from him.

When you clean the conscious and unconscious and create an effect, the hardware may not be able to hold and sustain that effect. If the master's initiation happens, the hardware also changes to hold that effect. In the absence of a living master, constant meditation and teaching can change the hardware. Our current hardware is like grooves created out of *samskaras* (stored past memories) in the brain. Once the new software happens, the hardware will slowly change. But if you wish to immediately change the hardware, the master's presence is the right thing. Straightaway it will change the hardware.

Sometimes, without even changing the software, the hardware can be changed and the person will directly start radiating the correct software! This can happen when a disciple is completely open to the master; if he is in love with the master for no reason. Sometimes a disciple falls in love with the master for no reason. He may not be attracted to his teachings or to his meditation techniques; he simply falls in love, that's all. In that case, straightaway, you can change the hardware. Those kinds of disciples will simply radiate the quality of the teachings and meditation without even going through all of them.

As of now, both hardware and software in you are outgoing, towards the outer world. If you get the right understanding. suddenly the software becomes ingoing; going in, towards spirituality, towards a cleansing process. The conscious portion is cleansed by the teachings and the unconscious portion by meditation. But even if the software turns inside, the hardware will not be able to handle it. Then naturally, the hardware will try its best to retain its current grooves. If the software is very strong and stays in the same tune, the hardware will slowly change. But immediately, if after the teaching and meditation is given, the initiation is also given, the hardware will also change and start holding the new software. It will get prepared to hold on to the new experience. This concept has to be understood clearly so that you may bring in enough awareness to allow the transformation to happen in you.

How does the mind work?

How does the mind work? Just look at this diagram here. It is a diagram to show how the information that enters through the eye is processed; actually, not just the information through the eye but information through all the fives senses - nose, ears, tongue, touch and eye. As an example, we are taking the eye. Let me explain it to you.

When you see something, first, the eye sees it. There is something called *chakshu* in Sanskrit, which digitizes the information seen by the eye. It is something like a digital signal processor – the DSP. The signal or the input is converted into a digital file by this *chakshu*. This conversion happens to the information received through all five senses, not just the eye.

Then the file goes to the memory. In Sanskrit, we call this portion *chitta*. In the memory, a little more work is done on the file. For example, if you are seeing me now, the file is processed through the *chakshu*, then taken to the *chitta*, memory and the memory starts analyzing the information. It does a process of elimination on the file received. It starts saying, 'This is not an animal, this is

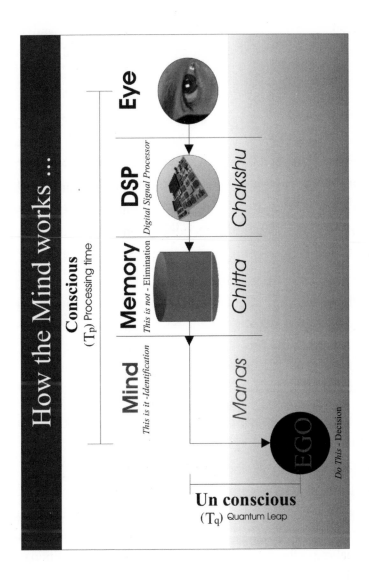

How the Mind works ...

Conscious
(T_p) Processing time

Mind
This is it - Identification

Memory
This is not - Elimination

DSP
Digital Signal Processor

Eye

Manas

Chitta

Chakshu

EGO
Do This - Decision

Un conscious
(T_q) Quantum Leap

not a plant, this is not a rock etc.' The process of elimination is done by the *chitta*.

Then the file goes to the mind or *manas*. The mind does the job of identifying the file. It says, 'This is a human being; a human being who is conducting a class.' The mind concludes, 'This is it.'

Next, the whole file takes a quantum leap to the ego and your ego decides based on your past experiences what your next action or decision will be. If you have past experiences with similar classes, say yoga or meditation, and they have been alright for you, if you think that it has helped you, you will decide to sit here, or else you will think it is better to leave!

Just try to understand this process: you are seeing me. The eye passes the information to the *chakshu*. The *chakshu* converts it to a digital signal. The memory then does all the elimination on the file – 'This is not...', 'This is not...' Then, the mind does the identification of the file – 'This is it.' Then the whole file takes a quantum leap to the ego. Here, you decide based on your past experiences, whether to sit here or leave the hall.

The process of elimination versus that of identification can be more easily understood by understanding this:

Let us say you want to find the word 'Home' in the dictionary. You start from the letter 'A' and you eliminate: not A, not B, not C, until you come to the letter 'H'. Until you come to the letter 'H', it is only an elimination process. Once you come to 'H', it is an identification process. You start identifying 'HO', then 'HOM', then you come to 'HOME'. Even in the identification process, there is elimination, but that cannot be considered elimination, because your whole attitude is changed during this time. Until you come to 'H', you don't even look at anything; you only eliminate. Once you come to 'H', 'H' becomes a standpoint. Then you start looking for HO, HOM, etc.

So, it is like this: you have thousands of files stored in your mind. Now let us say that you are seeing me. You will first start eliminating: this is not a stone, this is not a tree, this is not an animal. Then you come to the conclusion, 'This is a man.' Once you come to man, you start identifying: saffron clothed, my master, Nithyananda etc. So through elimination you find the right classification. In identification you go in-depth into that classification. Elimination is breadth, identification is depth. The elimination process is like handling many files. The identification process is like going deeply into a file.

Now, the process between the eye and the mind is logical and conscious. You are completely aware of this process. It happens with your awareness.

Now, the quantum leap from the mind to the ego is mostly unconscious. That is the time when the actual decisions are made and is mostly an unconscious process for you. It happens without your awareness. During this time, you decide illogically. You make an illogical decision.

Why does this happen? Why do you decide unconsciously and regret it later?

The reason is, this unconscious zone is filled with negative memories and restlessness; all your past memories which we call *samskara* in Sanskrit. All your past thought patterns are stored in this zone as files. In the field of psychology they use the word ito denote these stored memories. There are so many files stored in this zone. Without any logical connection between them, these memories or incidents are stored here.

What happens is, when the file takes a quantum leap to this zone, there is so much data stored, which causes so much restlessness in you, that the file does not even reach the ego properly for a decision. These stored engrams simply start playing upon the information received. They just impose themselves and cause havoc in the decision making process.

As a result, the ego just makes a hasty decision - purely at the instinct level, and passes the file back. The decision is taken through an unconscious process.

For example, according to the data that you have collected, you know that smoking is injurious to your health; it is not good for your body or your mind. You hold on to this decision as long as you are in the Tp level. But once the mind takes the leap to the ego, the engrams just instruct you to smoke; you simply decide to smoke! The conscious process says, 'No, it is not good for health.' But the unconscious process says...actually it doesn't even say, it *just* takes the decision and you execute it! It is a pure instinct-level decision.

This unconscious area is very powerful. It can be used in three ways – at the instinct level, at the intellect level or at the intuition level. As long as the unconscious is overloaded with negative memories and restlessness, it works at the instinct level, as we just saw. You simply decide instinctively, unconsciously.

When you are at the instinct level, you always end up regretting most of your decisions. You wonder, 'Why did I behave in that fashion? This is not me! How did I allow this to happen? How did I make that decision?' This happens because the unconscious is working at the instinct level. At this level, you just associate things without any logical connection and jump to a conclusion unconsciously.

For example, if you have been disturbed by somebody who was wearing a white dress, the moment you see somebody wearing a white dress, the past memory simply comes up without your knowledge and you feel anger. This is the instinct level. Without your conscious mind, without even you understanding, just like that it happens.

In the mind map diagram, when you have to plough through many files in the quantum leap to the ego, you are at the instinct level. When the file goes to the unconscious, the decision is made with many distortions. You will be continuously passing judgment on the pending decision. Your unconscious will be overloaded with your memory files. When you function this way, you will also feel tired.

It is something like this: when your hard disk is loaded with all high-resolution photographs, there is no scope to work further on your hard disk. In the same way, when your unconscious is loaded with many past thoughts, it becomes inefficient and makes superficial and illogical decisions.

The next is the intellect level. Here, you are conscious; you make decisions logically, but you do not have any extra enthusiasm or energy. You are not creative or innovative; you don't take big steps; you don't grow. You are like a faithful servant. Einstein says, 'The intellect is a faithful servant.' You can be a servant throughout your life. You can be just a servant, but nothing more or big can be done through you.

At this level, you will just be collecting the data, processing it and delivering it; you will be nothing more than a computer. You don't make wrong decisions out of restlessness; you make decisions in a logical and conscious way. You are in a break-even state. At this level, you are still not using your potential to the maximum – the extent to which it can be used.

The next level where you can actualize your entire potential is the intuition level. If you can infuse a deep silence and awareness into the unconscious zone and replace your engraved memories or files with silence and awareness, you can be at the intuition level.

If you can be free from your memories, be empty and blissful in this unconscious zone, if you can be alive and fresh every moment without the burden of your past, without the burden of these engrams, the energy of your being will express itself in its purest form. When this happens, we can say that your intelligence is at its peak, because energy IS Intelligence. Then, you make decisions out of an energy called intuition, where you simply *know* with tremendous clarity. Understand: The past memories are themselves not the problem. The bondage to them is the problem.

When you are at the intuitive level, you will make decisions from the energy of your intuition, from deep awareness and peace, from bliss!

This concept needs a deep understanding. You need to go deeply into the whole science, only then will you be able to understand what I mean by the word, 'intuition'. Intuition is something which happens in you beyond your intellect.

The power of intuition

What is intuition?

Let me explain. Suddenly you know for sure that something is the right thing and you feel that you have enough energy also to do it, but you don't know the steps involved in doing it. You don't know the steps that led you to the conclusion but you know for sure that your conclusion or decision is right. This is intuition.

This energy of intuition is needed when you are faced with a situation with no precedent. When you are stuck with minimum data and you need to make decisions, or you have many choices and you are not able to decide, in such situations, the energy of intuition helps you. Not only in such situations...if you can be in this zone of your being continuously, you will be totally present in every moment and you will give birth to future moments also in the same fashion.

If you try to assimilate what I am telling you now, if you can just spend a few minutes sitting with yourself and feel how your stored engrams are causing havoc in you and burdening you, if you can just see the truth in what I am saying, you will slowly know the knack of how to get out of this cycle and move to a higher plane of your being.

One more thing with intuition: it gives you the energy not only to make the decision but also to execute what you have decided. When I say this to people, they ask me, 'Swamiji how do I find out whether I am having an intuition or I am just being intellectual.' They tell me, 'Swamiji, I am confused about whether it is intellect or intuition.' I tell them: be very clear: if you are confused, it is only intellect. The very confusion shows that it is only intellect! When you have intuition, you will be so confident and brimming with energy that there will be no room for confusion.

With intuition, the potential power which is inside your being is simply unleashed. You open up and start expressing it, executing it. If you read about scientists and CEOs who have been involved in major breakthroughs in their fields, again and again they say their success came from something beyond their intellect, that something gave them the energy or the guts to make those decisions.

Each and every one of you has the power of intuition in you. Let me ask you: how many of you have experienced at least once in your lives, that when you are thinking of a particular person, the phone rings and that very same person is on the line? Or you enter a place and you feel you have been to the place before? Or similar intuitive things?

(More than 80% of the people raise their hands.)

44

You see, these are the moments of intuition that you have experienced accidentally in your lives. During these moments, you are accidentally in a meditative state. In these moments, your being tries to relate with you. But what do you do? You brush these things aside as coincidence and ignore your being. You completely ignore the higher dimensions of your being. How can something that has happened to 80% of you be a coincidence?

Be very clear: these moments of intuition are clear signs of the latent power in you. If you recognize and encourage it, you can express the higher dimensions of your being.

The other day I had an opportunity to have a meal with Dr Charles Townes, Nobel laureate in the field of LASER and MASER. I asked him, 'How did it happen? How were you able to do this?' He answered in a beautiful way. He said, 'I was just sitting in a park in Washington DC and suddenly something happened in me. Suddenly the conclusion was revealed to me. I immediately wrote down what I got. I then realized that I had a difficulty. I had the conclusion but not the steps! I was not able to present it to anybody because I knew only the conclusion; I did not know the steps. Then when I sat down, I was able to get the logical steps.'

Not only with Charles Townes, even Albert Einstein the famous scientist says, 'Whatever new understanding happened in me, came through intuition, not through intellect.' He says beautifully, 'The intuitive mind is a sacred gift, and the rational mind is a faithful servant.' We have created a society that honors the servant and has forgotten the gift.

Whether we believe it or not or accept it or not, there is something called intuition in us. Of course, even Einstein calls this a gift because he didn't know whether it could be consistently had. He was not sure *when* it would happen and whether it would happen or not. But *yogis*, the great eastern mystics, again and again say that you can very well have it all the time. You don't have to think that intuition is a gift. You *can* work for it. It can become a part of your life.

When intuition happens beyond your intellect, your whole being is integrated. You are at your peak. When you are at your peak, something opens. You may call it a revelation or an intuition or something else. *Yogis* have again and again said that it is a science. If you can tune yourself to this energy of intuition which is continuously available in your being, you can use this in your regular life.

Intuition is the energy of your being. When this pure energy starts flowing out from the unconscious level, it also heals you physically, mentally and emotionally. Apart from healing, it reduces stress and helps you to make decisions spontaneously.

Spontaneity has nothing to do with the data that you collect; it is something to do with the way in which you process the data.

The same data, the same information, can be processed in many ways. Intuition is all about how you process data and how you come to conclusions not limited by your intellect. We can prepare ourselves; we can tune ourselves to this energy of intuition through techniques and methods.

These techniques are what we call meditation. In the East, we use the word meditation to tune ourselves with the higher energy which is in our being, and which continuously invites us to experience it.

Whenever you find time, just sit with yourself and observe yourself. We are always ready to give appointments to others, but never to ourselves...! If you just sit with yourself, you can always see that some part of your being wants to express, wants to do something more, but you never give the chance or time to that portion of your being.

We are so caught up with our intellect. We think that our intellect is the ultimate, but again and again *yogis* have proven that something more than intellect is possible.

Energy centers within our body

If we understand how the mind works, how to unload the deeply engraved memories in our unconscious, how to prevent further loading and how we can awaken the latent power of our being to move into the zone intuition, we can live like a master and not a slave.

Just take a look at this chart here. Here you are able to see a human form with seven markings on it. Are all of you able to see? Yes. These seven markings on this human form are called *chakras*.

The *chakras* are the subtle energy centers of our body. They are seven wheels of energy in our body.

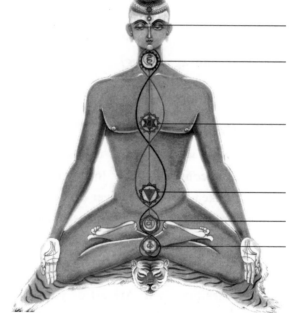

The Chakra diagram

Sahasrara
Ajna
Vishuddhi
Anahata
Manipuraka
Swadhishtana
Muladhara

We don't have only one body, as we think. We have seven bodies – energy bodies. I will explain the first three bodies now.

The first body – the one in which you have come here, in which you are moving, talking and writing – this is called the *jagrat shareera* - the physical or waking body.

The next body is the *sukshma shareera* - the dream body, the one that you use in your dream state. It is the body you use to travel from place to place in your dreams! In your dreams, you see yourself in various places. Sometimes you see yourself in places which you have not even been to in the waking state.

The third body is the *kaarana shareera* - the causal body, which you use when you are in deep sleep. This body does not move.

Now, the latter two bodies meet the physical body at seven points along the length of the physical body. These seven points are known as the *chakra*s. There are seven major *chakras* in our body. There are also a number of minor *chakras*, but these seven are the major ones that are responsible for our physical and mental well-being.

These *chakra*s were discovered a long time ago during the *vedic* age. In fact, in many of the spiritual chants, you will find reference to the names of these *chakras* very often. Today science has proved that there is a gland located near each of these *chakras* that is related to that particular *chakra*. These seven *chakras* supply energy to the glands.

These seven major *chakras* deeply influence our physical, emotional and mental activities. They have great power. They are energy centers and if they are kept in a cleansed and energized condition, they can cause us to live an ecstatic and healthy life.

Dis-ease is only an imbalance in any one of these *chakras*, because our body and mind are rooted in our inner consciousness. Keeping these *chakras* in a healthy state, we can see a transformation happening in us at the mental and physical levels.

Let me tell you a small story:

> After World War I, a biplane was abandoned near a remote tribal settlement in Asia. The tribal people had never seen an aircraft in all their lives. There was a lot of excitement and commotion about it and a big crowd gathered around it. They wondered what it might be and each one started giving some suggestion about it. They finally concluded that since it had wheels, it must be a bullock cart! News spread in the village about the new bullock cart. There was a lot of celebration in the village and the biplane was taken around the settlement yoked to bullocks, and it served as a bullock cart.
>
> Some weeks later, a young tribal boy who had returned from the city where he was studying, saw the biplane. He got into it and looked around. He saw all the gears and mechanisms in it. He fiddled with the switches and levers. Suddenly, the engine came to life! He managed to taxi the plane on the ground for a short distance and the villagers were shocked at what they saw. The boy had seen tractors being used and declared to the people that the biplane was not a bullock cart but some kind of tractor.

There was great celebration once again and the biplane started being used as a tractor!

Six months passed by and a retired army officer came to the village. He saw the biplane being used as a tractor and was shocked! He told the villagers that it was not a tractor and that the plane could actually fly.

They refused to believe him because the only things they had ever seen flying were birds! The army officer got into the aircraft, flew it for a short while and landed.

The villagers were wonderstruck. Then they understood its true potential.

Understand: man is a wonderful mechanism meant to fly. But we don't know our true potentiality. We have a very limited view of ourselves. Most of us operate only as a bullock cart, at the instinct level, surrendering to our emotions.

When we associate ourselves with mostly external things like a home, a car, a profession, and other basic things, we use our bodies as a bullock cart. We just operate at the instinct level and remain with an over-loaded unconscious mind.

When we additionally move into art, creativity, philosophy and such things involving not just the mind but the heart also, we use our bodies as a tractor. We will find a certain fulfillment in ourselves. A poet who has given birth to a poem will be happier than a woman who has given birth to a child. In the case of the latter, the womb is centered in the stomach whereas in the former it is centered in the heart, and so the fulfillment. These people will be able to operate at the intellectual level.

Finally, the man who enters into spirituality and develops a thirst for true knowledge and realizes that he is the ultimate existential energy in physical form, uses his body as an aircraft! Enlightened masters use their bodies as an aircraft. They are so ecstatic all the time. They rise beyond all the miseries of the bullock cart and tractor and just fly! They operate at the intuitive level.

What should we do to become an aircraft? What was the difference between the villagers and the army officer? The aircraft remained the same. Nothing was added to it or removed from it. No physical changes were made in it. Then what was the difference?

Knowledge. The knowledge of the mechanism of the aircraft. The villagers did not know that the device had such a mechanism that could be operated in a way that it could fly, whereas the army officer knew about it, that's all. The technique with which they handled the aircraft made it first a bullock cart, then a tractor and then finally an aircraft.

Just like this, there are mechanisms or gears inside us, called the *chakras*, which are boundless energy centers. Each of them is associated with a particular emotion within us. If we understand how to handle the emotion properly, we can function as an aircraft.

When we understand the science behind some of our basic emotions, we can become aware of our present deep unconscious state. Then we can free ourselves from the load of the unconscious and start moving to the higher dimensions of our being.

These *chakras* are not physical entities in our body. They are metaphysical representations because they belong to the auric body and not the physical body. Kirlian photography has enabled us to capture these *chakras* yand prove their existence on the metaphysical plane.

It has been proven that when a person is locked with a particular negative emotion, the *chakra* associated with that emotion shrinks to the size of a coat button. It becomes that small. But when the same person experiences the associated positive emotion, the *chakra* expands to the size of a cartwheel! This is the effect that our emotions have on these energy centers, our *chakras*.

Our energy flow in these *chakras* is blocked by our negative emotions and we are totally unaware of it.

Understand: man has not been designed to be a worm that crawls on the ground; he has been designed to fly in the air. Just as the villagers had no idea that the device could fly, man has no idea that he can fly. Man always thinks that enlightened people are gifted people and that he should stand at a distance and look at them with awe and respect. He never aspires to become like them. I tell you now: if you are really interested in achieving in the inner world, you will achieve it, come what may. The problem is, you don't believe that you can achieve. Just as the villagers refused to believe that the device could fly, you refuse to believe that you are actually designed for much higher things.

Don't learn from experience, learn from intelligence!

A small story:

> A young girl was learning how to play the piano.
> She was struggling to cope with the master's lessons.
> The man next to her was an expert pianist and was playing a song by himself.
> The little girl walked over and watched him play for sometime.
> She finally asked, 'Sir, do you by any chance have more fingers than I do?'

We always think that we are not gifted as we should be. The truth is, we have all that we need in us already. We only don't know how to use it effectively. Most of us express our potential like a bullock cart or a tractor. We don't know that it can transform into being an aircraft. The power to fly lies within you, but it can lie latent forever unless you learn the science behind these your own emotions.

In these few days, you will get a clear insight into your basic emotions.

A master is one who talks out of his experience of the ultimate truth. He talks with the ultimate authority because he has had the ultimate experience. We are all generally under the impression that only with age and experience, maturity happens and one can flower.

Masters are living examples to show that you don't need time to mature and flower. Let me explain this further to you:

When you were a child, you were very much attached to your toys, were you not? If someone took a toy away from you, how would you have reacted? You would have screamed and cried as if your whole life depended upon it, right? But now that you have grown up, if someone takes a toy away, will it matter to you? Will you feel upset? No! You are no longer attached to the toy. When knowledge descends on you, maturity happens naturally.

This kind of knowledge and maturity, although we feel can come only with age, actually have nothing to do with physical age; they are to do with what is called mental age. Research has found ways of detecting a man's mental age. They have found that the average man's mental age is not more than 14!

With a man's physical age, he needs to go through all possible experiences, make all possible mistakes, and become experienced and mature.

It is something like this:

When we touch the flame of a candle, we get burnt and learn that the candle flame burns. Next we touch the fire on the stove and learn that the stove fire also burns. Next we touch the cigarette butt and learn that, even that burns. Then we touch burning coal and learn that it too burns.

By touching various forms of fire, we learn that all forms of fire burn. By the time we learn this, it becomes time for us to go to the burning ghat ourselves! This is what we call learning by experience; acquiring knowledge with physical age. It takes you a lifetime to learn your lessons. With progressing age, you learn – at your own sweet pace.

On the other hand, just by touching the first fire, if you understand that all forms of fire burn, you are intelligent! This does not require age to learn. It requires only intelligence. This signifies your mental age. That is why we say that wisdom has nothing to do with physical age. It is a question of how intelligent you are, how much you have nurtured your inner intelligence to understand things.

Let me explain with things that happen in your own life:

During student life, when you are in college, you feel that you will be happy when you get a job. Once you get a job, you somehow don't feel the same happiness that you thought, you had expected, but you console yourself saying that you will be happy when you get married.

After marriage you feel that you will be happy when you have children.

You run after each desire thinking that you will be happy only when that desire gets fulfilled. In this way, you run to the end of your life and realize that none of your desires really gives you true happiness. Then you turn towards spirituality and meditation! This is the life of a man who learns with physical age, by experience.

A man with an advanced mental age is one who learns through intelligence; he is the one who clearly understands from his first desire, that no desire when fulfilled will give him true happiness.

There lies the difference. He will be able to see through the whole and analyze the whole thing. He will know that real fulfillment comes from inside and not from outer world things.

To attain this wisdom, you need not be aged, you need to be in the present, that's all. When you are in the present, Existence itself will teach you. Existence is the greatest master. When we are not in the present, when we are all the time running behind the past and the future, we take our own sweet time to learn, that's all.

Over the years, if you take the lives of enlightened masters like Buddha, Adi Shankaracharya, Bhagwan Sri Ramana Maharshi and Swami Vivekananda, all the enlightened people who created the history of India, they all attained enlightenment at a very young age. So understand that age is not related to spirituality or learning.

That is also why they say, 'You are as old as you are.' It means, you are as old as your mental age is. You are as old as your maturity is, not as old as your physical age is. You may be 70 years old but have the understanding of only a 20-year old. Or you may be 18 years old and have the maturity and understanding of an 80-year old. So you cannot claim superiority just because you are old by age!

A beautiful story about Swami Brahmananda, a direct disciple of Sri Ramakrishna Paramahamsa:

One day Swami Brahmananda was meditating in Brindavan. A devotee came and placed a costly blanket before him as an offering. Swami Brahmananda said nothing. He silently observed what was going on.

A couple of hours later, a thief came by, spotted the blanket and took it away.

Still the *Swami* watched in the same way, silently, with no reaction!

The gaining and losing of the blanket made no difference whatsoever to him!

There is a similar story in the life of Bhagwan Sri Ramana Maharshi:

One day, some thieves entered his ashram. They took whatever little they could find and before leaving, even gave him a blow.

It is said that not only did Bhagwan show no reaction, even the pace of his *breathing* did not alter during the incident! He was supremely unperturbed by the whole incident.

When we become a mere watcher, our mind becomes just a tool in our hands. We can then use it as we wish to. Otherwise, our mind can simply make us its slave. If you can use your mind when needed, you have learnt to drop it! And you have become a master!

So in these few days, we will see how to handle our emotions and become a watcher of our lives; how to center ourselves well inside us and function in the periphery in an undisturbed fashion.

We will see how to create a mental setup which is free from engraved memories that are responsible for our unconscious decision-making. We will see how to harness the energy of intuition in us; how to move from unconscious to conscious to super conscious; how to move from instinct to intellect to intuition; how to bring forth the fountain of bliss from within us!

We will meet for the next session.

Thank you.

Chapter 3

Be a source of love energy

hat is attention-need?

Before we move into subject of love, let us see what is meant by the word attention-need.

Whatever we do, whatever we think, we are subconsciously seeking concurrence and approval from the people around us in some subtle way. We are very keen that we should earn a good name from everyone. We may not do this in a very obvious fashion, but if you analyse deeply, you will not be at ease without the appreciation and endorsement of the people around you. This endorsement, this approval, is what we call 'attention-need'.

80% of our problems is due to this asking for attention or approval. If you just sit and write down, in a day, how many things you do to get a good name, to maintain your reputation in family and society, you will see.

You will find that all the 24 hours, all your lifetime, you are involved in getting approval from others. All your life, you are on a signature campaign, getting approval signature from family and society.

In a big register you make a column: *Good Father*, and for everything that you do for your children, you expect their signature of approval under that column! Then you go to your wife, to your boss, to your friends. You prepare columns with suitable headings like *Good Husband, Good Employee, Good Friend* etc. and wait for them to sign under it.

Of course, all these people also come to you for *your* signature! You too need to sign on their registers under the columns applicable to you!

Why do we bother so much about others' opinions about us? Why can't we judge ourselves by our own strength and continue to do our work? Why are we deriving strength from others? All this is because of two things: one, we don't know anything about ourselves. We know ourselves only through others' opinions of us, only through others' certificates. Second: when others give us their approval and attention, they are actually giving us energy to move on. Attention IS energy! That is why we feel so boosted when they give us attention.

Attention in any form is alright for us. In most of the houses, the mother-in-law and daughter-in-law will be constantly fighting with each other. They will be constantly complaining about each other to the poor man in the house. But for a few days, if one of them goes out of town, what happens? The other starts missing them! Although they are fighting all the time, they miss each other when they are not together! Why does this happen? When they fight with each other all the time, they are actually getting that much of attention upon themselves from the other person!

Don't think that only positive attention is energizing! Any form of attention is energizing. Both the mother-in-law and daughter-in-law subconsciously enjoy the attention that they get from the other when they fight. That is why they miss each other; they actually miss the attention! But when they start missing each other, they term it love! They say that they miss each other because of love.

Of course, it may be true; but I want you to understand that attention is nothing but energy, which keeps us in good spirits. It is a subtle form of energizing ourselves, and we are not even aware of this. When we *need* something, that something is not love; it is attention. You don't *need* love; you are love yourself. So when you say that you need love, when you say that you need to be loved, you are really in need of attention, not love.

People come and tell me that their sons and daughters don't love them enough in their old age. What they really mean is, their sons and daughters are not giving them the attention, the energy that they need in their old age.

Actually if you see, as we grow older, we should become more and more centered within ourselves, sensitive to the existential energy inside us. But what happens is, because we have been dependent on others for attention and energy all our lives, because the love that we know exists only in relationships, because we have lived with no awareness and sensitivity to what is inside us, when we get older, we start missing the love that came from outside or the attention that came from outside. The family becomes busy with other things and they don't interact with us as they used to. So we start complaining with age.

If you see, only because we don't understand that our energy source lies within us, instead of living life with more joy and energy, we live life with reduced joy and energy.

Certificates of energy?

When you are dependent on external sources for energy, you become psychologically handicapped. When you need physical support, you are physically handicapped. When you need psychological support, you are psychologically handicapped.

With a physical handicap, you know that you are handicapped because you can see it clearly, but with psychological handicap, you don't even know that you are handicapped. When you are not aware of it, you will not know the consequences that it can give rise to. When the real consequences or dis-ease happens, you will wonder what the reasons are.

If you have seen children play, you might have seen them building castles with cards. They will place the cards at a certain angle to each other and build several layers of such patterns in a pyramid shape. It will be beautiful to look at. But if you remove even one card from the castle, from anywhere, the whole castle will collapse! The higher the castle, the more the chances of collapsing.

Just like this, we build our own self-image like a castle, out of people's opinions of us. We collect certificates or signatures from our father, mother, boyfriend, girlfriend, teacher, friends and what not, and arrange all these certificates and build a castle to form our self-image. The image will look beautiful and we will feel happy.

But if even one person withdraws their certificate, what happens? The castle collapses! You start feeling miserable about yourself. You feel depressed. You feel that the whole world has come to an end.

65

At least in the case of the children, they build their castles with their own cards. But we build our castles with others' cards, with others' certificates! We don't have control over the castle because it is built with other people's certificates.

So what do we do? We start working hard in maintaining the castle; in guarding it well. We start behaving in such a way that people don't remove their certificates. We start doing things to get their continuous approval, because their approval has become our very survival.

A small story:

> A lady once went shopping with her husband because she wanted to buy a coat for herself.
> They visited many shops but she could not find what she wanted.
> The husband became tired.
> He asked, 'Dear, do you know the exact kind of coat you want to buy?'
> The wife replied, 'Of course! I am looking for a drop-dead coat.'
> The husband could not understand what she meant.
> He asked, 'What is a drop-dead coat, dear?'
> She replied, 'When people see it, they will drop dead!'

All the time we are looking to see how we can collect certificates from people! Every action of ours is unconsciously related to what people will say to it and how people will react to it.

For example, a bag may come reasonably within your budget and it may have a good utility value also. But unconsciously, your mind will say that people may not appreciate the look of the bag very much. You start choosing again! But you will not agree that you are searching for certificates, because it is an unconscious process in you!

We become almost like a centipede. A centipede needs 100 legs to walk. Like that, we need the synchronous approval of everyone for us to walk in life. What happens if even one leg of the centipede is not alright? It will be stranded. What happens to us when even one approval fails to be got? We fall into depression.

If we are so dependent on others, there is every possibility that we will fall into depression. People who suffer from depression are actually suffering from attention-need. Over time something happens; we don't get enough attention and we find it difficult to handle it. Just one word is enough to put us into depression. But we don't know the real reason for our depression. So what do we do? We start taking medicine to cure it.

How will it heal? The cause for the depression is inside you and you look at medicines for help. When people come to me with depression, I tell them to do the simple Mahamantra meditation to start with and tell them that slowly, we will stop the medicines.

You see, these people need to be shown that their energy source lies within them. Meditation can show them that.

Depending on the sincerity with which they do the meditation, they can simply harness the energy within them and come out of depression. Medicines will dull them even more. This needs to be understood.

I tell you: when you derive your energy from outside, it can simply play havoc on you. You just become a puppet.

Let me tell you a story. It is actually an experiment that was conducted in the University of Chicago in USA:

> A young, healthy and intelligent man wakes up and gets ready to go to work. His wife looks at him and tells him, 'You are looking tired; are you alright?'
>
> He feels irritated by her comment and tells her to stop imagining things and leaves.
>
> As he takes his car out of the garage, his neighbor is watching him and shouts out, 'Are you feeling well? You look out of sorts!' The man is surprised this time but tells him that he is alright and drives out.
>
> He reaches his office and as he walks in, the receptionist looks at him with concern and says, 'Sir, you look ill! Why did you come to work?'
>
> The man replies, 'Well, I think I am fine. Let's see....' And he goes to his office.'
>
> He starts to work and a colleague enters and says, 'Hey! You look awful. What's the matter? You have fever or something?'
>
> Now, this is too much for the man. He begins to feel uneasy and sick. Just then his boss calls him and he goes in. The boss takes one look at him and says, 'You look really unwell. Are you sure you can carry on today? Why

don't you go and see the doctor?'

The young man has had enough. He feels positively ill now; he says he would like to go home, and leaves.

As he drives home in his car, he feels his temperature rising. When he reaches home, his wife is surprised to see him back. She reaches out and touches his forehead and finds that he has high temperature!

A man who was healthy and happy in the morning became actually sick by afternoon! And how did he become sick? Just by people telling him that he was sick. The people were set up to tell him the same thing again and again. This experiment was conducted on several people and all the people fell sick at the end of it.

This is what happens when you are not centered in your own energy that is inside you. You will simply move from a high to a low just because of the influences from outside. When you become centered in yourself, nothing outside can shake you.

People tell me, '*Swamiji*, we don't do things for praise or approval; we do them because it is our duty.'

Be very clear: the moment you claim that you are doing your duty, you are doing it because if you don't do it, your people will stop approving of you. Your people will approve of you as long as you fulfill every small thing that is expected of you. Even if there is a small slip in what you are doing, you will be able to see the change in their relationship with you. You know this and so you do your duty.

You will say, '*Swamiji*, I am their father. If I don't provide for them, who will?' I am not saying that you should not provide for them. You have given birth to them; you have to provide for them until such time that they become independent and do things for themselves. But what you are doing, do out of no expectation whatsoever. Let it be an act which is an expression of the loving energy inside you, without any sort of expectation.

Right now, you might claim that you are not doing it out of any expectation, but when reciprocity from the other side dips a little, you will know; you will be able to observe the tension in you, the disappointment in you. This tension, this disappointment is the result of the expectation that was inside you when you did your duty. The degree of these may vary with each person, but it will be there at some level.

And when it is there, you are not doing it out of just an expression of the loving energy in you; you are doing it out of a lesser, limited quality called duty or so-called love.

 The Bhagavad Gita beautifully says:

Karmanyevaadhikaaraste maa phaleshu kadaachanah

It means, *Your job is only to do the work, not to be concerned about the result.*

Whatever you do should be an overflowing of the loving energy inside you. Then, you are not bothered about the results.

When I say you are not bothered about the results, I don't mean that out of a frustrated or cynical conclusion, you are not bothered. What I mean is, you don't even know to expect results because you are continuously moving and expressing your blissful inner energy. So we can't even say that you don't expect results. You are just flowing joyfully, that's all! This flowing energy is real love.

When you start expecting from other people, there will be no end to it. And let me tell you: the most difficult thing is to satisfy all the people around you. Do you think you can satisfy all the people all the time? Never. It is the most impossible thing to do on planet earth.

A small story:

> A husband and wife were celebrating their fifty years of marriage.
> The wife presented the husband with two shirts.
> He was very touched and declared that they would go out for dinner instead of cooking at home.
> It was a very tender moment for them.
> He freshened up and to make his wife happy, wore one of the gift shirts and appeared from his room.
> As he came down, she looked up and smiled, but soon her expression changed and she asked, 'So the other shirt is no good?'

It is never possible to make another totally happy!

First of all, try to satisfy yourself; find fulfillment in yourself. That is enough. And let this fulfillment have nothing to do with the people around you. Let it be just a bubbling energy inside you, irrespective of the conditions and people outside. That is enough.

It is good to do something for others; it is good to give attention, give respect – but out of a deep energizing love, not out of fear; not because we are afraid that they will take away their certificates. It is not worth investing so much in others' opinions that they become the center of your life. Don't make others the source of your energy.

As I told you earlier: because you don't know anything about yourself, you turn to society for an answer. And society happily puts its labels on you: *You are a good father. You are good-looking. You are a failure* and what not.

In the same way as a parcel without a proper address is pushed from place to place, we move around collecting all these labels. But we don't know that we are not the labels, but the stuff inside the parcel.

When you are dependent on others for your happiness, you are giving them control of your life. Be your own source of energy and inspiration! Come to a clear understanding that real joy is not possible when you place your center on someone else. If you understand this, half the problem is solved.

A small story:

> Brahma Sutra is a great book available to humanity.
> It is the unabridged edition of world philosophy, from which all other philosophies originated; it is the book of books.

It was written by Veda Vyasa, the greatest Indian scholar ever.

An enlightened master gave this book to one of his disciples, Vachaspati Mishra, and asked him to write a commentary on this book.

The master also gave his daughter Bamati, in marriage to him and died shortly.

Vachaspati Mishra started out on his task earnestly.

He was continuously engaged in writing. It became an intense and transforming meditation for him.

He wrote for months; soon months became years and years became decades.

He saw nothing else, thought about nothing else and heard nothing else during that time.

Finally, he finished the great work. Only the title of the book remained to be given.

He looked up from his work.

He saw an old lady, lighting the lamp next to him.

He was surprised. He asked her, 'Who are you?'

The lady replied, 'Never mind about me. Continue with your work.'

He said, 'I have finished. Tell me who you are.'

The lady said, 'I am your wife.'

Vachaspati Mishra was shocked.

He was simply shocked at what had happened.

For decades he had been writing the book without a single thought about his wife! He could not believe himself.

'Why didn't you remind me all these years!' he cried.

'What for?' She asked. 'You were immersed in the book. I felt no need to disturb you,' she replied quietly.

Vachaspati Mishra continued, 'You have sacrificed your entire life for the sake of humanity! What can I do to make up for it?'

Bamati replied, 'It has been a joy to serve you. I feel privileged that I was able to serve you while you wrote this great book. Nothing more is needed.'

Vachaspati Mishra shed tears of joy.

He paid his wife the greatest tribute. He named his life's work after her: Bamati.

Even today, the most outstanding commentary on humanity's most precious book, carries her name: Bamati.

Bamati has become immortal, because of her selfless devotion and love. She was enough unto herself. It is not that she did not want to disturb her husband; she did not *need* to! There is a big difference between the two. Most of the time we want attention but keep quiet thinking that we should not disturb the other.

But here we are talking of a person who did not *need* attention – that is the difference. She did not feel that her youth was being wasted; she was not making any compromise. She was being her natural self, that's all. And that was enough for her. It was not difficult for her not disturbing her husband. She was so centered in her own energy that it didn't matter to her at all.

Bamati lives even after she died. We are all dying every minute when we live. That is the difference.

Today, in our houses, can you read the newspaper for half an hour in peace? Can your wife watch her serial on television for half an hour? Just when you are reading the newspaper, your wife will think of telling you all the important things that happened at home the previous day. And she will complain that you are not giving her enough attention. She will say that you are with the newspaper all the time.

And exactly when your wife is watching her favourite television serial, you will feel hungry and want her to serve food for you. You will curse the television for showing the serials at the wrong times!

A small story:

> A man was sitting with his wife in a restaurant.
> They ordered for food and were waiting for it to come.
> The wife complained, 'Dear, ever since we entered the restaurant, you've been reading that paper.'
> The husband apologized, 'I'm sorry dear,' and signaled to the waiter. 'Can we have another newspaper please?'

You see, all of us are seeking attention all the time. And when we don't get it, we are upset. This is the root cause for all anger, disappointment and frustration in our lives.

We need to stop asking and start giving. We need to radiate energy instead of asking for energy. But we don't even know how to shift the focus from us to the other. We are so used to seeing ourselves as the center of attention. We need to start seeing the world outside as the center of attention. How to do this?

Shift that centre

For the next few days, I want you all to do this small exercise: Choose a partner from amongst yourselves, of the same gender. Look after that partner completely. Your first concern should always be for the other person's comfort. You should always look to see if he or she is happy and comfortable. Find out if they need anything. Instead of grabbing a plate for yourself first, give that person the plate and then you take one. If there is no warm water coming in your room, find out if there is warm water for them in their room.

And, I don't want you to pair up with your friends or relatives! I don't want you to choose people with whom you can exchange addresses with later on; with whom you can be friends later! Simply choose a stranger – the person standing closest to you. Just choose at random.

Almost all our lives, we worry only about ourselves. At the most, we worry about our close family, and that too because we feel that it is our duty-bound love. When you start doing this exercise, you will get a chance to see what selfless love is! It is selfless because you don't expect anything from the other person.

Real love

Real love is something so deep, so energizing, that you will not know it unless you experience it. Love is an expression of energy, not something that is transacted. Tell me one thing: can you love people when you meet them for the first time?

(From the audience: No Swamiji! We don't even know them, then how can we love them?)

76

Exactly! This is what you think. Let me tell you, with a little bit of intellectual understanding and meditation, you will realize that you can love anyone without a reason, causelessly! You can love the trees on the road, you can caress them and feel the energy flow from you. You can love people whom you pass by on the road without even knowing them. Love is actually your very being, not a distilled quality that you possess.

Nothing is as misconstrued as love is today. Today, love is more of a transaction. If someone says something nice to you, you love him; tomorrow if the same person falls short of it, you don't love him that much or you probably hate him.

Even your lifelong friend, with whom you chat everyday on the computer, will seem suddenly not-so-close if he says something that goes against your approval. Where is your love at this time? It has suffered temporarily!

It is just games that you play; a game in which love and hate surface alternately and interchangeably. And this love-hate relationship is not love at all. Be very clear. It is simply your reaction to a person or a situation, that's all. This is what *we* call love. This is not real love. It is subjective love, that's all.

Real love knows no object. It is simply there whether there is an object or not. Real love is the subject itself. It does not know any object. You are the subject and you have become love, that's all. Any object that comes in touch with it, feels it. Just like a river flows naturally and people enjoy it at the different places that they encounter it, real love exudes from a person and the people around him will be able to feel it.

There is absolutely no room for conditioning in real love. The energy in you should overflow and express itself as love. It is then that you can break through the highly knotted boundaries of relationships and express yourself beautifully, as a loving being!

In order to discover the quality of your being, that is love, two things can be done. The first thing: repeatedly listen to words like these so that they create a conviction in you about real love; so that a space is created in you for the process of transformation. Second thing: meditate so that the transformation can actually happen.

In practical life, when you go deeper and deeper into relationships, you will understand that all that you feel is not real love, but just some form of give and take. It is all just adjustment, some compromise, some duty-bound feelings, some fear, some guilt. It is all there in the name of love.

Meditation will take you beyond these mis-understandings of love. Meditation will work at the being level. That is why it is a shortcut! When you have to go through life and know it by yourself, it will take you a lifetime. But with meditation, a space opens inside you to experience these things clearly for yourself, whatever your age may be.

Just understand this one thing: when you are able to love without a reason, you will expand like anything. Your world will suddenly seem larger than life. It will be so ecstatic. You will become an energy source to yourself and to others. You will be so overflowing that the energy in you has to touch others. There is no other way. Others will be naturally drawn to you.

1 11-07-07 0
4x6-67900-8_01.JPG (10157)

Q: What about love between a mother and a child? Is it not self less love?

Even motherly love comes with expectations. Many times, people have confronted me with arguments when I say this. Let me tell you, a mother loves her son alright. But at the end of the day, there is an unwritten expectation written on that love. If the son causes a little friction, the first words that would come out would be telling the things that she had done for him since childhood. A small dent in the relationship is enough to bring the whole thing out.

Real love is the expression of the Existential energy in you and this love can never think of any such arguments. It only knows to flow causelessly. It doesn't know to maintain any track record. The moment you cite incidents from the past, it means that expectations were always there hidden behind your love and when it is this way, it can never be real love.

It is the same way when it comes to the son also. The son loves the mother, expecting her to look after him, expecting her to get up at five and pack his lunch for him, expecting her to maintain his clothes for him, without missing a single day. He adores the mother because he enjoys the care, the luxury.

A small story:

> A boy was learning fractions in his school.
> One day the teacher asked him, 'If there was a cake and we divided it into 5 portions and gave them to each of your family members, what fraction of the cake would you get?'

The boy replied, '2/5 Ma'am.'

The teacher asked, 'How? Haven't you studied your fractions well?'

The boy replied, 'Ma'am, my mother will give her piece to me if I like the cake.'

Mothers want to sacrifice for their children, alright, but the attitude with which they sacrifice is what we are talking about. They should do it out of simply an overflowing in them, not out of any hidden expectations. Events will never get recorded in them if they do it out of an overflowing. And even if they get recorded, they will not surface with a vengeance when things like this happen.

Common love always thrives on expectation. No one can deny this, although everyone may try to. The expectation in love is so well woven into it that it is difficult to perceive it. That is the problem.

Actually, as long as things go smoothly, it is difficult to believe what I am saying. But we hear of so many cases where sons and daughters are written off from the family for simple reasons! Simply because they married outside the community, or because there was some feud in the family. Where did all the love disappear suddenly?

Until such incidents happened, the son or daughter would have been loved very much. What happened suddenly? How can it suddenly disappear if it was real love? Real love can never be stopped because it is not bound by any cause-effect cycle.

Even in subtle family issues, if you look carefully, you will understand how bound your love is. Just try to re-arrange a few things in your life, and watch how your own family will react to it.

With your children, as long as you provide for them in the name of love, they also enjoy you, in the name of love. As long as you don't rub each other the wrong way, it is alright. If either of you behaves in an unexpected fashion, the mood of the love changes; the flavour changes.

Love which is always under threat is not real love. It is just arranged love. And anything arranged cannot be total. And when something is not total, it is always under threat. Love needs to be a total celebration, not a duty.

Respect is not love

One more thing: we all confuse love with respect. When you love totally, nothing that you do can appear disrespectful. You see, when you closely observe respect, you will find that when certain people do certain things, it appears absolutely normal, while the same thing, when some other person does it, appears disrespectful. The energy behind the person doing the act is what causes the act to seem respectful or disrespectful.

When the energy behind you is total, when you are just a loving energy, you can get away with anything. When you are not sure of yourself, you will get caught with the problems of respect. I am not asking you to be disrespectful. I am only saying that when your being resonates with love, your body language will be such that your actions can never seem disrespectful.

But if you get caught with respect instead of love, you are missing the whole thing. Then instead of being loving, you will start pretending, and when you pretend, you are not total.

When you are centered in respect, you will pretend because respect is societal and it keeps changing in its definition. But if you are centered in love, then respect becomes a pleasant by-product. So center yourself in love and respect will automatically happen.

Remember: Respect is dead. Love is alive. Respect creates a distance; love knows no distance.

People are trained to be so fearful and respectful of God. They are never taught to love God. They are not allowed to touch the idols in the temples. They are expected to stand at a distance and bow down. They are taught to be wary of God. Understand, the first thing that children should be taught is to love God.

If you cannot embrace God, there is nothing left to embrace, because God is everything! When you teach your child that you cannot embrace God, you are actually teaching him that God is different from the rest. By putting God on a pedestal, you are actually alienating the child from the whole of Existence.

Just have some social intelligence and play the game of respect in an intelligent way when required, that's all. Mind you, this kind of respect will happen with deep awareness and intelligence. It will not cause you to be less loving.

A small story:

> A mother went with her child to a public function.
> Somehow, she lost track of the child and they got separated in the crowd.
> The mother got very panicky and started searching all over for the child.
> Suddenly she heard behind her a voice, 'Maria! Maria!'
> She turned around and saw her daughter.
> She ran to her, hugged her and asked, 'But why were you calling me Maria instead of mom?'
> The child replied, 'That would have been of no use. There are so many moms around here!'

Children are still centered in themselves and they are more alive and alert than us. Their innocence, their love, their body language speaks for them, not their words. Because of this, whatever they say or do always seems innocent, never disrespectful. Once the mind steps in with societal conditionings, this innocence disappears. Then we have to make it up with words and pretensions.

When love becomes a duty, it becomes a burden. And when it becomes a burden, it is not more a celebration; you will be under pressure always to keep it up.

Love that liberates

Parents teach children reasons to love. From a young age, love is taught with a reason. Do we ever teach them to love the earth? Do we teach them to love nature? No. But we teach them to love our relatives. We teach them to love us. We teach them to love everyone who will be of some use to them in some way.

If you teach them to embrace nature, you are sowing the seeds of real love in them. I have seen many parents who will teach their kids to throw garbage in public places and destroy the beauty of nature. The same parents who teach the children to love the family will teach them to abuse nature. If you have real love in you, you will not abuse nature. You will embrace nature and people alike.

You have to sow the right seed. Only then the desired plant will grow. When you create the right conditions for love to flower inside the child, the child will blossom. Meditation helps in sowing the seed, in creating the right space inside. Nothing can be imposed from outside. The moment it is imposed, it will be met with resistance and carried out as a compulsion, what you call duty.

The love that we all talk about is actually psychological slavery. You enslave the person in the name of love, and he feels compelled to behave in a particular fashion. With physical slavery, you at least know that you are being enslaved. With psychological slavery, it is so cunning, that you will not even know that you are being enslaved.

Why do you think there is so much guilt in all of us? It is because the love that we know always puts us in guilt. When love is total, when it is pure energy from your being, it can never bring guilt. You feel guilty only because you always feel that you have not loved enough, that you have failed somewhere. And why have you not loved enough? Because you have been taught only love that has reasons, never total love.

If you see, when you have loved totally, you will never feel guilty or sad when a person dies. You may feel sad at the physical separation, but you will never feel that you have missed anything when they were living. When I say total love, I don't mean that you should have fulfilled all others' expectations of attention and wants. I mean, you should have been centered in yourself well and exuded that kind of energizing love towards them, seeing and respecting them as part of Existence.

If you had been this way, you would have experienced them in a total way and you will not feel any guilt when they pass away. Family always instills guilt in you so that it can have control over you. Guilt is nothing but a hangover of many kinds of emotions because you did not explore the emotion in totality. Never allow guilt to possess you.

I am not saying that you can do what you please and not feel guilty about it. I am saying, live totally, from your center, with deep awareness and understanding. Then there will be no room for guilt.

True love always gives without asking. It does not know any 'take'. It knows only 'give'. And you cannot create it either. It is like this: you can create a plastic rose but will it have the fragrance of the real rose? No! In the same way, true love can never be created.

For the real rose to happen, you need to create the right condition, the right soil, the right amount of water, and then it will happen on its own. Likewise, for true love to happen, you can create awareness, clarity and a deep understanding within yourself, and it will blossom from inside you.

In a college gathering one girl asked me, 'Swamiji, was it failure in love that caused you to become a sannyasi?'

I told her that it was success in love that caused me to become a sannyasi! Failure in love will create only a Devdas not a sannyasi! Only when you can love the whole world can you become a sannyasi. Only when you can love the whole world, it is real love.

Real love happens with no relationship. Only ordinary happens only when there is a relationship. In ordinary love, you love your father because he provides for you. You love your mother because she takes care of you. You love your boyfriend because he gives you sensual pleasure.

Real love is not like that. It doesn't say Oh! This is my father. I must love him...No! It knows to keep loving everyone and everything, that's all. Ordinary love creates bondage while real love liberates. With ordinary love, there will be failure and success. With real love, there is no success or failure, it just IS, that's all. The success is in finding it!

People think that when nothing works out for you, when all love is lost, you become a sannyasi. No. People think sannyasis are renunciates who are driven by frustration. I tell you: I feel so sad when I think of the people who say these things. They are in such deep ignorance. They continuously pass judgment from such a state of ignorance. Understand: *sannyas* is the ultimate marriage... to the Divine!

A true *sannyasi* is one who is so loving and compassionate that it is said that where he walks, the grass doesn't die! This is not a story. It is true. A true *sannyasi* is one who exudes compassion and love towards Existence. A true *sannyasi* is one who knows that prayer is love and love is prayer.

When you have found real love, your prayer will be just an expression of it. What are the Meera Bhajans? They are the loving outpourings of Meera, an enlightened being from India. She just resonated with Krishna who is Existence Itself, and she poured from her being. That is why the Meera bhajans are famous even today. The energy behind them can never fade because it is the Existential energy. Ordinary love cannot be felt over so many years by so many people. Only pure love can radiate that kind of lasting energy.

And for Meera, her *bhajans* were her prayer. When you have found real love, there is no other way. Prayer becomes love.

The ordinary love that we know is nothing but expecting someone to satisfy your psychological image; someone who can give you psychological support.

You need someone to take care of your needs. You need someone who will boost you up when you are down. You need someone who will sympathize with you and confirm your worries for you. This is what you call love. But true love is beyond names and forms, body and mind. Only a person who can love the whole world beyond all these can become a *sannyasi*. Only he can become a Vivekananda!

How we complicate love

When Vivekananda says, *Arise! Awake!* Does it mean that we are sleeping? Of course! We are sleeping even without knowing that we are sleeping. And we pass judgments while we are asleep. We criticize when we are asleep. We condemn when we are asleep. We think we are awake and we criticize. We think we know everything about everything including love.

A small story:

> A man had a wealthy old aunt whom he visited regularly.
>
> He coveted her wealth and went out of the way to please her.
>
> She had two cats, which she loved.
>
> The man knew this and would look after the cats religiously hoping to win her over.
>
> His secret wish was that she would make him a part of her will when she wrote it out.
>
> He would come everyday, feed the cats with milk, play with them, spend a lot of time and go back.
>
> The old lady was very pleased at the way he looked after the cats.
>
> Soon, she passed away. In her will, she had left him the two cats.

You can imagine the disappointment in the man! He must have felt cheated!

With ordinary love, there is every possibility that you will feel cheated. People love for wealth, for the favors that they get done, for the words of advice that they get, for other people's forgetful ways, which they can exploit... and what not. Love always comes with a reason.

But people will never accept this for a fact. They don't accept it because they are deluded by their own ordinary love. They think that that is the way love happens. And they think that while they are so loving, I am simply bringing down their love.

Honestly, if you sit and think by yourself, you will understand that what I am saying is true. Do an honest enquiry on yourself and see. Just sit down and try to visualize how you would react if your father or mother or sister behaved in a slightly different way towards you. You will then understand what I am saying.

We are all the time in need of something from someone and so we are continuously paving the way to get it from them in a smooth way. This smooth way is what we call love. Don't think that this applies to getting only material wealth. Even when you expect a person's behaviour to be in a particular fashion, you behave accordingly with them. As long as both of you are behaving in this fashion, you love each other. If someone misses it somewhere, your love takes a momentary dip!

Take me for example. You all claim that you love me very much. Each one of you has got a particular idea of how I should behave towards you. I simply behave towards each of you in the fashion. That is what I am doing now actually. What happens? If even once I don't smile at you or I say something to you that does not fit me into your frame, you start thinking that I don't love you any more.

You start thinking that maybe I am not so loving after all. You start imagining about why I said a particular thing to you, or why I did not smile at you.

I might have been talking to someone else, or I might have simply not smiled at you, just to allow your ego to settle a bit, that's all! But you miss the whole game and start interpreting my actions with your own dictionary of love. What will happen? You will land up in deep misery.

This is how you simply complicate love. At least when it comes to me, there is no complication added to it from my side! Imagine what will happen when two of you start relating with each other in this fashion? There will be total chaos! You will simply be moving from low love to high love to low love, that's all!

People tell me, '*Swamiji*, we love our children...'

When it comes to putting up with their naughty behaviour, how many times have you sworn at them? One girl was telling me at the ashram, '*Swamiji*, my mother loves my children only if they behave themselves well. She wants me to bring the children to show them off as her grandchildren to her friends and then scolds me for the chaos that they create!'

When you see children, you are pulled by their innocence. That is one thing. The second thing is, it gives you a feeling of pride, an ego boost, when you see that they are your creation. And of course, you provide for them and make them happy. But what I am saying is, this love also comes with limitations and preferences. It is highly subjective to the ways of the children.

A small story:

> A man was laying a concrete road.
> He had just finished laying the road when a group of children from the neighborhood came running onto it leaving footmarks.
> The man got very angry and swore at them.
> His friend asked him, 'Hey, what is the matter? I thought you liked children.'
> The man replied, 'Yes I do, but not on concrete.'

Ordinary love always comes with some condition somewhere! With some fine print somewhere. This is what I am trying to say. We love people subject to name, place, moods and situations.

The love of an enlightened being

A small story from the life of Vivekananda:

> One night, Vivekananda woke up at 2 am and awakened his disciples. His disciples were anxious and wanted to know what was happening. Vivekananda said that he was feeling a lot of pain and that in some part of the world there was a natural calamity that was happening which was causing him

the pain. The papers the next morning announced a terrible earthquake in Fiji islands that had consumed many lives.

He was sensitive to a calamity that happened in some corner of the world, thousands of miles away! Do you think normal humans can be this sensitive? Even if our neighbor is sick, it will not have any effect on us!

A small story:

> A man called up his family doctor and said, 'Doctor, I think you should visit us and do a check-up on my wife.'
> The doctor asked, 'Why? Is she unwell?'
> The man replied, 'I think so, doctor. Yesterday, she got up at her usual time, had a bath, cooked food, sent the children to school, cleaned the house because the maid did not turn up, washed our clothes, brought the children back home, attended to their homework and went to bed. Around midnight, she was complaining that she was tired. Maybe she needs to be checked up.'

We have become so insensitive today! We are not able to connect to the other person who is living with us 24 hours a day and 365 days of the year. Enlightened beings on the other hand are deeply sensitive to the universe surrounding them.

What happened in Vivekananda is what you call empathy. Mind you, it is not sympathy; it is empathy. Sympathy is a very superficial word. We are all capable of sympathy. When someone tells you about their suffering, you just confirm their suffering for them; that is sympathy! If someone tells you that their husband is ill, you tell them, 'Oh! How awful, you must be very unhappy. Don't worry, everything will be alright.' In the name of sympathy, we confirm their suffering for them and they in turn tell us that we are so caring and loving.

Actually, they love us because we have agreed that they are enduring suffering; it is a subtle ego boost for them. They feel good that we are acknowledging that they are managing such big worries. This is what society calls sympathy.

What masters feel is not sympathy; it is empathy. Empathy is when you feel another's suffering in your own being. Then, a person does not have to tell you his suffering, but you simply know because the Existential energy in you feels it.

Masters are one with you, because they are one with Existence, and you are a part of Existence; only you see them as separate. And because they are one with you, they feel *your* pain in *their* heart. They don't know any other way. And they have the capacity to witness the pain that comes with it also.

Ordinary love gives birth to children while real love gives birth to your own real self. You give yourself a new birth, a transformation. Like how the caterpillar becomes a butterfly, man becomes a realized soul. You awaken to the energizing love that is lying dormant in you.

A master transforms you with his love. I always tell my disciples, 'When I am compassionate, I cheat you and when I fire (scold), I teach you.' Either way, you grow! Sometimes I demonstrate my compassion in a very loving way so that you are more malleable to my transforming fingers! Sometimes I show my compassion by simply firing you so that you are jolted into deeper awareness. In both cases, pure love for you is the only reason.'

A master is an ocean of infinite love and knows only to give. If you approach him with a bowl, you will take back a bowl of him with you. If you approach him with a pitcher, you will take back a pitcher of him. It all depends on how thirsty you are, that's all. The thirstier you are, the bigger the vessel you will approach with.

But he is there always, watching you walking up to him with vessels of various sizes and laughing to himself at your own uncertainty, at the play of your mind which you project on him!

Be very clear: I am not asking you to love God or any Master. It is very difficult for you to love something you haven't seen. But you can love all that you can see, can you not? You can love the animals, the plants, people and what not. Simply love them for no reason except the joy of loving.

Feel a deep connection with them and love them. Once you start doing this, you will develop a certain faith in Existence because Existence is the common thread that runs through all these things. Faith is something that cannot be imposed upon you. If it is imposed, you will harbour a deep vengeance towards the object of faith.

When faith happens, slowly, your love will become love towards the whole of Existence. Then, the ultimate religion will take root in you – the religion of gratitude and love.

Gratitude and love are closely related. When you experience gratitude at the core of your being, there will be only love in you, nothing else. The first step towards feeling real love is feeling gratitude. As long as there is discontentment in your system, there cannot be real love. Gratitude and love go hand in hand.

Just disappear! That is love

Some people tell me, '*Swamiji*, I love the whole world. I don't do harm even to a small ant...'

Why do you want to delude yourself by saying all these things? Can you even love your neighbor whole-heartedly? I tell you: it is easy for people to say things like they 'love the whole world', because they don't have to do anything tangible to prove it! They can continue to say that they love the world and not do anything about it! They don't have to do anything special to show it. The world is after all an intangible entity; it is not a clear representation.

But when you say that you love your neighbor, the problem starts! You have to see his face everyday. You have to do something tangible to prove your love for him! Then it becomes a problem!

And how can you feel great in not doing any harm to an ant? Is the ant capable of violating your property or person? Is it capable of testing your love for it? It is not even visible to the eye and you talk about it to me. These are all ways to escape from the truth.

Just try to understand one thing: your inherent nature is love and love is permanent. All other emotions simply come and go, that's all. You are caught in thinking that all the other emotions are real and that they are destroying love. Love can never be destroyed. If love could be destroyed, it would have become extinct long ago.

Also, when you really love, the opposite emotions cannot enter into you. They will simply be excluded. When there is bright light in a room, can darkness be brought in? No! Only when you dim the lights, darkness can enter. In the same way, only when real love has not happened in you, the other emotions can enter. When you are brimming with love, there is no way another emotion can enter.

You might have experienced that when you do something intensely, you forget yourself. It can be anything - as simple as coloring or painting or reading....or anything. When you go deeply into it, you forget yourself. When you have an intense headache, just try doing some activity very keenly. Your headache will go away!

Because you are continuously aware of your head, your headache continues. The moment you go deeply into something else and lose awareness of your head, your headache will simply disappear. Only when you remember your head, you can have a headache. When you go deeply into any emotion, only that emotion remains and *you* cease to exist. This is what we mean by 'totality'.

This moment of 'you' disappearing, you may experience for just a few seconds. But if you work on being intense and total in everything, this experience of 'you' disappearing will happen more often to you and for longer periods also. Soon, you will master the art of doing work intensely, and being absent!

In the same way, when you are brimming with love, you don't feel yourself, you feel only love; you *become* love. Only when you become love have you found real love. When you become love, you automatically exude compassion towards everyone and everything around you. You take up a lot more responsibility around you. This responsibility is not out of ego of serving people, but out of the overflowing love energy in you.

Love and responsibility

Love and responsibility always go hand in hand. When you truly love, you will take up total responsibility as well. People think that *sannyasis* are those who run away from responsibility. Understand: When you forego responsibility towards your own family, you are taking up responsibility for a much bigger family, for humanity at large, for a family which is millions of times bigger than your own. People don't understand this and they simply criticize.

Responsibility is something that can be easily shrugged. The more responsibility you take up, the more you expand and the divine energy will automatically flow in you! I always tell my healers to take up as much responsibility for the suffering and pain around them as they can and to continually heal people.

When you feel that you are responsible for the pain around you, you will automatically stand up to help reduce it in some way or the other. People often think that it is enough if they do things for their own family. This is a way of contraction, not expansion. You need to expand for growth to happen. Existence will automatically flow through you when you take up responsibility.

People tell me, 'Swamiji, it is enough if I am able to feed my family properly.' Be very clear: this is just an excuse to draw a tight boundary around yourself; a way to contract yourself.

You might have heard of the famous lines of Bodhi Dharma:

> Buddham sharanam gachami
> Dhammam sharanam gachami
> Sangam sharanam gachami

It means:

I surrender to Buddha;
I surrender to *Dhamma* - the teachings of Buddha;
I surrender to the *Sanga* or institution created by Buddha.

It is very easy to surrender to Buddha or any master. You don't have to do much for it. Masters are so alluring because of their divinity. It doesn't take much from your side to do this. People tell me that the moment they see me, they feel a certain belief and faith in me. I tell you, it is not a big deal. The Existential energy that is flowing through this form simply pulls you, that's all!

The next statement: *I surrender to the teachings of Buddha*, is a little more difficult to follow than the first, because the moment you say this, you have to show that you are following it! For example, I say to you, '*Be blissful*'. That is my teaching. What do you then say? 'No, no *Swamiji*, it is not practical...' Be very clear: I say *only* practical things. You start thinking that I am enlightened and that I don't know anything about your so-called practical life.

I say only those things that you can *become* in day-to-day life. I am sharing my experience with you when I say, *'Be blissful.'* I am not just preaching the words. Understand that first. When I say, *'Be blissful'*, I am drawing you to experience the bliss that I am in. And it is perfectly practical because I am alive here in front of you, experiencing it!

The third line says: *'I surrender to the institution created by Buddha.'* Here starts the real problem. This requires a tremendous responsibility to be taken upon oneself.

Understand that masters live in their mission more than in their body. Only 33% of their energy is in their body. The remaining 66% is in their mission and teachings. That is the kind of responsibility they taken up. I always tell people that I get my energy from my *movement,* not from the food that I eat.

Masters never take up birth to fulfill any *karma* or unfulfilled desires in themselves, because they don't *have* any *karma* to be fulfilled. They take birth out of sheer compassion, sheer love to kindle divinity in people.

Masters live more in their words and movement than in their body. That is why I always tell you to drop my form and become sensitive to the energy in my mission instead.

But what do you do? You try to keep holding my elbow all the time! Instead of doing my work, which is your own flowering, you tag behind me wanting to be around me all the time. You never understand when I say this to you.

Understand that when you do the work of a divine mission, you are doing two things. One is meditation for your own spiritual growth and the second is service to society which is the greatest responsibility. The second is only a by-product. The transformation that happens in you while you are doing the work is the actual mission of transforming you!

So just take on responsibility with joy! You will feel selfless love growing in you. The whole world will become your family. When you are confronted with seemingly high responsibilities, simply nod your head to them. Mere nodding without resistance is enough. The rest will be taken care of by Existence.

Have you heard of the *mysore pak,* the famous Indian sweet? It will look and feel heavy, but the moment you put it in your mouth, it will melt and dissolve and give you a renewed source of energy. Likewise, when you simply nod your head to any heavy responsibility, you will immediately get the energy to execute it. The very act of taking up responsibility will bring the necessary energy into you. This is the loving energy of Existence that you need to discover in you.

To take up responsibility, you need to love the whole of Existence without discrimination. When you love without discrimination, you can take up responsibility without discrimination. Responsibility is nothing but the ability to respond spontaneously. When you can respond without a thought, without a plan, ready to take on anything, you have arrived!

Q: I want to be loving but I am unable to let go...

To be totally loving is a big challenge for the ego. To be totally loving is to merge oneself with the Whole. This is great trouble for the ego. You are right now fragmented; you are not integrated. When you are fragmented, you simply play with your different fragments and escape, that's all. To become loving means to become integrated. But you are scared because when you become integrated, you grow as a whole. Your parts have to die and become a whole.

You are so used to being fragmented that you feel threatened when you have to integrate yourself. Your ego refuses to allow it to happen. When you become loving, you are melting your ego. Earlier your ego was hard; it was solid and you felt good. What will happen when your ego melts? You will feel like you are losing your whole identity, your grip.

If you just decide to let go at least once, you will feel such a tremendous freedom, such liberation inside yourself. You need courage to let go and become loving. As a first step, at least become aware of this deep inside; the rest will automatically happen. Awareness is the key to open any lock.

When you start loving beyond names and forms, you are not losing anything, you are only losing what you are *not*; the illusion which you need to lose. What you have gained is reality. So just have faith and don't fear when you find yourself merging with the whole.

Just let go and watch the inner transformation happen in you. You will then realize how foolishly you were holding on to the ways of your ego; you will realize how much you missed because you were behind the mask of ego.

And understand that real love never calculates. Real love is from the heart and the heart never calculates. Only the mind calculates. It is time to move from the mind to the heart. You have listened enough to your mind. Decide now and listen to your heart. When you live with your heart, you will never regret anything in life because there will be completeness in anything that you do.

You can never experience true love with your mind. You can experience it only with your heart. Love needs to be experienced at the very center of your being. The center of your being is totally silent; it does not know any words or thoughts. No thought can ever penetrate it.

That is why time and again masters tell you to go deep inside yourself to discover your real nature. Your center is your true nature. This is actually *you*. But you seek to find yourself in all other places – in relationships, in material things and what not. You continuously miss seeing the truth. It is now time to look in.

We continuously talk about love, simply because we are missing it; simply because we have not had a taste of it. When a person is thirsty, he talks and dreams of water all the time. The moment he has quenched his thirst, he will stop talking about it. We need to let go and experience true love, the love that merges you with the whole. Then we will stop talking about it.

Love is actually surrender. But it becomes a fight for most of us. When I say surrender, I don't mean surrendering out of acceptance. I mean surrendering out of a deep understanding.

When you surrender out of acceptance, you are compromising. Love can never be a compromise. The moment you compromise, it is not love. Only when you understand and dissolve, it is love.

When you are with a master, you have a lifetime opportunity to discover love; you have the opportunity to die and resurrect with true love. The alchemy process that happens in the presence of a master will give you no option but to die and be born again with true love. All you need to do is be willing to dissolve in his presence. When you have the courage to do this, you are ready to take a leap into higher consciousness that is called love.

Love is not an object, it is the subject. It is *you*. *You become love*, that's all. Then you will start loving without a reason. You will love the trees, the flowers, the earth and what not. You will simply radiate love and merge with Existence.

The root is love

You see, when you grow in love, you learn to include everything and everyone. When you see a master, you will understand how encompassing he is. He never excludes anything or anyone. He sees no imperfections in anyone. He is just pure love, that's all. And pure love sees no imperfections.

Existence is pure love. Society is *always* against pure love. Deep inside, society is actually against Existence or God. All its worship is mere hypocrisy. It hides in the name of worship. The best way not to follow anything deeply is to start worshipping it! Society escapes in the name of worship. When you worship, you don't have to do anything else! And people will not trouble you because you are worshipping! But what happens to your inner space? It remains where it was.

Society never approves of letting go and loving every plant and animal with love. It would tell you that you are mad. It will approve only of love that is governed by give and take; love that comes with a reason.

But I tell you: don't give up. Keep on loving with all your heart. See Existence in everything. Feel the plants with tenderness in your heart. See the animals as if they were your own. See every person, stone or tree as a part of God. *That* is real worship. It is easy to worship God in the temple. The real worship is seeing everything as God. Start with your neighbor first.

People never go to the root of anything; that is the problem. The root of God is love. The root of God lies in seeing Him in everything. People are afraid to go to the root and so they delude themselves in superficial layers. They don't have the courage to explore beyond a certain point in anything in life. That is why they don't allow you also to explore. They tell you what they have found is the truth. They tell you that it is enough if you follow what they are saying.

Have the courage to go deep inside and love. You will start feeling the common thread of Existence in all that you see. You will understand that all that you see are illusory happenings held together by the real thread that is Existence. Automatically, you will start loving everything in the same way without any trouble because you will see only Existence in everything. This is the real shift in consciousness.

You can talk for years about Existence or God, and still not have any experience of it. Of course, your ego will be nice and solid because you will feel that you know so much about God! But if you look in, there will be no solid experience. And because you have no solid experience, you will keep getting caught in words, because if you stop talking, there is nothing left; there is no experience.

So start feeling love towards everything simply for what it is. Understand: because all of you are here, I am talking to you. If you were not here, I would be continuing to talk to this banyan tree, to these plants, to these animals! Every leaf here talks. That is the language of love!

For years people have been telling you that you are an advanced species of animals. Be very clear, even animals are not merely animals. Each and every atom on this earth is divine, a part of Existence. If you understand this clearly, you will be able to start feeling for everything around you.

Your mind does not need love, but your being needs it. Love is an adventure where you go into dissolution. When *you are not*, love *is*. We don't have the courage to 'not be' and so we hold on; we pull back from unconditional love.

Those who are ready to take the adventure into dissolution, into experiencing the whole, are the brave ones. The ordinary love that you know is like fighting within four walls. Real love is like fighting in the cold on the open streets. The courageous ones will fight on the streets and win. When you fight within four walls, you feel good, but you are missing reality. When you are ready to fight on the streets, you are in reality and alive!

You need not have any fear of fighting in the open. If you fight knowing that you are fighting under the compassionate eyes of Existence, you need not fear because even if you fall you fall into the very lap of Existence! But you have to have the courage to stand up and fight. That is the step that you take on your side. The rest, Existence will take care.

This will happen if you are just a little more than curious to know the truth. Mere curiosity is not enough. If you are just curious, you will come, flirt and get away. If you are more than curious, if there is a burning desire in you that surfaces at least once in a while, you can start knowing and experiencing the truth. If you are merely curious, there will be no devotion or dedication. If there is a fire, there will be devotion and dedication. Dedication is what brings you here, again and again.

Try as you might to run away from here, you can't! You might stay away for a few days, but the burning desire inside will draw you again and again. To discover true love, you have to have this intensity within you.

Love makes you beautiful and rich

Love as much as you can, without asking for anything in return. Loving for a reason is not love; it is just a business deal. When you can love without a reason, when you can love anything and anyone that comes your way, you will release tremendous energy and beauty. You will appear beautiful irrespective of whether you are physically beautiful or not.

Don't think that unconditional love will not get you back anything. It will get you back things in more than one way. But you should evolve to an extent where you see these things coming to you and continue loving, for the sake of loving. Your intelligence will make you see the things that you get in return, and the same intelligence will keep you blissfully untouched by them also!

There will be a revolutionary change in your heart and you will be a new person. Others will see a beautiful change in you. They will develop a new respect for you. They will see that you are flowering in a way incomprehensible to them.

To be able to love unconditionally, you need to feel free. What do I mean by free? Not being bound by caste, creed, sect, religion, family, relatives and any such thing. Because when you are bound by all this, your love will remain bound, and bound love is not real love. How can you love with boundaries? It is against the very definition of love!

I am not saying that you should forget your family, religion etc. Just don't see love in the context of all this, that's all. Free your inner space from these bondages. When you feel that you belong to the whole of Existence, you can love without any boundaries.

I always tell people: If you are able to feel the love that you feel towards me to each other, then you have had a glimpse of real love because, as I told you, it is very easy to love me! But if you can feel the same love that you feel towards me towards the others also, then you have caught the thread of real love; then you have started feeling Existence in everything. Then slowly, you will move on to embracing everything and everyone as part of Existence.

We will now do a simple and very effective meditation technique called the *mahamantra* meditation, for experiencing the energy source within us. This meditation is also good for energizing the *anahata chakra* that is located in the heart region.

Emotion: Love

Chakra: Anahata chakra

Location: Heart region

In Sanskrit, *anahata* means 'that which cannot be created'. Pure love can never be created. It flowers on its own.

This *chakra* is locked when you seek attention and love from others, and it flowers when you express selfless love without expecting anything in return!

Meditation Technique to be a source of love energy:
Mahamantra Meditation – a Tibetan Buddhist technique.

Mahamantra Meditation

(Total duration: 30 minutes. To be done on an empty stomach.)

The *Mahamantra* meditation is an ancient Tibetan Buddhist technique to help you feel the energy source within you. It will create a good energy flow in you. It will fill you to the brim with energy so that you stop seeking attention from others and start giving energy and love to others as a result of overflowing energy in you. This technique will awaken the *anahata chakra* located in the heart center.

This will also make your mind firm and stable. Your mind is mostly oscillating with thoughts. This meditation makes your mind still by making it enter into the zone of no-mind. It is like a jumping board into infinity.

While doing this meditation you may wear your *mala* (rosary) around your neck. It will serve to store the energy that you create during the meditation.

This meditation should be done on an empty stomach, preferably early in the morning, or two hours after any meal. It can be done either alone or with a group. When done with a group, it effectively energizes the place where it is done.

Let me explain the technique to you:

Sit cross-legged in a comfortable position on the floor. Keep your head, neck and spine in a straight line. Those of you who are not able to sit on the floor may sit on a chair. Feel relaxed and close your eyes. Even after we close our eyes, we see forms and images from behind the eyelids. To handle this, imagine that your eyeballs have become stone-like. Just harden them with mental pressure; then the images will die. The movement of our eyes is very closely related to the movement of thoughts in our mind. That is why you are asked to arrest the movement of your eyeballs. Don't be too worried about keeping them arrested. Just proceed with the meditation.

Keep your lips together and produce the sound 'mmmm...' from inside. If you were to put your face inside an empty aluminum vessel and make a humming sound, the sound generated would be like this. Note that this is not 'Hum...' or 'Om...', it is simply keeping your lips together and producing the sound 'mmmm...'. This humming should be as lengthy as possible before taking the next breath. It should also be as deep as possible, from the navel center, and as loud as possible.

Don't make an effort to take in a deep breath after every 'mmmm'; the body itself will take breaths when needed. Don't become tense. Put in your whole being and energy into creating this vibration. Just become the humming. Let your whole body be filled with the vibration of the humming. After some time, you will feel that the humming continues without your effort and that you have become a listener to it!

At the end of 20 minutes, stop the humming. If you are playing the CD, you will hear 'Stop!' and you stop as you are, abruptly. Don't wait to finish a breath, just stop abruptly.

After stopping the humming, keep your eyes closed and remain silent and inactive for 10 minutes with a smiling face and blissful mood. If any thought comes to you, let it come. Simply watch your mind as if you are watching the television. Do not resist your thoughts or pass any judgment on them. Remain silent and blissful. During this time, the energy created by the 20 minutes of humming will enter all the corners of your being and cleanse them deeply.

At the end of 10 minutes, slowly, very slowly, open your eyes. Try to talk very little for the next half and hour at the least.

Thank you.

Chapter 4

Live without worries

hat is worry?

Let us analyze what 'worry' is.

Can anyone tell me what worry is?

(a lady answers...) Swamiji, we get worried when we think of our business problems or when we think of our children or of our health...

What you are saying are the *reasons* for worry. I am not asking you the reasons for worry. I am asking you 'what IS worry'? If I ask you the reasons for worry, this session will never end! Each of you will be ready with a long list –

Swamiji, my business is down...

I have no peace of mind at home!
I have so many problems that you can't even imagine...!
I don't have children, that is my worry!
My children are my worry!

We all have so many worries all the time. And if we can't find any worries, we will worry about *not* having any worries! When we have no worries, we start feeling insecure! Some retired people come and tell me, '*Swamiji*, we don't know what to do.

Our children are married and settled in their own houses. They don't ask us for anything; there is nothing to think about. There's no point in living anymore *Swamiji*. We want to die peacefully.'

They don't know what to do because they don't have any worries! They try their best to think of something to keep their minds occupied, but there is nothing coming up! And this is new to them because they have all along been occupied with some worry or the other, with some thought or the other.

Before defining worry, I just want you to recognize that whatever be our culture, financial status, age or anything else, we all have one thing in common, and that is worry!

If I ask you why you worry, you will list so many reasons. You always think that worry is caused by external matters and you always blame the people around you for it.

If the cause for worry were external, there should be at least one person who has beaten all these causes and is free from worries? But is that the case? Anyone you meet has got some worry or the other, is it not? Whether they are rich or poor, married or unmarried, with children or without children, working or having their own business – everyone seems to have worries.

This is because, although we think that the cause for worry is external, actually, the cause for worry lies deep within ourselves. That is why everyone has some worry or the other all the time.

So we come back to the question: what is worry?

If you look deep inside, you will find that worry is nothing but *your response* to an event. Whether a situation makes you worry or not, depends entirely on how you choose to react to the situation.

For example, suppose your friend gets a new job and comes and tells you about the perks and benefits of it, how will you react? Unconsciously, you will be chattering inside yourself: *Oh, he's got a new job. He is enjoying so many benefits. What about me? What will my wife say if she hears these perks and benefits? Better not allow this guy to meet my wife, or else I will get into trouble. Should I start looking for another job? What if I don't get it? Nothing ever works out for me ...*

This is worry! An unwanted but continuous stream of words happening inside us all the time.

Why and How we worry

Worry is what happens when you constantly compare yourself against external frames of reference and continuously chatter to yourself about it. Over time, this sets in as your mental make-up. Your very mental make-up becomes worry.

You will think:

Am I doing as well as my neighbours?

How can I impress my boss?

What will my children think?

All the time, we need to get approval from others – whether it is family or work or society. This is a major portion of our worry. Our whole life is nothing but a process of collecting certificates from others. If others don't keep giving us certificates like *Good Husband, Good Employee, Good Neighbour*, we worry that our life has become worthless. We form our personality only from others' certificates. We have all stopped trusting ourselves; that is the problem.

As a child, each of us is strongly centered in our own being. Have you ever seen any child worrying about what people will think of him? No! A child is beautiful because he has no worries. He is not worried about what others will say about him.

As we grow up, society teaches us to evaluate ourselves by the ideas and opinions of others. Society makes us dependent on external support, certificates from others, for each of our actions and words. This is why we are all the time worried about what others will say about us.

Also, when you worry about something, you feel you have a definite point of reference against which to run your life. That is why worrying gives a direction to your life. Without worry, you feel as if you have no axis about which to move. And so you actually nurture your worries.

Let me tell you a small story:

> Three men were sitting abandoned on an island.
> They did not know for how many years they had been there.
> Suddenly, one of them found a bottle and picked it up.
> He rubbed his hands over it, and suddenly a genie appeared out of it.

They were shocked.

The genie told them, 'Thank you for freeing me from this bottle. Each of you may ask for a wish and I will grant it for you.'

They were very excited and they thought for a while.

The first man said, 'I want to marry my girlfriend and live happily.'

The genie said, 'Alright, your wish will come true.'

The first man disappeared from the island and the genie looked at the second man.

The second man said, 'I want to become a wealthy businessman.'

The genie said, 'Alright, your wish will be granted.'

The second man disappeared and the genie asked the third man what he wanted.

The third man said, 'I am going to miss my two friends who have been with me all these years. I want to be with them!'

The genie said, 'Alright,' and it disappeared, leaving the three men just as they had been on the abandoned island!

The third was actually attached to his worry which is being marooned in the island! This is what I mean when I say we are so fond of our worries! We claim that they give us misery but we are so attached to them.

People come to me and say, 'Swamiji, my business is going from bad to worse. Last month I suffered heavy losses and the next month I know it's going to be even worse.'

I ask them, 'If you already know that, why don't you close down your business right away? Why should you suffer?'

But they are shocked. They ask in disbelief, 'What are you saying, *Swamiji*? What will I do then?'

The moment I give a solution for your worry, you are shaken because without a reason to worry, your ego loses its reason for existence! That is why you choose to remain in the dimension of worry. When you are in worry, you feel you are someone. You feel solid.

Whereas, when you are free from worrying, you are in bliss, but in this dimension you are nobody! There is no material to keep you occupied. There is nothing to solve. You feel insecure, like a non-entity. That is why I tell you, to enjoy a worry-less state, you need to first drop your ego about wanting to be a solid entity.

And the thing about worrying is, first of all, worry itself is your decision to give food to the mind and keep it occupied. On top of this, each person thinks that only *he* has got a lot of worries and that only *he* is unhappy, and everyone else is very happy! But the strange thing is, every one thinks this way! How is this possible?

A small story:

> In a certain kingdom, it came to the king's notice that everybody in his kingdom was depressed, because each person felt that they had the maximum worries, and no one else had any such worries.
> So the king announced a 'Worry Exchange Offer', where people could bring in their big worries, and exchange them for someone else's small worries.

A big space was made ready, and in the center of it a huge 'worry pot' was placed.

Anybody who wanted, could come and dump his own worries inside it, and pick up any other worries they wanted.

The only thing was, they had to pick up *some* worries.

The whole kingdom gathered for the event.

The people moved around and met each other and started talking to each other about their worries.

After a long time, the event was declared open for the worry exchange.

A lot of time passed and not a single person came forward to drop their worries in the pot.

The kings asked his ministers what was happening.

The ministers replied, 'Your majesty, after all that interaction, everyone thinks that their own familiar small worries are much better than everyone else's worries!'

If we get down to the bottom of our so-called worries, we will understand that we are simply magnifying things that are not so bad at all. We simply talk in the air without getting down to the actual facts. If we get down to the facts, it will be not even 1/10th of what you worry about.

Speaking in and speaking out

Alright, now let us analyze what actually happens inside the mind when you worry.

Just watch your mind when you are worrying about something.

You will see that a continuous stream of thoughts is being generated in your mind - totally disconnected thoughts and usually negative thoughts. An influx of negative and repetitive words will be like a current in your mind.

You see: we all use two kinds of speech – *speaking out* and *speaking in*. *Speaking out* is speaking to others, what we call speech or conversation. *Speaking in* is speaking to ourselves. Actually, this *speaking in* is a continuous process that goes on inside us. This *speaking in* is called 'inner chatter' and this is what is called worry also.

Worry is nothing but this continuous, uncontrolled inner chatter happening in your mind. This inner chatter becomes your master and takes control of you.

Whatever words you speak out, you speak carefully because if not, society will ask you to be careful. But your 'speaking in' is not controlled in any fashion. When words that you speak out, can be controlled, why can't words that you speak in be controlled?

You don't control what you speak inside because you don't have self-respect. You simply say what you wish inside you. Do we throw garbage on a plate of food? No. We throw it only in the garbage can. You treat others like a plate of food and yourself like a garbage can. Because of this, you become indigested.

The dangerous this is, with outer conversations, there will be breaks when no conversation happens. But the inner chatter is continuous. It can drive you mad! Actually, many times, you speak outside only to escape from your own inner chatter. That is why so much talking goes on in the world! People are afraid to be

121

silent because there is a madhouse inside them. So they meet up, socialize, talk, and keep themselves occupied.

What exactly do we mean by this inner chatter?

Just try this small exercise when you are by yourself. Just sit for a few minutes with your eyes closed. Keep a pen and paper with you. Don't focus your mind on anything. Just witness your mind. Just see what is going on in your mind. Almost as soon as you close your eyes, you will see that there is a continuous stream of thoughts flowing through your mind. Write down honestly, whatever thoughts are there. Just write whatever is going on, however unconnected the thoughts may be. Do this for five minutes.

Now, sit down and read what you have written on the paper. You will be shocked! Whatever you have recorded on the paper is your inner chatter. If you read it, you will see how disconnected, how irrelevant your thoughts are! One moment you will be here; the next moment you will be in America; the next moment you will be in your office; the next moment you will be thinking of your children!

This is the mind you have entrusted your life to! This is the mind that generates all your worries. This is the mind that is living your life for you. If you understand this step, the rest is easy.

A small story:

> One day, there was an accident on the road.
> People gathered around and saw that a brand new car had crashed against a wall.

They asked the driver, 'Why are you driving the car if you don't know how to drive properly?'

'Of course I know how to drive,' replied the man, 'I only don't know how to stop.'

The man knew how to drive but did not know how to stop! You are also driving a vehicle which you don't know how to stop. It is a very dangerous thing. Your mind is a like vehicle that you don't know to stop. Just try to stop your inner chatter, even for a few seconds. Can you? When you try to control it, the number of thoughts increases. And you will have one more worry that you have to stop your mind!

You are not driving your mind; your mind is driving you.

To understand worry, we need to have a deep insight into the nature of our minds.

The way to worry is through the mind, and the way out can also be only through the mind. But we keep searching for answers in all the wrong places. We search outside all the time. We think, *If I had more money, all my worries would be over! If I was more good-looking... If I had a better job... If... If... If...*

The solution cannot be found in outer world things. It can be found only inside ourselves.

A small story:

Buddha had ten thousand disciples whom he used to address every morning.

One day he brought a tightly knotted rope and placed it before them and asked, 'Can someone untie this knot?'

The disciples came forward, pulled and pushed the knot but could not undo it.

One intelligent disciple came up, looked at the knot for a while and undid it easily.

You have to look at the knot and see how it has been created, then you can undo it. Instead, if you simply pull and push, you will never be able to untie the knot; it will only become tighter.

The same thing applies to our problems also. The problems, diseases, emotions you are struggling with, are nothing but knots in your system. Once you clearly understand how the knots have been created, you can take the right steps to untie them.

Worry is closely related to the *manipuraka chakra,* the energy center which lies in the navel region. Negative thoughts directly attack the *manipuraka chakra*.

Just do this small test: Whenever you feel negative thoughts coming up, look into them and see where they are rising from. You will find that they always rise up from the navel.

Whenever you feel worried, whenever a situation arises that you simply can't handle, the first thing to get affected is also your navel region, your stomach. You can physically feel depression as a weight in your stomach. That is why we always say, 'I can't stomach it; I can't digest it.' This expression is there in all the languages. It is universal. Constant worrying locks the *manipuraka chakra*.

So, what is the way to be worry-free?

Create only positive words

If I ask you how to be worry-free, you will say, '*We should never get worried in any situation Swamiji.*'

Just try telling yourself that you should not get worried. What will happen? You will create one more worry of not wanting to worry. Never say, 'Stop worrying'; it is utterly impossible. The only thing you can do is, *Stop worrying about your worries!*

What do I mean by not worrying about the worry? Just see the worries and don't get perturbed by them, that's all. It is only when you start repeating your worries to yourself, does the actual worry take root. This is what I mean by, 'Stop worrying about your worries.' Don't give life to your worries. Don't feed them with flesh and blood.

When you say, *Control the mind, Don't think negatively* – it is just like tightening the knot in the rope. Your mind becomes more tense and constricted. This will not help in untying the knot.

When you suppress, the memories of the suppressions go directly to your worry center. When the this center is poisoned, all your actions will have an unconscious violence. You will pluck leaves from trees, you will destroy things, you will misbehave with your body, you will fight with yourself and with others.

These are all subtle expressions of suppression. That is why people say that their stomach is burning with anger or they are feeling heavy in the stomach. The suppressed anger gives rise to more negativity.

What is negativity?

Supposing you suffer from a business failure due to some reason, how would you react? You would feel sad that you met with failure; that is ok. But you will not stop at that. You will allow all sorts of things to enter into your head.

Oh, this is my bad period!

Everything I touch is sure to be a failure!

I am good for nothing!

Why am I always so unlucky? And and so on!

This is negativity. This is the root of worry. 99% of our worries are never true. It is just negativity, that's all

Gradually, this negative chatter solidifies in your being and becomes a negative influence in everything that you do. And you are so unconscious of this solidified thing in you; that is the danger. To make you acutely aware of this in your system itself is a big task because it has become your very nature. You don't see it as something different from you. You feel that is the way.

The clinical name for this negative attitude is depression. Some people are less depressed, some people are more depressed. The more you allow this chatter to consume you, the more depressed you become. The people who are less depressed feel it only occasionally and that too at a lower degree whereas the people who are more depressed feel it most of the time in a severe fashion. But the current is flowing for both.

So depression or negativity is nothing but a collection of negative thoughts, which you speak to yourself. And once you allow such thoughts to enter into your mind, the same thoughts will keep playing back every time you suffer a small failure. It will keep reinforcing this attitude. After all, worrying is only a highly reinforced habit.

But it is a mere habit and so you can kick it like any other habit! But you don't think it is only a habit; you think it is a solid reality. That is the problem. That is why you are not able to kick it.

Remember: the mind is an excellent recording system. It stores your negative thought patterns, your complexes and your worries. Whatever you teach the mind, it learns and repeats faithfully. This is how you create a solid mental make-up of negativity. So be very careful what you tell your mind. We always take so much care in how we speak to others, but we never care about how we speak to ourselves.

Just like poor eating habits cause cholesterol to accumulate in your arteries, constant worrying causes worries to solidify in your being. In the same way as cholesterol creates blockages in your arteries, worry creates energy blockages in your energy.

Over a period of time, worrying becomes part of your nature; it becomes an unconscious act. Even if you reason your worries out, the low mood still remains. Why? Because all your worries, all your anger, you have suppressed over the years, and they are still there as an invisible layer in your being. Worry is the wave that rises from time to time, but depression is the water itself.

How do we go beyond depression or negativity?

Just be aware and alert. Whenever you become aware of a negative thought surfacing, just visually scatter the negative words and see them disperse. If you keep doing this, you will not allow the negative patterns to settle, and with time your mental make-up, your mental programming will change; it will not be negative any more.

If you go beyond inner chatter even for a few moments, you will become more aware, more alive. You will understand that worry is unreal, unnecessary.

Q: *Swamiji*, are thoughts a part of the mind, or are they an expression of the mind?

Your mind and your thoughts are one and the same. There is no difference between mind and thoughts. Mind is thought and thought is mind. The mind is nothing more than the collection of your thoughts, the continuous flow of ideas. And thoughts are no more than the words that you speak to yourself continuously.

When you worry, allow yourself to enter deeply into it, with acceptance and clarity. Don't be afraid to enter into it. Remember: acceptance is not impotence. Acceptance is a great meditation technique. Acceptance releases a great energy that gives you great clarity and liberation.

When you accept your worries, when you enter deeply into them, you will come to a tremendous understanding that all your worries are just your own creations. You will be able to see how your mind plays and causes tension in you.

When I tell you worry is unnecessary, you can understand it only intellectually. When it becomes your own experience, you will go beyond worries. Then depression cannot touch you. You will go beyond misery.

A small story:

> When I was staying in Calcutta, taking classes on the Isha Vasya Upanishad, a man came to see me.
> He said, 'Swamiji, I have a problem. I don't sleep well at night because I live in an area where there are many street dogs. Every night they start barking, and keep barking till sunrise. I am already a very light sleeper, and I am unable to get any rest because of this noise.'
> I told him, 'Go home and try this tonight. When you hear the barking, just drop the anger, the negative feelings that rise up in you. Just listen to the barking sound without resisting. Tell yourself that the dogs are barking, that's all. Don't allow yourself to react to it. The problem is not the barking, but your resistance to it.'
> The man went back and tried what I said. After a few days he came back to me and reported, 'Swamiji, I tried dropping my resistance as you said. Instead of thinking, how dare those stupid dogs spoil my sleep, I just relaxed thinking,

The dogs are barking. They are spoiling my sleep...

The dogs are barking...

Some animals are creating some sounds...

By the time I came to that sentence, I think I fell asleep.
Anyway, I've been having excellent sleep all these days.
Thank you *Swamiji*!'

This can happen with you also. Any situation can be dealt with, if
you know how to drop your negativity, if you know how to drop
your negative reaction to it.

But the mind is so eager to repeat familiar patterns of inner
chatter. It always looks to typecast things. It all the time compares
past, present and future and gives birth to worry.

Drop worry, enter into the moment

Worries are nothing but familiar dwelling patterns for our mind.
These familiar patterns are called *engrams* in the field of human
psychology. Engrams are the engraved memories of the past,
which serve as an undesirable resource inside us for all our
present and future actions. Because of these stored engrams, we
react illogically in the present.

Why can't we take every moment as it is? Why do we need to
link the present moment to the past and future? Why should we
look for consistency in everything? And when there is no
consistency, why is it difficult to digest? This is because we are
always looking to frame things with the help of our mental make-

up, with the help of our stored engrams; and when we can't, we get worried.

Have you seen me worrying any time? How many of you have asked me how I am able to be blissful at all times? The reason is, I simply live in the moment, that's all. I don't carry the past as a reference in my mind. I don't burden my mind with the future either. Things happen from spontaneity, not from patterns.

Many of you would have seen the river Ganges flow in the Himalayas. It is so beautiful. It appears serene at certain places, turbulent at other places, crystal clear at times and murky at other times. *Where* a person encounters it, *that* will be the experience he gets from it. That is spontaneity.

Can two people who encounter the river ever compare notes and complain? How foolish it would be! The river simply flows, that's all! It has no plan. Enlightened masters are like a river. They flow without a plan, just spontaneously, without a worry.

But people come and tell me, '*Swamiji*, what you say and do are so contradictory!' People pass judgment on me; they say I am inconsistent. How many of you here have complained at my inconsistent words and behaviour? Come on, raise your hands!

(*after a long gap, a few venture...*) I am sure most of you would have had this thought at some point in time, just that only these people have had the courage to raise their hands.

Can you say that the Ganges is inconsistent? Can you say that the Ganges should flow in a more orderly fashion? No! That is the way it flows, that's all; you can't pass judgment on it. In the same way, a master also flows. You can't call me inconsistent. I live moment to moment. You live with interconnected and complicated moments. What is the result? You feel burdened and worried.

When you have so many moments weighing on you, you will definitely feel heavy. In the same way, when only the moment is on you, you will feel so light. All your worries are because you connect the present and the future with past patterns. In the whole process, you miss the present, which is actually a gift for you. You continuously miss the present for the sake of the past and the future. Finally, only the future and the past remain, never the present.

These patterns that cause the current of worry have become a life-sustaining element for you.

A small story:

> Two friends went to a cinema theatre to watch a newly released film.
> One of them noticed that the other was frequently looking at his watch.
> Finally he whispered to him, 'Are you not enjoying the film?'
> The friend replied, 'I am. I am just wondering how much more time is left to enjoy.'

Most of us are like this! We are so tuned to worrying, that even if there is nothing to worry about, we worry about how long this state of no-worry is going to last! When we are enjoying ourselves, we worry about how much time is left to enjoy. How will we ever enjoy then? When you are continuously thinking this way, you are keeping yourself in the future all the time. When you do this, you have missed the pleasure of the moment!

Everyone feels important and productive when they harbor worries. Actually, the more a person worries, the more he feels good about himself because he feels he is managing so much worry! That is why most often you will see that when you talk about your worries to someone, they will say, 'Ah! This is nothing; listen to my problems; then you will know what worry is.' People feel superior in shouldering big worries!

By thinking of worries all the time, what is going to happen? Nothing. With your ten worries, an eleventh worry called depression will happen, that's all.

We worry while we work. When there is worry, you cannot work and when you are really working, you cannot worry. Where there is worry, there cannot be any creativity and where there is creativity there cannot be any worry. Creativity is God's job. When you create, you are close to God. Creativity comes from the heart. Worry comes from the mind.

Past is an unwanted baggage. Drop it.

By going behind the past or thinking about the future, you miss the present. Spirituality is all about dropping the past and living in the present. Right now, you are accumulating the past. You feel bogged down because of this.

You don't know how to unload your past. You feel that you have to carry it with you. Society has taught you that you have to carry it with you. You are taught to feel guilty if you try dropping it.

Society tells you that you are ungrateful if you drop the past. There is absolutely no need for you to carry your past with you. The people who tell you these things don't know that gratitude is something that you have to feel continuously in you towards Existence and everyone as a whole, and not something that you feel towards isolated incidents in life.

When you drop your past, the present will take you by surprise. Society always teaches you to enjoy the present as past, never as present. It teaches you to make everything a past and then enjoy it.

I have seen people who go out on holidays – they are all the time with their still camera and video camera. In the most scenic of places, instead of enjoying the nature surrounding them, they will be scrambling with their cameras to capture all the scenes.

They will then go home, wash their film rolls, sit on their sofa inside four walls and enjoy the same scenery through the camera. And they will show all the photographs to family and friends just to tell them that they have visited the places seen in the pictures. But they never enjoyed the places when they were there!

You enjoy the present after making it a past. That is why people say, 'Those were the golden days.' When the days were actually there, you would have surely not thought they were golden. At that time you would have been saying that the earlier days were golden days!

When you are in the present, every moment will become a celebration and you will not be searching for past incidents to celebrate.

Also, it is such a waste of time dissecting the past for worries because you are a new person every moment. Every moment you are evolving; every moment you are getting updated. You are a part of Existence and Existence changes every moment. Then how can you dissect past incidents with your updated intelligence? It is totally irrelevant and meaningless.

Never analyze the past with updated intelligence. It is a totally foolish thing to do. It will only lead to more worry and guilt. Every moment you are dying and becoming a new person. This is the truth.

Have you seen any buffalo or cow worried? Have you heard of any plant that is worried? Are they not conducting their lives without a hassle? Why do *you* worry then? I tell you: worrying is the most unproductive habit of man.

Words are the unit of worry

All our worries are nothing but a collection of words in the languages that we know. And they cause so much confusion and misinterpretation in us. But what to do? Words are the only form of communication man is familiar with.

I always tell people: when I say something, you understand it as something else. And that is where the problem starts. Each one carries his own dictionary and interprets the words in his own way.

A small story:

> One man told his wife, 'You know, it is said that over 5000 camels are used in a year to make paintbrushes.'
> The wife replied, 'Oh God! Is it not amazing to see what they can make animals do!'

The husband says something and the wife understands it as something else. This is how most of us relate. That is why I say, words cause confusion. Sadly, the only form of communication that man knows is words. He gets caught in words and more words.

You see, words will always give rise to more words. But there is a silence or a gap between one word and the other – a tiny gap not perceivable by us; this is the gap we need to be aware of! This is the gap that holds what we are seeking.

This gap is so microcosmic that although we go through it all day, we are blissfully oblivious to it. When I talk, you become intensely engrossed in my speech. Sometimes, I give long gaps between words. I give those gaps for you to absorb and witness the silence, which holds what you are seeking. But invariably what happens? The moment I give gaps, you start getting restless. You start fidgeting with your things or you start looking around and talking, collecting words again!

Real silence is that which is flooded with only awareness and nothing else. It is not just keeping your mouth shut.

Now your mind will start asking, 'How can I stop this inner chatter and thoughts? How can I experience real silence?' This thought will start haunting you and it will become one more worry!

Try to understand: you can never stop the thinking. The thought that you have to stop your thinking itself is another thought! If you forcibly try to be silent for a second, that silence is not the silence we want to achieve; it is just a forced and dead silence. The silence that we want to achieve is a vibrating and blissful silence, the silence of Existence.

So what is it that needs to be done? Simply watch the mind, that's all. Be an observer. Don't pass any judgments; don't resist any thoughts. Watch it with the deep gratitude that it is God's gift to you. Automatically, silence will happen.

Your awareness will slowly grow and make you centered in yourself and increase the silence in you. When I say increase the silence, I mean your inner chatter will reduce and you will be more of a watcher. With that increased silence, there will be more awareness in you and it will become a cyclic process.

With greater awareness, you will be able to enjoy the beauty that surrounds you. It is not that the beauty came in suddenly; it was always there! But you were not aware of it. You were too busy within yourself. Now with your awareness, you will be able to celebrate it! Suddenly, nature will start revealing itself to you as very beautiful. Your inner self will transform, and along with it, the outer world will transform too!

When you learn to be in awareness, you can use your mind at your discretion. It becomes a vital tool at your disposal. You can use it just when you want to. From being a dangerous enemy, it becomes a reliable friend.

Bring down the number of thoughts per second

When your inner chatter comes down, when your TPS or Thoughts Per Second comes down for even a split second, for that split second you are totally in the present and for that split second, you have the ability to access your past and future like an open book! When your inner chatter is high, your TPS is high and you are all the time either in the past or in the future; never in the present.

Let me explain to you what I mean by being able to access your past and future. Sometimes you might have experienced that when you are at a lecture or at a party, or in any other place, suddenly out of nowhere, you feel that the whole scene has happened before. The voices, the conversation, the place, even a few curios in the place, all will look like a replay of a scene that you have witnessed earlier. You are shocked.

Or, suddenly you think about a particular person, a friend whom you haven't contacted in a long time, and that person calls up on your phone. You are able to predict what is going to happen in the next few moments. You feel jolted when these things happen to you. Be very clear: in these few moments, you are accidentally completely in the present. Accidentally, somehow, you fall into the present.

You are never consciously in the present. You are always in the past or future. You move from past to future without touching the present. This is the truth. But accidentally your thoughts per second come down for a moment and you are jolted into the present.

When you are completely in the present for even a second, your past and future become transparent to you. That is why you see these kinds of intuitive things happening in you.

Our thinking is never clear. It is always just association; it is never real thinking.

Let me explain what I mean by association. You wake up in the morning and see a rose that has bloomed in your garden. Immediately your mind goes to someone who gave you a rose sometime in the past. Your thought then goes through your reaction at that time to the flower, or you start thinking about that person. You then start thinking about incidents that have happened with that person. In the end what happens? You miss the rose that is in front of you!

This is how you run behind the past and miss the present. This is what I mean by the word association. This is the nature of your current mental set-up. As long as your mental set-up is mere association, you will continue to go behind the past or the future, creating words and more words within yourself.

Enlightened masters live always in the present. That is why they have access to the vast ocean of the past and the future. For you, it is an accident. It is a split second when this happens to you. You even feel scared when this happens! You are so used to living unconsciously, that when you are jolted into consciousness, it is too much. Reality becomes too much!

Your TPS plays a major role in determining how far you are from the present. When your TPS is high, you live unconsciously; you are so far flung from reality. When your TPS is low, you come close to the present. Meditation and awareness is the way to bring down the TPS.

People tell me, '*Swamiji*, we went for a vacation and it turned out to be hell.' I tell you: hell is inside you; you carry it with you everywhere. Obviously you will find it anywhere you go! When you live, you give hell to others. When you die, you get hell! Wherever you go, you want to carry your hell with you. You are so familiar with hell that even if you are shown heaven, you will feel a misfit there!

A small story:

> Three fisherwomen went to sell fish one day and it became late that night when they were returning home.
> They decided to spend the night in some house on the way. They entered the house of a lady who sold jasmine flowers for a livelihood and they requested to spend the night there. The lady agreed and they went to sleep in the room given to them.
> The house was filled with the fragrance of the jasmine flowers.
> But however hard they tried, the fisherwomen could not sleep.
> They were tossing and turning, and they did not know what to do.

Then suddenly, one of them got up, brought in the empty fish basket and kept it by their heads. They went to sleep in no time!

We carry our worries with us everywhere we go and feel comfortable nurturing them! But we also complain that we are so worried all the time! We want to be free from something but we are not willing to transform and be free from it. This is what I mean by being self-contradictory. If we don't want to worry, then we should not worry. On one side we don't want to worry but on the other side, we want to worry all the time!

Stop reacting

How can we be free from this? What should be our attitude?

Both questions have only one answer: *whatever* you do, do with a feeling of bliss, that's all. Your inner space decides the quality of your life. This space should be pure and blissful always.

It has been proven that the consciousness of a scientist plays a major role in the experiment that he conducts. It has been observed that the same experiment when done in the same controlled environmental conditions produce different results when done by different scientists. They have clearly proven that a person's thoughts control his actions and the results of his actions.

Bliss attracts fortune. This is a great truth. When you are blissful, automatically, Existence showers on you. Material wealth comes to you. Be with a sense of gratitude always. The rest will happen automatically.

Simply decide not to feel miserable about anything. If any worry or guilt or sad incident comes to your mind, just look at it, smile and say, 'No, I am not going to be affected by you. What will you do?' Automatically the incident or guilt will not have any effect on you. By allowing it to attack you, are you going to gain anything? No. By looking at it and saying that you will not let it attack you, you are only avoiding misery. I am not saying to run away from the problem. I am asking you to look at the problem and decide consciously not to react to it.

If you try to suppress the thought, it will keep lurking at the back of your mind and threaten to come back at any time. So allow the thought to surface. But just look at it and say that it is powerless; you will see that it automatically dissolves.

Knowledge – the culprit

Anything that gives you strength through the body, mind or spirit is spirituality and will automatically take you towards bliss. Anything that weakens you is not spirituality and therefore, just don't pursue it. This is the thumb rule to be followed. Never forget that bliss is your true nature.

One more thing: anything beautiful that you see, experience it instead of just naming it with your knowledge. Have you seen the sunrise and sunset in the ashram or anywhere else? Have you ever stood and watched the beautiful transformation of colours across the sky? Most of us either don't know that the sun is setting or simply say, 'Yes, the sun is setting; so what; it sets everyday anyway!'

Knowledge can mar the innocence and make life dull. When you see the sunset or sunrise, it can be such a beautiful meditation. If you become a part of it, you will see that you are a speck of this tremendous Existence that is celebrating every moment. You will then participate spontaneously in the celebration!

But we are dulled by our so-called knowledge, which is nothing but again a collection of words. We have collected so many words and we think that these words are the ultimate, and therefore nothing surprises us. Even if God comes to us and says that he is God, we will ask, 'So what?' Everything is taken for granted because of knowledge.

The whole of Existence is taken for granted because of the so-called knowledge. We run behind worldly things that give only more and more greed, worry and fear. These things only disconnect us further from our inner core; they make us look outside instead of inside. They make us sway between depression and joy alternately, instead of being centered upon permanent bliss.

We feel that everything is happening outside and that we have to run to catch it before it is too late. That is why we are always in a hurry, always chattering inside ourselves.

Knowledge is simply data, facts, statistics; it is just dead. Collect knowledge, but don't let it control you in any way. Learn to keep it aside and look at life with awe. The mind always tries to conclude, summarize, judge, and collect information with whatever it sees. It wants to collect words and more words, that's all. Of what use is it?

I took a couple of devotees to Mathura, the birthplace of Lord Krishna. It was so beautiful. We went in the boat on the river Yamuna, reliving the days of Krishna. I was sharing my joy with the devotees - a pack of highly intellectual people. Here I was recalling the days of Krishna, showing them where *Ras Leela* happened, and I was filled with such ecstasy, and these devotees were telling me that the tiles in the place look as if they had been renovated! I was shocked. I told them that I should have brought a few people who had lesser knowledge and more awe left in them so I could share my joy with them!

Knowledge is dead at the end of the day. Somehow, people use knowledge to measure a person's worth. The more knowledge you have, the more you are respected.

With knowledge, you are constantly living with your mind. You can never know Existence with your mind.

Existence is beyond Logic

Spirituality is all about understanding the perfect harmony, the deep connection between man and Existence. When you understand this and drop your struggle, you will just flow like a river. The river will take its course and join the mighty ocean. You just need to let go, that's all.

I don't mean that you can sit in a corner and you will be swept along by some river. I am saying, just do your work with undaunted faith that there is a life force that is conducting this universe that is taking care of you also, that is making the breath in you to go in and out. That is enough.

Simply shift the responsibility to a higher authority and relax. You will then live like a king! You will then start listening to the synchronous music of the flowing river, of Existence taking you, of the harmony between you and Existence. This harmony is what you need to tune into. And then, all your worries will disappear!

Of course, there is no proof that Existence is taking care of us. Certain things cannot be proven. Can you prove that this direction is East? No! Can you prove the phenomena of sunrise and sunset? No! You can only experience it. Because you cannot prove it, can you disprove it? Can you prevent the sun through science from setting and rising everyday?

Understand that Existence is the only thing beyond logic. If you can prove Existence with logic, it means logic is greater than Existence, and this can never be!

One man asked me, 'Swamiji, should I become a Hindu to become spiritual?' I was shocked at the question! I told him that he did not have to become a Hindu. Be very clear: anything that curbs your field of perception is clearly not related to spirituality. Spirituality is always all encompassing.

Drop all your notions of 'I am this' and 'I am that'. Keep your life open. This is the basis for spirituality. It is like this: a person who stays continuously in a locked room will not know about the open air and breeze. He will be having such clannish thoughts. The moment you impose this kind of restriction upon yourself, you will not know about the infinite love and compassion that lies within you. You will only worry and complain. You will not blossom.

Buddha was once asked what kind of hell was given to people who were not compassionate. He replied, 'You cannot put them in hell because they are already in hell!' Only when you are in hell, you will create hell for others, because you can give only what you have.

A small story:

> A mother and a son were having a heated argument and she asked him, 'Do you have any brains?'
> The son laughed.
> The mother asked him why he was laughing.
> The boy replied, 'Only when you don't have something, you ask others for it!'

Real peace

We should work with our mind again and again to see what it is that gives us joy or bliss. Be very clear, happiness is different from bliss. Bliss is a beautiful and intense feeling inside you that makes you feel that you are on a different plane of existence. Happiness or pleasure are most often related to outer world objects and create pain continuously for us as well.

Happiness is relative while bliss is absolute. Bliss is something that has no opposite. When you are in happiness, sadness is just around the corner. When there is a lot of pleasure, you are on the anvil of pain. But when you are in bliss, you simply *are* and there is no opposite to it. Happiness and pleasure are like pendulums that are bound to sway and reach the other end before coming back.

But bliss is not a pendulum; it is beyond duality; it never sways. It just IS.

Again and again, scan your mind and see what it is that gives you joy. Then, start following it. Once something inside you tells you that you are moving towards permanent joy, once you find conviction in yourself, re-position and adjust the matters concerning your life, orienting them towards this bliss. Every action or thought of yours should be towards feeling this bliss. Energy spent will then be energy gained. You will be always energetic.

Some people say that they want to be left peaceful without worries. The peace they are talking about is not a living peace; it is a dead peace. It is a lifeless and dormant peace as a result of not knowing how to handle the richness of life. It is a peace that they crave because life is too much for them to handle. It is like saying 'sour grapes' and moving away.

Real peace is something that is in you all the time irrespective of what is going on outside; you are simply happy unto yourself; you look at anyone and anything like a passing breeze that kisses you and moves. Whatever may be the person or thing is in front of you, your peace remains with you. People or circumstances do not alter it in any fashion.

Peace is nothing but the bliss that is felt inside yourself. When peace is born out of bliss, it keeps you and others in a peaceful state. Once you have found this peace within yourself, you will never say things like, 'Leave me in peace, I want to be in peace,' etc. The moment you say these things, it means that you are trying to be peaceful at others' mercy, which is not peace at all.

Peace is a solid center that develops within you that keeps you happy unto yourself always. Anything that happens outside will be just another incident. You will not even relate it with your peace. The moment you relate an incident with your peace, be very clear; real peace has not happened in you.

Complaining - a byproduct of worry

In our yearly trip to the Himalayas, some of the participants complain about the hardships and unhygienic conditions. I have told people time and again that just *being* in the Himalayas is a blessing that not many people get and that they just have to enjoy that and leave the rest as trivia. Somehow, people get perturbed and talk about these things.

On one such occasion, two of the younger disciples were telling me, '*Swamiji*, these people are talking about the hardships here and they try not to bother about it, but we can't even see the hardships! We are just enjoying ourselves all the time!' This is what I mean when I say that when you are happy unto yourself, there is no such thing such as 'my peace' or 'your peace'. Whatever is, *Is*, that's all. You are there, it is there and nothing is related. You simply move on in the same state of peace and bliss.

Complaining is worry-related because you are uneasy and caught up with words. If you see the wandering mendicants in the Himalayas, with just a small water jug and two sets of clothing, you will know that you don't really need anything more than what you have and therefore there is nothing to complain about.

Why do you complain? Actually, the people who complain are the ones who have been blessed with too many things; they don't know what else to talk about and so they complain! When you have enough and don't have to fight for survival, you will have the time to complain. When your survival is at stake, you will concentrate on your work and not complain, because if you start complaining, who will do your work?

In the Himalayas, it is the survival of the fittest. You have to be alert and aware all the time. There will be landslides that may descend upon you at any time. Suddenly snow will fall and cover up the familiar trails; food and other rations will be suddenly restricted due to non-availability.

Under such circumstances, you should watch the people there. They are such innocent, welcoming and warm people with not a care or complaint. There is a lot to learn from them. They don't see anything amiss; they just live happily that's all. They just re-arrange their activities in accordance with what's happening around them. They don't worry and they don't complain.

Why don't you just carry on with whatever is available and keep moving? People who have been born and brought up in India, when they go to America and come back, complain about the conditions in India. Starting from the bathrooms to the roads, they complain about everything. It only shows that all your exposure has made you more finicky and complaining, instead of giving you vastness and making you blossom the way you should.

When you understand that you are showered not because you are worthy of it but because Existence simply showers on anyone and

149

anything, you will stop complaining. You complain because you feel you are worthy of something and have not been given that.

Be very clear: no one is worthy or unworthy; no one is a saint or sinner. It is all in the understanding and moving in tune with nature that makes you a receiver of Existence and its gifts. It is always a deep understanding that gives you a shift in consciousness.

If you are open, Existence showers. Existence is continuously showering, only we don't know how to receive it. We are so busy collecting words!

Learn to be with yourself

When you learn to be with yourself, you can commune with Existence. But we are never with ourselves. We are all the time with people, with noise. We identify ourselves with others, not with ourselves. We feel alone and scared if we are with ourselves.

You were alone in your mother's womb and that *is* your true nature. But what happened after that? You started thinking that you needed people to make you happy. You laughed with people, cried with them, talked to them, suffered because of them and what not. You don't know how to celebrate with just yourself.

The moment you find yourself alone, you start scrambling inside. Your inner chatter takes over, your worries take over and you start thinking of how to create noise or whom to call up and talk to or whom to chat with on your computer.

You are afraid of looking inwards and so you look outwards. When you become a meditator, you will slowly understand that you don't need to depend on relationships to make you happy. You are enough unto yourself. When you cannot be in peace with yourself, you will remain at the periphery of your being, caught in the so-called relationships.

You need to have a relationship with yourself first. When this is strong and steady, relating to others will become just incidental. Right now, what needs to be at the periphery is seen as the core and what should be the core is treated like the periphery. You have to reverse the situation, for which you have to turn your gaze inwards.

Go behind the mind... & beyond it

To have a relationship with yourself, you need to have the courage to go behind your mind. You are ready to give appointments to everyone but not to yourself. You give appointments to others because it is ego-fulfilling. You don't give an appointment to yourself because you are afraid that the truth might surface and you might not be able to take it. You are comfortable searching for bliss in the wrong places and complaining that it is eluding you. If you really want to find bliss, you will find it. But you need courage.

Actually, we are all searching for the same thing... that is bliss. But we are continuously searching for it in the wrong places. If I ask a youngster what it is that gives him happiness, he might readily say 'drugs'. He is also searching for bliss, for everlasting peace, but in the wrong direction!

We have moved so drastically away from our path, that our original thinking system has been completely replaced by negative thought patterns. Our life is drastically different from what it is supposed to be. By consuming drugs, can you find bliss? By consuming drugs, you are escaping from yourself and also, your health will be in trouble.

Taking drugs might sound obviously foolish to you because it is something drastic. It hits the morality scale and so it hits you. But your other subtle activities aimed at finding happiness, are also similar attempts but on a different scale, on a not-so immoral scale, so you don't think they are foolish. Whenever you get time, if you do housekeeping of your mind, you will know what I am trying to say.

Worry can cause you to make a lot of false assumptions. For example, when your son comes home late on just one day, you assume that he has probably been with some bad company and that is why he is late. This becomes a recording inside you. The next time, even if he comes home late after attending classes, this recording in you will surface and you will accuse him.

Your son will not only get frustrated but he might also resort to truly wayward ways simply to defy you. You need to understand that everyone is evolving and fluid and that it is not going to help if you are in your own frame of imagination.

It is easy to live with imagination. But I tell you: 98% of what you believe is wrong. You will realize that there is a big screen between yourself and the other person. If you wear spectacles tinted green, you will see the whole world as green.

Mohammed Nabi says, 'When you see the world as something, that something is *You*.' You complain to me about someone claiming that you are worried and so you are telling me these things, but actually you are clearly showing your own mind because you see things only as you want to see them, never as they are. When you see only what you want to see, you miss so much.

Let me tell you something that actually happened:

> A few years back, I used to travel everyday with the same driver from the ashram to the city center in Bangalore.
>
> One day, I wanted to go to a particular street and recalled the street to the driver by referring to a mosque that was near the street.
>
> He claimed that there was no mosque in that place.
>
> I tried recalling to him a famous hotel near the mosque, but that also he failed to acknowledge.
>
> I finally told him that there was a Hanuman temple in that place.
>
> His face immediately lit up with recognition.
>
> He then went to that street and I showed him the mosque that was right there next to the temple and five times as big!
>
> He was shocked.
>
> He was such a staunch Hindu that he had not even seen the mosque in all those months.

Don't be with a single frame of mind.

Just think of a river: when you put your leg in the river the first time and take it out and put it in the second time, is it the same river? No! The river has changed faces; the same water is not there anymore; fresh water has flowed, has it not?

So don't strive to identify yourself with anything; life is ever changing. Because of your narrow scope of beliefs, your spiritual growth gets curbed. You become like a horse that has only a limited angle view of the road ahead of it. A broad perspective is needed in life.

Our forefathers gave us a lot of food, but not the tongue to taste it. It is up to us to experience this world with joy. The joy is in the way you experience it, not in the outer world objects themselves. This has to be very clearly understood. Your mental set-up is what makes your life joyful or miserable.

When you have a clean mental set-up, you will never worry. Only when you are confused with complex thought patterns and words, you will be worried. I always tell people: when you are not sure of yourself, you will be worried about where the planets are! You will start analyzing which planet is centered where and how it is influencing you. The actual problem is *you* are not centered.

Work on your mind when you have time. Look in and house-keep it. After all, you are with your mind 24 hours of the day, are you not?

I have seen people who maintain their houses so beautifully. They use the vacuum cleaner and clean the carpet till it gets a hole in it! What about cleaning the house in which you are living 24 hours - your mind? You are with it 24 hours; every single thought or action of yours involves it.

You bring in *Vaastu Shastra, Feng Shui* etc. which are all sciences to keep the space inside your house in a pure and energized condition. But you fail to understand one thing: you need to continuously energize your home only because *you* are contaminating it with your negativity.

When you contaminate the space in your house with collective negative thoughts, with your worries, the space starts radiating the negative thoughts back to you. You get caught in a vicious circle of negativity the moment you enter your house.

How many times have you felt that you are perfectly alright until you entered your house? The moment you enter, you feel gripped by a force of familiar negative thought patterns. This is nothing but your own thoughts that you have managed to fill your house with. What do you then do? You call an expert in *Vaastu shastra* to change the layout of the house, or call a temple priest to perform some fire ritual and cleanse the house or you apply *Feng shui* ideas to your house.

When these things are done with sincerity, they will no doubt be useful. But you have to understand one thing: these are only supplementary methods. The actual thing is, to clean your own self and radiate a blissful mental set-up so that automatically, the space in which you live radiates that.

A man was asked what the difference was between his past and present.

He replied, 'Earlier I used to sit on the floor on a mat and eat. Now I sit at a table.'

You see, in the past and the present, his mouth is the same. If there is no radical change in you, your life will seem only this much different. Just as beauty lies in the eye of the beholder, taste lies in the tongue that experiences it. Your mental set-up defines the taste of your life.

Most often, we know that we need to change but somehow we fall back comfortably in the present set-up of ours. We get caught in the same wheel again. One side of us tells us that we need to change and the other side unconsciously slips into the familiar patterns again. Even if you are presented with many opportunities to change, you feel cozy in your present state and choose to remain there.

Help your children too

If you live with a solid mental set-up, there is a great danger in it: There is every possibility that your children will imbibe it from you.

I am reminded of a joke:

> A husband and wife were both pick-pockets by profession. They would often discuss that if they had a child, it would be very prosperous!
> Soon, they had a baby.
> The newborn baby however had its right hand closed very tightly. They could not get it to open it.
> The doctor attending to it tried all sorts of things and finally took out his gold chain and dangled it in front of the baby's eyes.

The baby slowly opened its hand and inside it was the midwife's gold ring!

This is only a joke, but understand that as parents, you have every possibility of passing on your mental set-up to your children. So be aware every moment and work on your consciousness; work on cleaning the inner chatter and framework inside you.

We always try to control children and make them into puppets. Children are wild energy. We try to box that energy so that it becomes convenient for us to handle.

A small story:

Two dogs were walking down the road.
The first one said, 'My name is Sandy. What is yours?'
The second one paused awhile and said, 'I think mine is No, No Roger.'

The dog's owner must have kept telling the dog, 'No, no Roger,' for everything that the dog did! The dog had started thinking that its name was *No, no Roger*! Just like this dog, children also start absorbing and learning from our words and body language. When children are very young, they refer to our words and actions subconsciously and take them to be the truth. So when you are with children, be even more aware, try to keep their intelligence alive instead of trying to blindly control them.

Mothers are continuously trying to do this. For example, if it rains, the mother will tell the children to get into the house because they might catch a cold. If she does this a few times, automatically the child will think of a cold when it sees rain. Even if it drizzles, the child will start sniffing.

Actually, man's body is the most intelligent, self-correcting, auto-immune system. But somehow, we trust our mind rather than the inherent intelligence of our body. There starts the problem and all our worries.

A small story:

> A father camel was explaining to the son camel the body structure of their species.
> He said, 'You know, we have humps in our body to store water for a few days when we are in the desert.'
> The son asked, 'Why are our eye lashes so long?'
> The father replied, 'To protect our eyes from sand storms.'
> The son then asked, 'Why do we have such bulbous feet?'
> The father replied, 'So that we can travel fast in the desert.'
> 'Dad,' asked the son, 'what are we then doing in this zoo?'

You see, our body has been designed so beautifully! If we just allow it to run on its natural intelligence, it will function well. The moment you impose conditionings on the body, you start experiencing difficulties.

In the Himalayas, the *sadhus*, wandering mendicants, live inside caves. They are the healthiest people ever. Come sun or rain or snow, they continue to live; their body adjusts itself to the

158

prevailing conditions. We just have to trust nature and our own immune system. But somehow, we keep imposing our worries and our mental make-up on our body. This is the root cause for all our diseases.

Be reborn with the master's presence!

A master is one who can give you a new mental set-up, a rebirth. He gives it just by his presence. If you are in the master's presence, it is enough. It will happen. When the master's energy floods you, your mental set-up changes, you are reborn. You enter into a space that you never even knew existed.

When you are reborn in this fashion, you will be free from the grips of all types of emotions. You will be able to handle them with such ease that you never knew before. You will become just an observer of everything that is happening around you.

I was watching the television the other day in a hotel where there was a meditation workshop. A particular Indian channel was showing a duet song from an old movie. Another Indian channel showed another duet song from a new movie. I was telling my secretary that these two channels only showed that there has been no real growth in human consciousness over the years.

The same patterns are repeated again and again like five people kicking a ball around in a closed room. Familiar patterns make our intelligence dead. Even our worries are nothing but familiar patterns stored in our minds, ready to impose themselves upon us again and again.

Be aware, become blissful!

When I tell people these things, they tell me, '*Swamiji*, I understand what you are saying but I am not able to overcome it.' I tell them, 'Just allow my words to penetrate you and create a new space in you; that is enough.' This is where meditation can help. What I do in my meditation camps is, I give you the intellectual understanding and then work on it penetrating you through meditation.

But people tell me, '*Swamiji*, we have our work to do, bills to pay, deadlines to meet; how do we then meditate?' I answer them with a simple meditation technique: Whether you have time to pay your bills or to meet your deadlines or not, you surely have time to breathe? Otherwise, you would not be alive! Now, you simply add awareness to your breathing, that's all. That is the meditation. Just watch your breath. That is the simplest and most powerful meditation you can do.

Every time you remember this technique, practice it. Soon, it will become a habit. When you infuse awareness into your breath, you will be in the present moment. Living in the present takes you to bliss. The power of NOW is the straight way to bliss. Simply add awareness to every inhalation and exhalation.

So to attain bliss, you don't need any separate time. You need not take time off and go to any retreat or meditation camp. You can continue with your daily activity. With the increased awareness that you will be creating, your deadlines and other targets will get done much more efficiently.

Meditation is nothing but a shift in your consciousness. It is an 'energy shift' in your being. It is not sitting in a corner, cross-legged and straight-backed, trying to control the mind. If you try doing this, you will only land up with neck pain and back pain! You will have one more worry that you are not able to sit and do meditation.

All you need to do is, try to live in the present, now and here. When you are in the present, you will move in tune with Existence. When you are in the present, Existence itself will teach you.

Existence is the greatest Master. This is what they mean when they say that life is a great teacher. When you miss it, you take your own sweet time to learn. You learn for lives together. When you take your own sweet time to learn, life gives some shocks so that you wake up and learn quicker!

Now, you are either running behind the past with regret or behind the future with anxiety. You completely destroy the present because of this pattern. What happens is, you never really act properly, you simply 'react' based on the regret of your past or anxiety of the future. When you react, you are not using your whole potential. You are simply behaving like a programmed robot; you function out of blind logic, not out of awareness or intelligence.

80% of your energy is locked in the past and future. Only 20% is available to you in the present. That is why you feel dull and sapped of your energy. With increased awareness, this situation can be turned around and your life can be lived on a higher plane, blissfully, joyfully, with excitement!

Q: So you are saying that simply by witnessing our breath, we can achieve bliss?

Yes. It is a very powerful technique. You see, when you watch your breath, your awareness is intense and no thought can escape you unconsciously. When every thought starts passing through your awareness, you will automatically not create negative thoughts for yourself.

You don't have to spend any time in correcting your thoughts; the awareness will do it for you. Your thinking system will automatically become restructured. The power of awareness is such that it transforms your thinking system to positive energy.

Integrate your thoughts, words and actions

Actually, we have been trained to think that only if we work and experience pain in some form, we are worthy of happiness. So we run until we get pain; we run until we hit the fence. We are so used to the concept of a fence that even if we are told that there is no fence, no boundary, we are not ready to believe it. We run and somehow hit a fence and feel pain; then we stop, satisfied in having felt pain. We always feel that we *have* to go through anxiety and worry in order to be worthy of being showered.

There are some other people who create worries for themselves and then drink to forget the worries! This is a very common thing today. It is something like this: a pig is not able to bear the smell of its own habitat and so plunges its nose inside it to escape from it. You think you have beaten all your worries by drinking, when in reality you have actually plunged headlong into more of it.

We want something but we work towards creating something contradictory to it..This is what I mean when I say you should integrate your thoughts, words and deeds, otherwise you will create contradictory results in your life.

A small story:

> An unwelcome visitor came to a man's house.
> The man screamed to his wife who was inside the kitchen to bring coffee for the visitor.
> The wife screamed back that there was no coffee in the house and that there was no money to buy it either.
> The husband got angry and started scolding his wife and finally gave her a slap for not being able to serve coffee.
> The wife started crying.
> The visitor saw what was happening and slowly got up and went away.
> The wife wiped her tears and triumphantly told the husband, 'Did you see that? I pretended to cry and sent him away!'
> The husband replied, 'Well! I pretended to be angry with you and made you cry!'
> The visitor joined them, 'I pretended to walk away and I have now come back!'

Our thoughts are different from our words, our words are different from our actions, so we invite contradictory things into our lives continuously! Ramakrishna Paramahamsa says, 'Uniting our thoughts and words is like doing penance.' But what do we do? We edit our thoughts and bring them out as words. There is so much calculation that goes on inside before the words come out. We see 'profit and loss' and go into the future to analyze before we start talking. Our personality never gets integrated because of this and we remain fragmented.

People ask me how I am able to talk for hours together without any preparation. You see, I talk the truth as it is, spontaneously, that's all. I am not worried about exposing the truth! I never edit my words. For me, thinking is talking. For you, first thinking happens; then editing is done on it and only then comes talking. The innocence is lost in the whole process and you are caught with so many words also.

You are able to listen for hours together to me only because I am talking spontaneously. Otherwise, you will get restless. The fact that you are here without being bothered about the time passing by is enough proof for what I am telling you.

When spontaneity happens, the flow happens and so it is interesting. Otherwise, you stagnate in a one-track mind.

A small story:

> A man was trying hard to sleep but could not, because his neighbor's dogs were barking persistently.
> This scene remained unchanged for a few nights.
> He finally decided to talk to the owner about it.
> He went to his house the next day and complained to him about it.

The neighbor was unmoved and said, 'Nothing I can do about it. What do you plan to do?'
The man replied, 'Well, tonight I will tie the dogs in my backyard and then you will know what it is!'

Just think what foolishness it is to do what the man suggested! He is again and again going into the matter with a one-track mind. How will he find a solution? When you are spontaneous, you will never be challenged for even a moment. You will come back with a solution instantly. When you are spontaneous, you will simply jump off any cliff and build your wings on the way down!

Q: What would you say is the root cause for so much worry and tension in our lives?

The fact that you are asking these words shows that you are ready for the solution.

You see, we are continuously having some imagination about everything – about the people around us, the places where we live, the situations that arise, and the lifestyle that we follow. We are continuously fantasizing or expecting things to happen in a particular fashion. But reality is always different from this imagination. The gap between reality and our imagination gives rise to tension in our lives.

We have created a virtual world inside us and are continuously looking to realize it in reality. There is a gap between our fantasy and reality. The more we have imagined, the more will be this gap and the more will be the tension.

We always think that we are getting to the point of realizing our imagination but when we get to it, we find our imagination has grown further and so we never really get to it. This creates disappointment, tension and worry in us.

The fact is, we are not even aware that we are working with imagination. Our imagination has become such a solid thing for us that we can't even see it as imagination. We are caught up in it. If working towards something is causing tension in you, then you are not working in reality; you are working in your zone of imagination.

Every moment, we are trying to fulfill our expectations in the world outside. The expectations could be to do with people, material comfort, name and fame, anything. If people don't react or respond in the way we imagined, our expectation suffers. From minor to major things, we are always looking for a match for our imagination. It is an unconscious process inside us. Because it is unconscious, we are not even aware that we are doing it, which is why we don't understand the cause for tension. The cause is so subtly woven into the whole thing that it cannot be made out.

If you bring your awareness acutely to this point and watch yourself for just a few hours, you will understand how your whole mind works. Just decide to be a watcher of your mind and the people around you. You will see how subtly your mind is continuously creating expectations in every small thing you see and do, and how reality sometimes matches and sometimes misses your expectations and how feelings of tension and worry arise within you when this happens.

Just by flooding awareness into this whole thing, you can see how your mind plays and creates tension for you. Once you learn to become the watcher, your worries will drop and you will also not internalize any of the outer world incidents. When you internalize outer world incidents, you create a larger database of words inside you, out of which new worries will arise.

When you plan chronologically and work towards realizing your chronological plan without loss of time, you are on the path of reality. If you find yourself worrying more than working and not getting anywhere, then you are on a path of psychological worrying. Then there is a gap between reality and yourself. It is time to look in and straighten your thoughts.

Thinking to plan chronologically is alright, but thinking about how you are going to execute your plan is not alright. It becomes psychological worrying and this is what creates tension and worry.

If it takes just 2 hours to plan for yourself, then the remaining 22 hours are available to you to execute the plan. Why then is the plan not getting executed? Because, you waste more than 80% of the remaining time on worrying about how you are going to execute the plan.

When you keep repeating the plan to yourself, you are in effect draining your own energy into it. Instead of using the energy to execute the plan, you simply waste it. How will the job get done?

One more thing: If you really want the job to be done, you will get down to doing it without worrying. Actually, tension and worry are mere excuses for running away from doing things. Under the pretext of worry and tension, you escape from responsibility.

Every problem is pregnant with the solution. If you really want to solve it, you will do it. All you need to do is look at the problem with deep awareness, and the solution will stand out. Only when you don't want to solve it, you will feel comfortable just talking about it. And you will feel great that you have so much to worry about!

The best way to shrug responsibility is to get into a state of worry and tension. Most often, people suffering from depression feel comfortable in that state because they don't have to take up any responsibility.

A small story:

> A man who was known to be a great healer visited a village.
> Very soon, a crowd gathered around him.
> He touched a man on his neck and the man who was suffering from chronic spondolosis became relieved of the pain instantly.
> He then touched another man on his head and the man's headache disappeared that very moment.
> He moved towards a man on crutches.
> But the man on crutches moved away and said, 'Don't touch me!'
> The healer was puzzled and asked why.
> The man said, 'I have just applied for my Disability Benefit Claim.'

We talk endlessly about our problems, but when we are offered a solution, suddenly we become too relieved! We have never thought beyond our problems, so we find there is a void when our problems disappear!

So drop all your imagination about your lifestyle, people etc and start living in the present moment and things will automatically happen. Remember: you can't live in this comfort zone for long. Some time or the other, reality will find you. So start living consciously, make conscious decisions and take up responsibility for every decision you make.

It is very easy to go by another's decision and blame them at the end of it. It is the most foolish and cowardly thing to do. Never blame anyone for anything. Remember, only when you are unable to handle something, you will allow to take the responsibility and also blame them for it.

Q: *Swamiji*, how should we be relaxed always?

When your consciousness is alert all the time, you will be relaxed all the time. Meditation is the key to achieving this state. At least at the intellectual level, understand this first. You will then start experiencing it for short intervals of time. These time periods will increase and become your permanent state.

I always tell people that to find out if a master is a true master, watch him when he is asleep. A real master will appear like a flower when he is asleep! He will be totally relaxed and beautiful to look at. He will radiate a child-like innocence when he is asleep. An ordinary man, on the other hand, will appear tensed and tight when he is asleep.

A master is always in a state of superconsciousness and he sleeps only to relax his body. When you are continuously in a state of heightened consciousness or awareness, you can never be tense. Only when you allow yourself to fall into unconsciousness, into a state of delusion, you will create tension for yourself. The only way to be relaxed always is to be aware all the time of every single thing happening inside and outside yourself.

Learn to relax with awareness. When you are with a master, if you allow yourself to relax, he will enter you; his state will penetrate you. If you are close and tense, he will not be able to enter you.

The word *Upanishad* itself means, 'Sitting at the feet of the master.' If you are able to sit at the feet of the master with an open and relaxed mind, his presence will enter you and work on you with all the compassion.

When you relax in a master's presence, you are actually settling down in your own body; you are settling down in your own individuality and you feeling relaxed in your own personality. Then there is no wedge inside yourself and you become integrated. So practice relaxing in the presence of the master.

Q: *Swamiji*, do you always feel blissful? Don't you ever feel the sway of emotions?

Yes! I am blissful always – 24x7 in your language! This is because plurality has disappeared from my being. When there is bliss, there cannot be plurality. Only when plurality disappears, bliss can happen.

In my being, there is no lust or fear, attachment or hatred or any of the opposing emotions. The only emotion is bliss! Unless it becomes an experiential understanding for you, it will be difficult for you to understand this. You might understand it at the intellectual level. As of now, understand that I am always blissful; that is enough!

The first step to bliss is to become a watcher. Simply watch life as if it were a drama. When you watch, your mind will become still. When it becomes still, you have caught the thread. When you experience that stillness at least once, you have caught the thread.

That thread will guide you into periods of longer stillness. The stillness is your inner master. The outer master helps to find your inner master. When you have found the stillness, you will understand that all emotions are a mere play of the mind.

Understand, you can never drop any emotion by consciously trying to drop it. The more you try to drop it the more you will fight with it. The emotion will haunt you. The only way is to watch your emotions. As you watch your emotions, the emotions will simply disappear.

Right now, you are so entangled with your emotions that you simply cannot see yourself as different from them. When you start watching, you will start creating a distance between you and your emotions. Slowly, the distance will increase and one day, the watcher will disappear from the scene.

Then, you need not put any effort to drop your emotions. They will simply drop on their own. You will no more be able to relate with them. They will disappear from your being. A shift in consciousness happens in you. You become a new person.

When you become a watcher, there will be no room for worries or pain. There will be only a beautiful energy within you what is called love. You will then understand the love of Existence, the infinite love that envelops you every minute.

A small story:

> A man was known to have a very weak heart.
> His family was always careful in telling him any drastic news.
> One day, they came to know that his wealthy uncle had died leaving one million dollars to him.
> They were very excited and at the same time did not know how to break this news to him. They were afraid that he might collapse hearing it.
> One of them suggested, 'I think we'd better call the family doctor and tell him to handle this.'
> They all agreed.
> They called up the family doctor and told him the matter.
> The doctor said, 'Don't worry, I will handle it. It is not so hard as you think.'
> He soon arrived at their house and went into the room and started talking to the man. He casually asked him, 'If you were suddenly told that you were given one million dollars in cash, what would you do?'
> The man replied, 'I would give half of it to you, doctor.'
> The doctor collapsed and died.

We are ready to see life as a drama when it comes to others but when it comes to us, it becomes hard to digest! We are always ready to give advice to others. I read in a book that advice is something which everyone loves to give but no one is ready to take!

You can watch your own life also like a witness. You can be like a lotus – untouched by the water although deep inside it. Then you have learned to play the game of life. Understand one thing: Existence is trying to express itself continuously in many ways. Our role is to understand and flow with it with deep awareness.

Understand that the whole of creation is flowing in accordance with Existence. Then you will automatically drop your worries and anxieties. You have to reach a stage where your core is untouched by what is happening around you. This will happen if you understand that Existence is continuously changing.

Outwardly, you may express different emotions, but in your innermost core, you must be able to continuously see that all the incidents outside are like beads that are strung on the common thread of Existence. The thread is what holds them together.

Q: But we don't intentionally worry. How do you then say that we bring worries upon ourselves?

Worry has become the unconscious state of your mind. You don't have to put any intention into it. It simply happens, that's all! You don't have to make a conscious effort; it is there in you all the time.

A small story:

> A woman called up the reception desk of a hotel and screamed for help.
>
> The receptionist came to her room.
>
> The lady screamed at her, 'I can see a naked man, across the way in the window of the other room.'
>
> The receptionist looked through the window and saw a man standing with his upper body bare.
>
> She said, 'Ma'am, only his upper body is bare. How can you conclude that he is naked?'
>
> The lady screamed, 'Get on top of the wardrobe and see!'

Even if everything is alright, we search with a torchlight for worries! We don't do this intentionally at all. We do it in the most natural fashion ever - that is the problem! Our state of mind has to undergo a 180 degree change.

Another small story:

> A policeman was going on his night rounds when he saw a cow dead in the middle of a lane.
>
> He started dragging the animal towards the adjacent street.
>
> A passerby asked him why he was dragging the dead animal all that way.
>
> The policeman replied, 'When I report this tomorrow, it will be easier because I know the name of that street.'

Because we don't know how to be spontaneous, we are worried all the time! We complicate things in our lives in order to fit them into our framework. We don't live in a fluid way. When you live in a fluid way, you don't have to work unnecessarily. You can simply enjoy and move on.

For example, if I now tell you that you should be blissful always, you will start worrying about how to be blissful! You know to start anything only with worry; that is the problem. That is why most of the time when you ask me something, I never tell you anything directly or in many words. I simply tell you a few abstract statements so that your mind cannot be put into any track of worrying but at the same time I give you the energy to understand and implement it.

Q: Then how do we start following what you are saying if we don't start worrying about it?

Just absorb the energy and inspiration behind my words and start living in the present, that's all. When you allow logic to come in, the trouble starts.

Just feel the energy behind my words, what I call the silence, the silence with which I am trying to enter you all the time. This silence will ultimately take you where it has to take you. Never try to get into the real meaning of my words. I have my own dictionary, while you have yours! It will not match. Just absorb the energy. Energy is intelligence. It will guide you.

Never collect words. Only intellectual nuts collect words and more words. They collect words and get more and more confused.

175

They collect words thinking that they will get clarity at some point in time, but it never happens.

Whatever I say, even if it seems contradictory, it is the complete truth for the moment that it is spoken. Whatever I say is the complete truth for that moment that I am speaking it. But you cannot infer from my words alone. So for that moment, simply take them in with a mood to experiment. That will give you the energy and intelligence to follow through.

So don't listen with your intellect. Listen with deep meditation. Whatever may be your emotion or path at that point in time, just go deeply into it and listen to me. That is enough. You will automatically be filled with energy and clarity. These are all the basic secrets that I am giving you.

When you cling to my words, you will be worried that you might forget them. You will start jotting them down. I tell you, the moment you start jotting things down, you miss the whole thing. You will neither have absorbed the energy behind the words nor would you have completely taken down the words. You will go home with scribbled notes and a few days later, even that will be lying in some corner of the house. Sometime later, even if you find them, you will not be able to make anything out of them.

It is something like this: Let us say you read a book and retained only the last two pages of it in your hand. With just those two pages, would you be able to re-compile the whole book? No! In the same way, don't try to jot down a few of my words and try to recollect the whole thing. Just be present completely when I am talking. That is enough.

These words will penetrate you and do the work if you give your whole presence here. So listen with your being, not with your mind. Don't bother about forgetting these words. When you understand something and transform, you will never forget it. If you have forgotten, it means that you have not understood!

Not just my words; don't cling on to *anything*. Every moment is going past; then what is there to cling to? Clinging will bring misery upon misery. There is no point in thinking about the future also. It is yet to come. What are you thinking about? The future will also come in the form of the present only. So focus on the present.

When you are in the present, you don't choose at all. Worry basically arises because you are in the past or future and choosing all the time. When you decide not to choose at all and just totally accept and drink in the whole experience, there will be no worry.

People ask me, '*Swamiji*, I am afraid when I think that the world might suddenly come to an end.'

So what if the world comes to an end? If the world comes to an end, everyone is going to be ending along with it. There will be no one and nothing remaining for anyone to be worried about! You were earlier worried only because there was something in the world to worry about. If the world itself is coming to an end, then there should be nothing to be worried about. But you worry about that also!

See how self-contradictory the mind is? It worries if there is something to worry about and it worries if there is nothing to worry about also. But it wants to be free of worry all the time!

Actually, all of your emotions are nothing but the play of the unconscious in you. When you live with total awareness, you can never be under the sway of emotions. That is why again and again I tell you to flood yourself with awareness.

You see, your worries, your words, really make or break your life. They have got that much power - to influence you and others. For example, when I utter the word 'cow', immediately what happens? A figure with 4 legs, 2 horns and 1 tail appears in your mind. A simple 3-letter word can bring to your mind a whole image! Words are that powerful. When we don't respect words and use them wrongly, we are asking for trouble.

A small story:

> Birbal, an enlightened master, and Akbar, his king, were walking together on the streets.
> They saw a sandalwood dealer and Akbar said to Birbal, 'I don't know why but I feel like hanging this man.'
> A month later, they walked past the same sandalwood dealer and Akbar this time said, 'It's strange but I feel like giving this man some endowment now!'
> Birbal replied after a long pause, 'A month back, the sandalwood dealer's business was suffering and when he saw you walking past, he thought to himself that if you die, the courtiers would come to buy a lot of sandalwood from him for your funeral pyre. He sent out these negative vibrations, which prompted you to feel hatred towards him. I immediately purchased a lot of sandalwood from him to make tables and chairs for our kingdom. Today, he feels

very grateful towards you and you have been struck by these positive vibrations from him and therefore you feel like giving him some endowment!'

Understand that your thoughts have a lot of power in themselves. It is therefore very important that you have positive thoughts and a worry-free mental set-up.

Q: There are books that say 'don't sweat for small stuff'. But small things do matter, do they not?

When you function with intelligence, you will not fall into the category of sweating for small stuff.

A small story:

> A young man went to visit his friend.
> He found him scraping the wallpaper off the wall.
> He asked him, 'Are you repainting?'
> The friend replied, 'I am moving house.'

You see, you cannot ignore the small things. But you should be intelligent enough to pay only the amount of attention it warrants, or else you will start to sweat. Never listen to people when they say not to pay attention to small things. Remember that small holes can sink a great ship. Just operate with your intelligence and awareness and you will know which the real small stuff is.

If you are convinced without self-contradiction that you need to do those small things, automatically you will find the energy to do them. When you are not fully convinced, you will not have enough conviction and energy to go behind them. Your intelligence will not be fully backing you, because intelligence is energy and energy is intelligence.

If you are sweating about the small stuff, then there is something wrong somewhere. Be very clear that all miseries arise because of self-contradictions. You yourself are not fully clear about what you want to do and so you are unable to do it. For that clarity to happen, you need to nurture your own intelligence.

When intelligence happens, self-contradictions disappear and you start becoming integrated. When you start becoming integrated, your intelligence grows more. This is the cycle you need to get into. This is the cycle that can clear your worries also.

If you are really interested in dropping your inner chatter and worries, you could try a small exercise. Think of all the things that give you joy. Make up your mind that you will allow your mind to linger on only these things and nothing else. Anything else, you will give just enough energy to get it done and then forget about it. Try this exercise and you will see that you conserve a lot of energy.

Understand that you have given a lot of power to your worries by simply talking about them more and more. For example, when a housewife picks up the telephone, she will start by telling her friend that the house maid did not turn up for the day. That is her depression for the day. If you are really depressed about the maid not coming and you are really interested in coming out of it, then you should simply finish doing the work yourself! Doesn't this sound more logical?

But what do you do? You keep on talking about it and expecting your friend to feed your depression as well. If she doesn't sympathize with you or if she tells you that is how life is and you have to move on, you will make a call to another friend and tell that friend about how inconsiderate this friend was! Just think, if you really wanted to move on with your life, you would appreciate the words of the friend, would you not?

But why are you reacting differently? The reason is, you are so comfortable just talking about your worries and not finding a way out of them.

If you start doing this small exercise, you will see that all your worries simply disappear and you acquire a new mental set-up altogether. You will find a surge of energy within you because all the energy that you previously spent on harboring your worries is suddenly available to you!

Do an honest check for yourself and find out if you are secretly nurturing your worries or whether you are ready to take on the transformation.

When you stop going behind your worries, you will be able to see how others are helplessly caught up in that cycle. You will be able to see how they magnify their worries by endlessly talking about them to people. This talking about worry is what I call 'worrying about the worry'! Only when you are able to watch this, will it stop. Until such time as you become the watcher, you are caught up in the emotions, giving so much of power and control to them.

I am not asking you to run away from your worries. I am saying, don't magnify them by talking about them. Don't expend your energy on them. Instead, address them for what needs to be done so that they stop worrying you. Address them without loss of time, that's all.

Check yourself to find out if you are starting to feel comfortable with your worries. This is the scale to see if worries are controlling you or you are controlling your worries. If you are feeling comfortable talking about them repeatedly without taking any action, then worries are controlling you. If you don't linger on them and address them correctly, then you are controlling them!

Q: *Swamiji*, earlier you mentioned about drinking. My husband drinks ever so often claiming that he drinks to forget his worries. What do I do?

As I told you, this is a common problem and if your husband were here, it would have been helpful. If you analyze the habit of drinking, you will understand how self-contradictory you are in this habit. Let me try to explain:

You drink to feel joyful, but you end up becoming miserably miserable.

You drink so that you can be called sociable, so that society will accept you, but you land up becoming argumentative!

You drink so that you will look sophisticated but you end up looking insufferable.

You drink so that you can sleep forgetting all your worries but you wake up feeling more exhausted than ever!

You drink to experience ecstasy and end up feeling depressed!

You drink to feel confident but end up becoming afraid of yourself.

You drink to maintain the conversation but end up becoming incoherent.

You drink to see your problems dissolve but end up seeing them multiply!

This is the truth and you know it better than I do! Now tell me honestly, is it really worth drinking? This is how self-contradictory you are in not only this matter but in all matters in life. If you clearly knew what you wanted to do and spent every ounce of your energy in that direction, you would grow steadily and experience joy. You would then never be self-contradictory.

Every time you drink, drink with complete awareness. Every time you drink, drink consciously, slowly, watching every movement of yours, tasting every drop of the drink, and watching the reaction of your body to it. Make it a process filled with acute awareness. I assure you, if you do this every time you decide to drink, you do not have to drop the habit, the habit will drop you forever.

Addiction to anything is an unconscious or mechanical process. It is not just addiction to drinks or tobacco. It is addiction to even religion. People who pray unconsciously and mechanically, following a routine, will find it very hard if they miss even one day's prayer. For them, it is an addiction and so it causes anxiety when missed. In the same way as an alcoholic who misses his evening drink starts trembling in insecurity, the mechanically religious person will feel a big void if he misses his routine prayer.

The key is to understand the difference between doing things with awareness and doing things mechanically, out of fear. Doing things in the former fashion will never bring you under any sort of binding. It will not bind you in space and time. You will be a master. Doing things in the latter way will bind you and cause misery to you. You will be a slave.

To drop an addiction, flood it with awareness. It will transform in the right way. Never think that you need to drop an addiction. Anything that you resist will persist. You simply need to transform it through deep awareness. When you understand the language of transformation, you are on the right track; you are on the path of openness.

What I say is most practical!

People tell me, '*Swamiji*, it is very inspiring to listen to you talking. Now we have to apply it in our day-to-day life and see if it will work.'

I always say only practical things. Never think that I say things that can't be done in day-to-day life.

If I am a person who is sitting in the forest and telling you these things, then you are free to think that I am saying impractical things. But here I am running a worldwide movement for transformation! Actually, all I am doing is repeating the same *vedanta* – ancient scriptural texts - but in different words, in the modern context, so that you feel comfortable listening to it; so that you feel that it is relevant to you and you follow it. If you read these ideas in a book, they will simply be moving from the head of the writer to your own head. There is no scope for any experience. But when you listen to these words from an enlightened being, from someone who comes from the experience of the soul, they will enter deeply into you and give you the desired result.

I am not sharing my knowledge with you. I am sharing my experience, my life, with you. When I speak from my being, it *has to* touch your being. It *will* transform your life. There is no other way.

Vivekananda spoke in Chicago in the World Parliament of Religions for the first time, 'My dear American brothers and sisters...' It is recorded that the auditorium thundered with applause! A lady wrote, 'It was not just the applause. He had won an entire nation. We felt as if a current of love was passing through us, through our being...!' She later asked Vivekananda how it happened and he simply replied, 'Because it came from within me.'

Vivekananda spoke from his being. When words emanate from the brain, it will touch the brain of the other person and this is called 'communication'. When words emanate from the heart, they touch the heart of the other person and this is called 'communion'. Communication is not enough. We need to know how to commune. I talk from the bottom of my heart, so that you will listen whole-heartedly.

When the speaker speaks with totality, the listener is bound to listen with totality. His life is bound to be transformed. If your life has not been touched by my words, I have no authority to speak. You are free to doubt the truth of my experience. If you feel that my words have not been able to transform your life, there is no need to hide your feelings. Come out with it. But there is no possibility that you will not be touched!

If you listen with your heart, you will see these words working out in your life automatically, when the time comes. Only a teacher who is unsure of himself needs to urge his disciples to go back and practice his words. When a master speaks, simply listening will do. Listen totally and the transformation will happen.

The Chandogya Upanishad describes this beautifully. The master tells the disciple: *tat tvam asi* - you are That. Just by listening, the disciple actually attains the spiritual experience! When both the master and disciple act with totality, this is possible.

When you are around a master, words are totally irrelevant. Just being around a master in silence and absorbing him is what brings about actual transformation in you. But what to do? You are so caught up with your inner chatter. So I use words to silence you. Because if I don't talk, you will talk continuously inside yourself, dissecting and analyzing the past, worrying about the future, concluding, judging and what not. If I talk, you will be intently absorbed in my words for fear of losing track of me and I can use that time to enter you!

When a master talks, he is actually silent within himself. But in others, even if they are silent, they will be talking inside themselves! The inner chatter will be there. That is the difference. Just observe what is going on inside you when you are silent. Your silence invariably is just inaudible scrambling. Inside you, you jump like a monkey from one subject to another without any correlation.

Now let us enter into a meditation technique called the *Manipuraka Shuddhi Kriya* that will cleanse the *manipuraka chakra*.

Emotion: Worry

Chakra: Manipuraka chakra

Location: Navel region

In Sanskrit, *manipuraka* means 'The City of Jewels'.

This *chakra* is locked when you constantly worry and it flowers when you stop worrying about your worries!

Meditation Technique to expel worries:
Manipuraka Shuddhi Kriya – a technique from *Christianity*.

The Manipuraka Shuddhi Kriya

(Total duration: 30 minutes. To be done on an empty stomach.)

The *Manipuraka Shuddhi Kriya* is a meditation technique taken from ancient Christianity. Known as *glossolalia*, the technique was further adapted by the Sufis as 'gibberish'. This technique will empty you of your deeply engraved negative mental patterns and worries. It will clear all your suppressed emotions of anger and worry. Once you do this technique, you will feel very light in the *manipuraka chakra*, the energy center located in the navel area, the area of your worries and complex mental patterns.

This technique **should be done on an empty stomach,** or at least 2 hours after a major meal.

Stand with your eyes closed. Go deeply into your navel region and feel how heavy the area feels. It holds all your worries. Focus on your this region for a minute. Just try to feel all the pent up anger and worry inside you due to various reasons.

Now, just start making nonsensical sounds from the navel area, as loudly as you can. Do not use words to shout. If you use words, only familiar and recent emotions will surface and also words will give rise to only more words without actually working on the emotions behind them. Shout absolute gibberish; only this will open out the unconscious in you; only this will open out the deeply hidden emotions. Wave your hands, shout, scream; if tears flow, let them flow.

Do it with all your might, to vomit out all your negative feelings. Recall the painful incidents. Visualise the persons involved and feel the emotions involved in those incidents. Bring out all the emotions. Become completely immersed in them. Be aware of nothing else.

At the end of twenty minutes, stop. With your eyes closed, sit down in silence for the next 10 minutes. Just be a witness to your thoughts. Feel the lightness in your navel region. You will find that it is light and blissful. Your whole being will be very light and free.

Slowly, very slowly, open your eyes.

Chapter 5

Transform lust to divine love

undamentals of lust

The most talked about, thought about and written about subject is sex. The most misunderstood, misinterpreted and confusing subject is also sex! We either try to avoid the subject, or we try to indulge in it. Sex is deeply buried in our unconscious minds. Right from the start, we rarely find someone who can enlighten us on the subject of sex.

Sex, more than any other subject, needs to be illumined with the light of consciousness!

Our condition right now is like that of a man walking in a forest on a pitch-dark night.

Somewhere there is a big pit that has been dug and kept.

The man who tries to avoid the subject is in total unawareness; he doesn't even know where the pit lies – then how can he avoid it?

The man who indulges in the subject is aware of the pit, but can't see any other way than to jump straight into it.

Can either of these be the solution?

One should know where the pit lies, and then take the right steps to move around it.

The topic of sex is always swept under the carpet. It is a taboo topic. Parents do not come out and discuss it with children. First of all, the parents themselves don't know the underlying facts of the subject! On any subject, you need to ask an authority, otherwise you will miss the right understanding and when you miss the right understanding, you mis-understand.

A small story:

> A lady received a letter from her son's schoolteacher.
> The teacher had written that the boy was unable to see the board clearly and therefore made mistakes while writing.
> The lady promptly took her son to the eye doctor.
> The doctor examined the boy and wrote out the prescription.
> It read, *'hair cut'!*

We laugh at this, but I tell you, in life, if you go to the right person in the first go, you will get the right solution; or else you will go around in circles advocated by so-called authorities and you will waste your life.

Still worse, you will be advocating these patterns to future generations also. This is how convention sets in. When you allow convention to set in, it becomes a Herculean task to break free from it because convention becomes the truth over the years.

When the master appears, his first job becomes to undo all that has been done to you. Only then he can start showing you what you really are. It is a tough job for him because you have advanced so much in your own track that you wonder how you could be on the wrong track!

Let us come back to the subject, 'What is sex?'

Sex is a tremendous creative energy. It is a meditative energy. The whole world has arisen out of sex energy.

Our ancient enlightened masters, the *rishis*, have given us great clarity on this subject. Do you know that Vatsyayana, the man who wrote the Kama Sutra, the book on the science of sex – was a *sannyasi*? He was a celibate!

In fact, he delivered the Kama Sutra to his own mother.

After his enlightenment, he came back to visit his mother one day.

She told him that since he was enlightened, then he should have insight into any subject on planet earth.

He agreed and asked what she might like to hear from him.

She told him, 'As your mother, I know that you have been celibate since birth. There is no chance that you would know anything from experience about the subject of sex. But, can you tell me something about it?'

Vatsyayana smiled and delivered the Kama Sutra – the science of sex!

Vatsyayana was questioned once, 'What authority do you have to speak on this subject?'

A natural question! I think many of you might be silently putting this question to me also!

The answer that Vatsyayana gave, I am translating into modern language for you, using a modern analogy.

194

An electrician who visits your home knows exactly what happens when each electric switch in the house is put on or off.

He knows the entire circuitry hidden beneath the wall.

If there is a problem, he can determine the exact cause and give a solution for it.

He understands the science of electricity.

On the other hand, you, who puts these switches on and off fifty times a day, have absolutely no idea about what is actually going on behind the walls! Am I right?

Many of us know nothing more than how to put on and off the switches. That's why we sometimes get an electric shock! So, understand that although we may be fathers, mothers or grandparents – we may know nothing about sex.

We are all under continuous hormonal torture. The television and other forms of media show lust in various forms and we watch this and think we know all about sex and love.

Only an enlightened person, can give you the science of sex.

India, over the years, has been looted of vast wealth and land. None of these were great losses to India and after every invasion, India came back and the society stood up. Finally, our Gurukul system, the olden days' system of learning at the feet of the master, was destroyed by the British and Kama Sutra - the science of sex was no longer taught to children. This was the greatest blow to India. This is when people stopped understanding the meaning of sex and started getting consumed by lust or *kama*.

Have you ever watched two people playing a game of chess? When you simply watch the game, very often, the right move will suggest itself to you – but somehow it never occurs to the two players! How many of you have observed this? What do you think could be the reason?

Because we are not involved in the game Swamiji?

Yes! Actually, the man who is witnessing is not under pressure to win. Pressure and stress make the mind dull. So, only the man who has come out of the game, who is a mere watcher, can give you the right idea about it. A master is one who knows the Whole. That is why he becomes the authority on any subject.

So what is sex?

Today, biology has proved that no man is 100% man, and no woman is 100% woman. A man is 51% man and 49% woman. Likewise, a woman is 51% woman, and 49% man; just a difference of 1%.

You have taken birth from the *muladhara* (sex energy center) of your father and the *muladhara* of your mother. Then, how can you be only male or only female? The qualities of both are bound to be there in you!

This is the basis behind the symbolic representation of Lord Shiva as *Ardhanareeshwar*, the figure that is half male and half female. Whether we accept it or not, we are an embodiment of both male and female energies. We are whole, not divided.

Tantra deals beautifully with the whole concept of sex. In the scriptures, Lord Shiva speaks to Devi Parvati on this subject. Those insights recorded several thousands of years ago are found to be relevant in biology today.

In order to be complete, to be whole, it is essential that we are able to accept and express both the masculine and feminine aspects of our nature.

But does it really happen? Are we allowed to express both aspects?

Right from the moment of birth, society labels you as either male or female. And it expects you to start behaving accordingly. Society does not allow boys to express their feminine side, nor girls to express their masculine side. Right from a very young age, one half of our being is suppressed.

Until the age of seven, before the social conditioning has taken a deep root inside, the child is not conscious of being male or female. That is why a very young child has a sense of completeness. He is centered and secure. He is so beautiful and joyful to look at! By around seven, the child comes under society's control.

A male child is not encouraged to play with dolls and kitchen sets. A female child is not encouraged to play with race cars and rockets. Even when it comes to colours of their clothes and other belongings, there is discrimination. You choose blue for boys and pink for girls, is it not?

In earlier days, the parents left the child in the *gurukul*, a residential school headed by *vedic* age masters. In the *gurukul*, the children were taught the Gayatri Mantra – an initiation chant to kindle the intelligence at the age of 7. If by 14 they had a spiritual experience of some kind, they were taught the Brahmasutra – the greatest book on world philosophies, or else they were taught the Kama Sutra – the science of sex, so that they learned the art of family life. If before the age of 21 they were enlightened, they were initiated into *sannyas*. If not, they were taught the *yoga sastras*. This is how a child was allowed to evolve in his own way under the guidance and love of the master.

But now, such strong conditioning goes into the child, which is so damaging for him. The child begins to suppress that part of himself which is not approved by society. We don't realize it, but this period is traumatic for the child. He suddenly feels uprooted, cut off from one half of his being. He starts searching for this suppressed half outside.

Man's inherent nature is fulfillment. He came from fulfillment and looks to attain it as well. So as a child, he begins to search for the lost half, the suppressed half, unconsciously. He starts looking at the outside world for a substitute for his own lost half. The male child starts searching for a female presence and the female child for a male presence.

This is where the whole idea of sex starts. This is how the idea of sex takes root.

In the period from 7 to 14 years, the child is closest to his parents. From the parents, the child collects images about how the

198

ideal woman or ideal man should be. For the male child, the suppressed half of his own personality is replaced with his mother's image and for a girl child, the suppressed half of her personality is replaced with her father's image.

That is why every boy's first heroine is his mother, and every girl's first hero is her father. This deep-rooted search is what is behind the Oedipus and Ophelia complexes of Freudian psychology. A boy expects care from his wife like the care he received from his mother and a girl expects the security and assurance from her husband that she enjoyed with her father.

In broken homes, where the child has been deprived of the mother's or father's presence due to death or divorce, the child carries a sense of incompleteness. Even long after you are an adult, no matter how many differences of opinion you have with your mother or father, you can never remove their imprint from your being. So when the proximity to parents is not there at that age, the child develops a void.

At fourteen, the child attains physical maturity. Naturally, social laws don't allow him to have the same intimacy as earlier with the parent of the opposite sex and also, their activities become diversified and they don't spend as much time with their parents.

So at 14, the search continues, but this time in the outer world. These days it is happening much earlier than 14. Children are exposed to the television and internet from a very young age. That's why they also grow up faster mentally. At about 14 years of age, the search begins in the outside world.

The child now begins to collect images from outsiders and media. The media is perfectly aware of this. That is why you will see that all advertisements always have sexual undertones.

Almost all motorbike ads show women although very few women ride motorbikes. Whatever the product may be, you will find a smiling woman recommending it. When you go to the market, you promptly pick up that product, forgetting that the woman does not come with it! That is the media's way of cashing in on your suppressed desires.

The matching game

All forms of media are nothing but dream sellers. We collect the dreams that they sell and keep running over them in our minds hoping to quench our thirst. Is it possible? Can your thirst for water be quenched by consuming salt? No! If you do this, your thirst will only increase.

If you are alert and aware, advertisement hoardings can never fool you. Of course, by seeing them, you can always be aware of the latest things in the market, no doubt, but they will not deceive you.

You will not be vulnerable to them. You will be able to see them objectively and leave it at that. You will not feel an instant and unconscious pull towards them. It is only when you allow your 'reactive' mind to be your deciding authority that you are in trouble. You need to replace the reactive mind with your intelligence so that you are with awareness all the time. This is where meditation helps a lot.

While on one side, the media feeds your imagination, on the other, society tries to suppress you. The more society tries to suppress your imagination and desires, the more your imagination grows, because society does not address the root cause of it. When you just cut off the branches of a tree and leave its roots as they are, what happens? The tree grows in a more flourishing manner.

During these years, from 14 years of age, we collect ideas from all sorts of media and build up an image of the perfect woman or man. From each person, we collect the best nose, the best eyes, the best personality, and create our own 'ideal person'. We follow a cut and paste method! In your computers, you cut and paste all the time.

This stage lasts for around 7 years, until we are 20 or 21. By then identification with the media wears off – but the ideas are already deep-rooted in our minds. Then a fresh search begins – to find that ideal person in our real life. This is the search with the idea of how our 'would-be' 'should-be'. This is where the expectations start.

For the next 7 years, this search continues. Person after person we try out, and get disappointed. A few intelligent people figure out after a while that dreams cannot become reality. Only because dreams cannot become a reality, they are called dreams! But most people keep searching.

A small story:

> A 90-year old man used to sit every day at the beach from morning to evening, watching the people going by.

Another man who noticed this went up to him and asked him, 'What do you actually do sitting here everyday?'

The old man replied, 'I am searching for a woman to be my wife.'

The man was simply shocked at this reply and asked him, 'Why did you not search in your youth?'

The old man replied, 'I have been searching since I was 30 years old.'

The man was astonished and asked him, 'What sort of a woman are you searching for?'

He replied, 'I am searching for a perfect woman.'

'And you haven't found one?' the man asked.

'I found one woman who matched what I had in mind but it didn't work out well with her,' replied the old man.

The man asked why.

The old man replied, 'She was searching for a perfect man!'

This is what happens when we try to get a perfect match for the image that we carry inside us.

But after a long search, we suddenly find a person who seems to match our mental image – from a distance. The picture in our mind is green – and the person, the image that we see also seems to be green – and then, all is green! A match seems to be found!

What happens at this point is what is called 'falling in love'. This is the science behind falling in love. Note that it is always 'falling' in love, never 'rising' in love! Because what actually happens is, because of our own strong needs and expectations, we see things as we want to see them. We project our mental image upon the other.

So anyway, the world becomes filled with greenery and music and life becomes poetry. At last, our search is over! This is the stage at which we begin to write poetry, make paintings and what not.

As long as this distance is maintained, things go on smoothly. We continue to project our imagination upon the other. But slowly, the person comes closer and then we feel that what we saw as green was not so green but only a pale green. But it seems alright and we move on. After a while, we come still closer and feel that it is not even pale green but actually a shade of yellow.

But at this stage, we don't want to accept that our imagination has turned out to be a lie, so we start making excuses for the situation. We say to ourselves, 'This is life! Everything can't be perfect!' and so on. It requires tremendous courage, tremendous intelligence to live with reality. So we use these excuses instead, as a buffer system.

Finally, when we get close enough we find that it is not even yellow; it is just white! What is inside us is green and what is outside is white. Fantasy and reality are totally different.

A small story:

> A man fell down from the third floor of the building onto the road.

A passerby ran up to him and asked, 'The falling must have hurt you.'

The man replied, 'No. The falling did not hurt me; only the *sudden stopping* hurt me!'

As long as we float and flirt in love, as long as we keep our distances and time short, we are fine; we are in a fantasy world; we are not at the functional level. It is only when the floating stops and the real relationship starts, when the distances reduce and the togetherness time increases, the problem starts!

The more fantasies you collect, the more your falling time is before you hit the ground, and so more the damage. The fewer fantasies you collect, the fewer the number of things there are to compare with and lesser the trouble. If you don't have any fantasy or imagination, you will immediately meet your soul mate. If you don't have fantasies, anyone you marry will become your soul mate.

We need to understand that no living person can live up to the image we carry in our minds simply because the image is not built from reality. The image is a cut and paste from various quarters of our dream world! Reality cannot be matched with it because at the end of the day, it is only an image, a fantasy!

It is alright if you collect your images from real life characters, from the people you see around you. But you collect from media.

The media itself is suffering from lust! How then can it provide any sort of guidance or relief to you?

That is why, all the so-called love most often ends in pain. We end up feeling cheated or exploited by the other. Our basic instinct is to blame the other for what has happened.

But is it the other's fault?

No! Because we expected something, and we tried to force our imagination upon the other, the problem staretd.

You see, there are some cases where one person starts behaving in an eccentric or irrational way. Those are exceptional cases where you have to decide if you want to continue to live together with such behaviour or not. You cannot apply what I am saying to that. Exceptions are always there.

But what I am saying is what is actually happening in reality in many houses where both the people are normal and yet there is unrest. But we never try to look into it. We never like to deal with the truth.

Understand what I am trying to say. Drop your imagination and start living with reality.

A small story:

> A man gave his friend a puppy as a wedding gift.
> Three months later, they met on the street.
> 'How is married life?' he asked him.
> 'Oh, just a few small changes over time, that's all,' replied the friend.
> 'What changes?' he asked him.

'In the beginning, the puppy used to bark at me, and my wife used to bring me the newspaper. Now, my wife barks at me, and the puppy brings me the newspaper!' the man replied.

Once the honeymoon is over, what happens? No wonder it is called the honey*moon* and not honey*sun*! The happiness invariably lasts only a fortnight! I tell you, even if you marry a supermodel, her beauty will fade in just 15 days in your eyes because you are already fantasizing about someone else! And you keep on fantasizing because you are actually looking for fulfillment within yourself but searching outside for it through these built-up images.

One lady was advising her daughter on the subject of marriage. 'Listen dear, when you love someone, it should be for life; only then it is real love.'

The daughter was listening to what she was saying.

The lady continued, 'Take my word of advice. I know what I am talking about. After all, I have been married three times.'

The problem is, everyone is ready to give advice, but there is no one to take it!

Anyhow, at least when we find out what is outside is white, if we accept reality, there is no problem. But do we keep quiet? No! We take out our brush and paints, and try to paint the white into green! We try to change the other person to suit our mental image. We try to sculpt each other in the way we have imagined him to be. We try to possess the other and convert them into matter. We degrade energy into matter. Here starts the problem!

A small story:

> One man was a painter by profession.
> He was telling his friend, 'You know, one day a girl walked in with a chip that was a kind of blue-black colour and wanted me to paint a model house with the same color. I thought I would give up my profession in trying to match it. Nothing seemed to satisfy her.'
> The friend asked, 'Did you finally match it?'
> He replied, 'I was lucky. She got a call on her mobile phone and I quickly painted the chip while she was talking!'

All through the day, in every home, just listen carefully to the husband and wife talking to each other. You can hear the chiseling going on! I think that for marriages, we can gift a chisel and hammer along with the sacred thread or wedding ring!

Another small story:

> A man and his friend were having a cup of tea together one evening.
> The man told his friend, 'I am planning to divorce my wife. She has not spoken one word to me in the past 6 months.'
> The friend said, 'Think carefully before making any such decision. You won't get another wife like that.'

In life, if we drop the images inside us, we will find endless possibilities!

If you are unmarried, drop your fantasies so that you can choose your life partner and not a dream partner. When you select a person, just remind yourself that you are going to be spending your entire life with him, not just a few months. It is not just a fling. It is a life-long matter.

As of now, any black jeans or blue T-shirt will fall within your fantasy world and you will be attracted to it. But understand that the black or blue will fade away in six months' time!

If you are already married, drop your fantasies; only then can you start a real relationship with anybody. If you move about with a chisel and hammer, a real relationship cannot happen. What happens in chiseling is, you start chiseling and when you think that you have finished chiseling, your imagination has changed; it has become something different and so you have to do more chiseling to match the changed imagination! It becomes a never-ending cycle.

A real relationship can never happen as long as you have fantasies. If you notice, even if you stay for twenty-four hours in the same house with the other person, you don't look into the other's eyes, because you live with fantasy and not reality. You don't actually live with the real person. You see all that the other person does through your imagination and conclude that your life is a punishment to you from God.

If you are unmarried, drop your fantasies and your blood will cool down.

If you are a widower, drop your imagination and you will not suffer the pain of loneliness.

Try your best not to allow children to watch the duet songs on television until they have learnt not to build fantasy. If they only enjoy the music and dance along with it, it's alright; but they invariably internalize all that they see. This is where the problem starts. Everything gets stored in the *muladhara chakra*, the sex *chakra*. Then a mere suggestion is enough and the *muladhara* will be ready.

The sheer load of expectation leads to disturbances in the *muladhara chakra*. This is the way this *chakra* is locked. When you try to fulfill your fantasy through another person or by watching the television, when you try to impose or project your expectation and imagination on another person, this *chakra* is locked.

It has nothing to do with the outer conditions of life. It has nothing to do with so-called celibacy. It is to do with your inner fragmented self.

What is celibacy?

What is celibacy?

Celibacy is nothing but not craving for the suppressed half that is inside you, that's all. If you are a male, you need to experience such fulfillment unto yourself that you no longer miss the suppressed female inside you. And if you are a female, you are so enough unto yourself that you don't look outside to experience this fulfillment.

If this is achieved, you can live with or without the female in the outside world. If this is not achieved, even if you get married, you will continue to be under the torture of your hormones. Your hormonal torture is nothing but a yearning for the fulfillment that you are actually supposed to get from within, not without.

When you achieve this fulfillment, whether you are married or not, there will be peace in your mind. It is then that you can be celibate even in married life! This is true celibacy.

Instead of this, people go out of their way to become celibates and become more suppressed and neurotic.

Comment: *But* Swamiji, *we don't even realize that we are carrying an image within us...*

Yes, because we have never looked in. We go everywhere but inwards. Up to 80% of our energy is locked in this energy center! This energy center doesn't even need to be energized. It simply needs to be opened and activated, and the flood of energy flowing from it can transform your whole life!

If you look deeply inside yourself, you will understand that you are suffering because you always feel there is some mismatch between what you see and what you want to see. This 'what you want to see' is the image that you are carrying inside.

At least from now on, try to watch with awareness, the play of your mind in whatever you see. Try to catch the scenes as they are before your mind steps in and passes judgment. You will then see how subtly and seamlessly your mind plays in whatever you see, causing you to believe that there is something always wrong with what you see.

In Sanskrit, there are two phrases that teach us reality: *dhrishti shrishti* and *shrishti dhrishti*. *Dhrishti shrishti* means seeing the world as it is, taking it as it comes; to welcome what *is*, as reality. *Shrishti dhrishti* means seeing the world as we would like it to be, through our own colored lens, through our fantasies. The former leads to a peaceful life while the latter leads to suffering.

A small story:

> Once a man came to me and said, '*Swamiji*, we are just two people in our house, my wife and I. Still there is no peace!'
> I told him, 'Who says there are only two people in your house? You are four people.'
> The man was simply shocked.
> I told him, 'You are you, your inner woman, your wife, and her inner man! That is why I say you are four people. Just learn to drop your inner man or your inner woman – and see the change that happens in your house!'

The man went away silently.

Q: *Swamiji*, we experience disturbances in other relationships also, like between parents and children...

Yes, in any relationship there are expectations. I don't think we have any relationship without expectations.

Parents try to chisel children, and children try the same with parents.

Parents try to live out their unfulfilled desires through their children. Parents dream for their children to become a doctor or an engineer. Why not find out from the child what he wants to become and then dream to fulfill *that*? That would help your child immensely.

The day your child starts back-answering you, *that* day he has become a man. You have to deal very carefully with him. Spend time with him, talk to him, be a good friend and find out what he really wants to do in life. Guide him with deep love and trust. Then, make his ambition your reality and help him in achieving it.

So many children tell me, 'My father wants me to become a doctor,' or 'My father wants me to become a lawyer.' Of course, if the child is unable to decide for himself, and he asks you what he should do, you can tell him what he could do based on your observation of his talents and capacity.

You can always suggest, but don't stuff anything down his throat. Also, make the child understand that you are giving him freedom and maturity in doing things and make it clear to him that there can be no blaming at the end of it. He needs to understand that clearly.

For homework today, I want you all to write down your ideas on how a perfect husband, a perfect wife, a perfect father, a perfect mother, a perfect child and a perfect friend should be. Choose any five relationships relevant to yourself, and note this. Do it honestly. When you read your paper, I am sure you will find, deep down in your unconscious, all your ideas are drawn from popular media.

You watch a television serial and start liking a particular character. The character becomes a solid reality for you. You unconsciously start expecting to see that kind of behaviour in certain people associated with you in real life.

People even carry the image of the 'ideal guru' in their minds. Usually it is the image of an old man, with grey hair and a flowing beard – what you see in books and television serials! And when they come and see me, they are unable to accept that such a young person can be a real master. So I too face the same trouble! I too have to free people of their expectations about the Guru, before they accept me!

Q: But sometimes we feel that we have to chisel... like when we are handling our employees at work. What do we do then?

Do your chiseling consciously. Be aware of what you do – then you will not do more than necessary. See if your expectations of your employees are realistic. Check if there is any alternate solution. Only when it is absolutely necessary, should you try to mould the other person.

When power has been given to you, learn to use it with awareness! Even anger and lust are great energies given to you by God. When you have respect for that energy, you will not waste it or misuse it.

Do we ever misuse money? You never misuse money, because you respect it. If a person does a job worth ten rupees, will you pay him one penny more? But with anger, you always 'overpay'. If a person makes a mistake worth 'ten rupees of anger', you always pay him with 'fifty rupees' worth anger! Why? It is because you use your anger unconsciously, not consciously like with money. If you use your anger consciously, it will pay off and you won't feel guilty about it also, I assure you.

You should never get disturbed by your own anger. If you get disturbed, it means that you have not gone through anger with awareness; you have allowed anger to overtake you. This is the scale to see if you have used anger properly!

A small story:

> Once a *sadhu* – a wandering mendicant - was passing through a village, when he received a complaint from the villagers about a cobra that was playing havoc with their lives.
> The *sadhu* was known to have the power to communicate with animals, so they begged him to convince the cobra to spare the villagers.
> So the *sadhu* spoke to the cobra, and the cobra promised not to bite any of the villagers anymore.
> A few months later, the *sadhu* was passing through the

same village when he came upon the cobra, badly bruised and almost dead.

'What happened to you? Why are you hurt?' Asked the *sadhu*.

The cobra cried, 'O *sadhu*! It is you who made me promise never to bite the villagers! I have kept my promise to this day. But the villagers, who were earlier in fear of me, took my mildness to be weakness. Seeing that I don't bite, they started torturing me everyday. See what a state I have been reduced to!'

The *sadhu* replied, 'My poor foolish friend! I only asked you not to bite. Did I ask you not to hiss?'

You need to use anger in the right way in the right quantities. Anger is a tremendous energy if we know how to use it rightly.

Knowledge about anger reduces anger.

Many people come to me and tell me, 'Swamiji, I love my wife so much. That is why I want her to change for the better! That's why I fight with her.'

I tell them, 'You don't love your wife; you love the image that you carry in your mind.'

You love your image and whenever your wife matches the image, you love her. Your real love is not for your wife; it is for your mental image. If you really loved your wife, you would change your image to suit your wife. You would not expect her to match the image.

Most of us love our images. That is the beginning of unrest in our homes. That is the beginning of an intimate war! Honestly I tell you, lovers are intimate enemies. They are intimate but constantly on guard. They are constantly trying to dominate each other.

Real intimacy is when you are totally relaxed with the other. That is real intimacy.

Q: *Swamiji*, what you are saying is that we should accept the other person completely, with all his faults?

No!

Even the word *accept* carries a feeling of condemnation. When you say the words 'accept him with all his faults', it is like a silent complaint. It is like saying, 'What to do, we have to live with it.' No! I tell you, *welcome* the other person into your life, just as he or she is. There is a difference between accepting and welcoming. Accepting is like making a compromise. Welcoming is opening out your being to the other person without any expectation, unconditionally.

The whole of creation is a gift to you from Existence. Receive it with grace and humility. When you do this, the tremendous energy of the *muladhara chakra* is opened to you. To awaken this *chakra* is to touch a perennial source of energy. The tremendous energy that is usually locked in imagination, expectation and greed can be made available for creativity, for business, for life, and for reality!

Not only that, you will find your house becoming a *kshetra*, a shrine of peace. Our houses are meant to be *dharmakshetras* - abodes of righteousness - but they have become *kurukshetras* - abodes of war! And why have they become abodes of war? Because we are chiseling human beings. If we chisel idols or wood, we can make beautiful forms and furniture, but if we chisel human beings, only suffering will follow.

One man asked me, '*Swamiji* can you please tell me a way to find a connection with the eighteen-handed Devi.'

I told him, 'First you try to find a connection with your two-handed wife and then we will see how to establish a connection with the eighteen-handed Devi!'

Another man came to me and asked for blessings for a divorce.

I told him that I would give blessings for marriage but not for divorce.

I asked him what the problem was and if I could sort it out.

He told me, '*Swamiji*, this morning, I asked for coffee. She came with the coffee with such haste that she spilled it on my clothes.'

I was shocked and told him that the incident seemed too trivial to ask for a divorce.

He went on to say, '*Swamiji*, you don't know. Today she poured coffee, tomorrow she will pour acid.'

I was shocked. I told him, '*Ayyah*, why do you want to move from coffee to acid without any reason? All she did was spill coffee in some anger and haste and in any case, she is going to be the one who is going to wash your clothes!'

He continued, '*Swamiji*, during our marriage ceremony, there is a custom wherein three pots of water are kept and the couple are meant to leave their hands in all three of them to try and find a ring which has been dropped in one of them. As early as that time, she scratched my hand with her fingernail!'

In order to zero down the distance between the couple, small games such as these are played during Indian weddings. The man had been keeping a 10-year track of such trivial incidents!

I asked him, '*Ayyah*, if you maintain such a police track record, how can one live with you?'

You see: there are two things that we do: One is, presenting arguments and looking for a judgment, while the second is, forming a judgment and then collecting arguments to support that judgment. The second is what we do *99%* of the time.

There are many things happening around us but we register only what *we want* to register, never what is really happening. Because of this, we miss reality. Reality continuously exists but we see only what we want to see. In marriage, within the first few months, the man or woman forms a judgment about the other and from then on, whatever the other does, he or she sees from the point of view of the judgment. They search and collect arguments to maintain their judgment.

That is why, if you decide that your wife is a fool, she will always look like a fool no matter what. If you decide that your husband is the type who controls you, he will always appear in that way to you, whatever he may be doing.

If you do this, you will never be able to see the real aspects of your spouse; you will see only those aspects that feed your judgment. This is like when you are hungry, only restaurants hit your eye on the road. In the same way, before killing a dog what do we do? We call it a mad dog and then kill it.

Drop this attitude. Only then you will find a certain freshness in every person and thing that you come by.

A small story:

> A man walked into a police station to complain that his wife was missing since three hours.
> The policeman asked him, 'Can you give me details about her height, weight etc.'
> The man said, 'Oh! I don't know.'
> The policeman asked, 'What was she wearing when she left the house?'
> The man said, 'I did not notice, sir. But wait, she took the dog with her. I know that.'
> The policeman asked, 'What kind of dog is it?'
> The man replied, 'A dalmation breed with grey spots instead of black; he weighs 50 lbs and has a pure white tail with no spots on it; he wears a brown collar with a silver chain. His name is Spot.'
> The policeman said, 'That's enough. We will find them!'

A husband and wife live with each other with a certain freshness for probably a few months after marriage. In those few months, they collect judgments about the other. After that, they don't relate with each other at all. They don't actually see the other person itself. They relate with the judgments, that's all.

The husband relates with the judgments that he has collected about his wife and the wife relates with the judgments that she has collected about her husband. The actual husband and actual wife are different! They become four people in one house.

Just do an honest check. How long is it since you looked into the eye of your husband or wife and spoke to him or her? A very long time I am sure. And we feel that the early days were golden days and that life has become boring. If you really see, it is your attitude that makes it boring.

You give absolutely no room for a person to evolve. You are in such a hurry to typecast them. You don't want to take in anything new on their account. I tell you, you don't even see your wife or husband after a few years of marriage because you are happy relating with your image of them.

What will happen then? You will land up like this man who was clueless about his own wife's particulars! Not knowing a wife's particulars is a very superficial level problem. The understanding I am trying to express goes deeper than that. You actually miss the real person who is living with you. You live with your *idea* about the person.

For just 24 hours, make up your mind that you will see your wife or husband as if you are seeing her or him for the first time.
220

Receive every word or action of hers with a freshness and innocence without jumping to conclusions. Feel lovingness in you towards her. Even if she says things that provoke you, listen to those statements with awareness and respond in a calm and loving way, instead of in the usual resistive way. You will see that you are actually opening out new avenues for both of you; you are giving the two of you a new space to relate.

Suddenly, you will realize that all along it was your attitude that made things look miserable. Of course, you might say that the other person too must reciprocate. You have the power to transform yourself and others. With just a change in your mental make-up, you can do much. When you decide to change, the other person will automatically change their ways too.

A small story:

> A man was walking past a cemetery one day when he heard a loud cry from inside.
> He felt obliged to stop by and see if he could offer help.
> He walked in and saw a man crying loudly near a tombstone.
> He was repeatedly saying, 'Why did you have to go? Why did you have to go?'
> The man felt really sad for his suffering, so he went near him and asked, 'Sir, I am sorry. Was it your wife?'
> The man replied, 'No. It is her first husband.'

Relationships turn out to be a trauma because of a sheer mismatch between one's own imagination and reality. Still worse, people move from one relationship to another thinking that the next one is going to match their imagination. They go with it for some time and find out that there is something lacking there also and move onto the next. It never occurs to them that there is nothing wrong with the other person.

Today, it is becoming increasingly difficult for youngsters to tolerate one another and marriages are breaking up so easily. It is such a pity to see these things happening. An awakening is needed now. Only a deep understanding can bring about this awakening.

If you read all the love stories written until now, you will find that nowhere have the man and woman stayed with each other on a full- time basis at a functional level, in reality!

In a story about eternal lovers written by Rabindranath Tagore, the hero and heroine decide to live as eternal lovers on the two sides of the river Ganga. Periodically, they come by boat, meet each other and get back.

If they do this, obviously they will be at peace during the time they meet. Every time they meet, there will be freshness in the air because they know that they will be together for only a few hours; the moment becomes precious!

All eternal lovers, be they Romeo and Juliet or Laila and Majnu or Ambikapathi and Amaravathi, never really lived together!

The problem is, life doesn't have background music! When you watch the love stories on television, they all come with background music and so you easily enter into a fantasy world. All the scenes that you see, especially the love scenes, come with background music. You enjoy it so much because of the background music. You are completely mesmerized by the atmosphere created in the television box.

In real life, you search for that music and don't find it! But if you find that music within yourself, then you won't look for it outside. Finding it within yourself is nothing but creating the beautiful space within you where everything is experienced as wonderful part of Existence.

Remember that your husband or wife is a creation of God. Your creation cannot compete with God's creation! Only His creation will win!

Today, there is a very large instance of pornography, fantasy, dreams and perversion in society. People have started going to other poor substitutes to fulfill their fantasies. Pornography does not fulfill sexual life; it creates more fantasies and perversion, that's all. But there is such a compulsion for fantasizing. Understand one thing: unless you are weak, nothing becomes a compulsion for you. When you are strong, you can drop anything.

(A lady shares her views) Swamiji, you ask us to be as we are. But how can we live in society just as we are? I think we have to change according to the family, the society.

Yes, everybody faces this problem on a practical level. You say, 'Swamiji, I have to act according to the other.' I ask you, why not also make sure that others act according to you? True, in society, we have to be dependent on each other. There is no other way.

But be very clear of your limits.

Be independently dependent!

Be very clear, which is your space and which is the other's. Try your best to enrich your own life, without disturbing one another.

Q: Can't the other person's muladhara chakra be opened, so that he drops his expectations?

How will you do that? You can only make sure that your own expectations are dropped, so that from four people sharing one house, you at least come down to three!

How to change the other person...? These days marriage counselors suggest even hypnotism!

The other day, I read about a case where a woman wanted to bring down her husband's anger levels. I read that the Chicago University once performed an experiment where they implant electrodes in a person's brain and completely control anger. When they asked for volunteers to participate in this research, it seems hundreds of women forcibly brought their husbands!

After the experiment, 72 women – this is a fact – 72 women came back and told the university, 'Please remove these electrodes. I want my old husband back! I want my old angry husband back!' When asked why, they say, 'Life has lost its taste! Unless we fight, there is no interaction. He pays me no attention!'

Everybody needs attention! Behavioural psychologists say that a normal man can survive without food for up to 90 days, but without attention from others, only for 14 days! He will start going insane.

What has happened is that we have forgotten how to love each other and care for each other. Love is a forgotten language! So the only interaction and attention we can hope to have is by fighting with each other!

I think even the people sitting here and complaining that their husbands or wives are not spiritual... if their spouses become spiritual, they may come back and complain that they want their old partners back!

Carry heaven with you wherever you go

The beautiful thing about this *muladhara chakra* is, if this one *chakra* is opened, you will find that 50% of your problems have disappeared! This one *chakra* manages more than 50% of your life. In whatever you do, you will find a trace of this *chakra*! Even in your signature, you'll find a trace of this *chakra*! What I mean is, even the way you put your signature shows what kind of emotions are pent up in you. When the *muladhara chakra* is activated, even your signature will look different. If you pluck a flower, the way you do it will be different. It will be so soft and gentle, with no violence.

There are a set of Tamil saints called the *Nayanmars*. There is a song which says about them, that when they pluck a flower, the tree will not feel the pain! What do we mean by that? You become so sensitive and loving, when this *chakra* is opened.

225

When the energy of this *chakra* is transformed, it will overflow from you as love!

Sex is carbon, love is diamond. Sex is mud, love is the lotus that blooms in the mud. It is the same substance. But the thing is, you should know how to process it. Just drop your expectations, and you will find a tremendous upsurge of energy.

Today I want you all to try this technique when you go home:

Sit down and concentrate on your *muladhara chakra*. If you notice, your *muladhara chakra* is always tense. It is always tight.

For five minutes, mentally forgive your husband or wife for anything disturbing that they have done. Really forgive them. Go to the root of all your misgivings and drop the feeling of resentment. Do it totally. Just welcome them as they are. Give them your deep love.

After just five minutes, you will see that the *muladhara chakra* is totally relaxed.

If just five minutes can give you this result, just imagine what will happen if you change your entire attitude! What a tremendous energy flow you will experience!

The way you are living now, it is as if you have got 100,000 rupees, but you have locked away ninety thousand in some place where you can't recover it. You try to manage your whole life with the remaining ten thousand. Then naturally you will feel that you are poor!

In the same way, all your energy has been locked away in this *chakra* – in anger, in sex and what not. You don't have enough energy even for your day-to-day living! Once this *chakra* is opened, your life will become rich. You will be able to think better, understand better, plan better. You will feel this energy consciously working in you. It will open a new dimension that you would not have experienced before. You will actually realize that your husband, your wife, and everyone in this world are spiritual beings!

You need to understand that heaven and hell are not geographical places. You can't locate them on a map. They exist only psychologically. It's up to you to transform your life into heaven or hell.

When you are full of expectations, you carry your own hell in you. So wherever you go, you will find that your personal package of hell travels with you! Like how a circus troupe carries and spreads its tents everywhere it goes, so also you carry this hell with you to any place you go to. And when two such people meet, there is a great clash of hells, not bells!

Why do you want to carry this load around with you? Just drop it!

Just think of all the energy you waste in trying to chisel the other person to suit your expectations. Isn't it much easier to just drop the chisel? If even 10% of that energy is channeled into meditation, your life can be transformed into true living.

Living is 'life led with awareness, with freedom'. We have a choice! We have a chance to become conscious. It is up to us to decide.

227

Lust to love, the alchemy process

Lust, like anger, is a tremendous energy. Actually, until such time when you understand what lust is and how it can be transformed, any action that you do is lustful. Even if you pick up a pen, it is lustful; if you are petting a small child, it is lustful. There is a certain animal nature in it because your energy is still driven by greed. It has not transformed into higher energy.

In the same way like how knowledge about anger reduces anger, so also, knowledge about lust reduces lust, because both are the same energy! The problem with lust and sex is, they have been magnified and imagined to be much more than what they are. Because of suppression, sex is made out to be much more than it is. There starts the whole problem. It has been contaminated to a great extent by media.

When your lust is not accepted by the other, it turns into anger against that person. That is why you read newspaper reports of teenage boys throwing acid on the faces of girls who have rejected them.

Society has always made divisions like lower humans and higher humans. Any one with passion or lust is said to be a lower human. There is no lower or higher; a transformation has to happen, that's all.

The people who go about setting these moral standards are simply people who pretend to be moralists. They are either afraid to go behind these feelings or guilty to go behind them and so they pass off as moralists. They become the ones who set standards like low and high in society.

Just understand that there is no low or high. The moment you think that you are low, you start fighting with that feeling and it becomes very difficult for you to overcome it.

When people try to impose the inferior and superior feelings in you, remember that every individual is a part of Existence and no one is inferior or superior to anyone. It is only when you forget this truth that you will use these kinds of words.

Lust is a result of deep ignorance. The process of changing lust to love is an alchemy process. Alchemy is the process of changing any base metal to a higher metal. Similarly, changing our base emotion that is lust to the highest emotion we are capable of, that is love, is an alchemy process. It is the ultimate alchemy.

Let me narrate to you something that actually happened to me when I was wandering in the Himalayas:

> In the Himalayas, I used to simply walk anywhere I felt like. My belongings were very few and I used to wander and sleep anywhere at nighttime. I used to simply grip the branches and roots of trees and climb! I met many sages during that period.
>
> On one such occasion, I met a sage, very barely dressed, with matted locks and with a fierce expression. He was a*Naga Baba,* belonging to the *Naga* sect of sages.
>
> I was somehow attracted to him and went near him.
>
> At that time I did not know much spoken Hindi, but I managed to converse with him in my broken Hindi. I was with him for a few days.

All day long, he would smoke his hookah. I was watching him and was amazed at what he was doing.

He would drop two copper coins in his hookah, smoke for some time and then empty his pipe and two gold coins would drop out!

He would then sell the two gold coins and get more copper coins and repeat the process!

I asked him how it happened.

He did not answer but simply gave me the pipe. Somehow, the smell of tobacco or alcohol never agreed with my system at any time, so I just took a few steps backwards.

I told him that I had come to the Himalayas for meditation and enlightenment and I was not interested in smoking or gold coins.

He looked at me and spoke in Tamil for the first time: '*Angam pazhuthaal thangam pazhukkum*' which means: 'When your being ripens, gold will ripen.'

I was speechless. I wondered how he knew that I knew Tamil.

He playfully blew smoke rings into my face.

I was in deep bliss for three days after that.

Changing copper to gold is an alchemy process. It is an alchemy process in the outer world. The alchemy in the inner world is all about changing our base energies to higher spiritual energies. When you master the art of transforming your base energies to spiritual energies, you can transform copper to gold; it is no big deal. When you master the inner alchemy process, the outer alchemies are nothing. They become just child's play.

I have narrated this incident to you only to make you understand the concept of alchemy and not for you to pursue any outer world alchemies! Outer world alchemies are ordinary. The inner world alchemy is the one that makes you a real master.

What is it that actually happens in the process of alchemy with metals? First, the impurities from the base metal are removed. Then some components are added and the whole thing is taken through a process. At the end of it, the base metal becomes a higher metal.

Our animal emotions have to be changed to divine emotions. We all have lust, which is an animal emotion. At least animals have pure lust. They simply forget the whole world when they are having a relationship. But for us, even our lust is not pure. Lust is mixed with feelings of guilt and unsure desire all the time.

Either our conditionings from the past make us feel guilty and we withdraw, or intense desire to continue into the future makes us indulge, only to feel guilty again. It is a vicious cycle of pulling and pushing as a result of which the lust is contaminated. It is not pure.

Always if you notice, the moment you fulfill your imagination, you are engulfed by guilt. That is why sex makes you feel guilty. Family instills the first sense of guilt in you when you are a child. Then, you master the art of creating guilt for yourself!

Understand guilt first

Understand guilt first. Anyone who wants to have a control over you, first instills guilt in you. They make you feel you are inferior in some fashion. Then automatically you follow what they are saying.

Society knows to control only through guilt. Rules are alright for children and it is good to start with rules. But it is important that as you grow, you are led by your own intelligence. When you integrate yourself, guilt cannot be instilled in you and you become intelligent also.

Actually, an incident itself does not cause guilt in you. The effect of the incident is what causes the guilt in you.

People blindly pass down rules from one generation to another and with that is passed the guilt also. Like a crown, the guilt is passed down – grandfather to father, father to son, son to grandson and so on.

All the beauty products tell you repeatedly that you are not good enough. You start feeling guilty about your own inadequate body. What do you do? You go and buy their products and use them. You automatically fall under their control. Once you use them, you are engulfed with one more feeling of guilt, 'Did I go through all this trouble for this after all?' The moment you achieve something, the first feeling that engulfs you is guilt.

Drop the cerebral layer

Coming back to lust, you create a solid cerebral layer with all the imagination collected from all that you have seen on television, internet and books. You live mentally in this layer all the time. Even when you are in a relationship, you are relating with this layer; you are not relating with the actual wife or husband. The actual wife or husband becomes a poor substitute for the images in your mind. Your lust is then contaminated.

When you indulge in this fashion, you are caught in a vicious cycle and that is why you don't go into it fully and come out, but keep going in with more and more craving. If you go deeply into it, you will flower out of it!

That is why, in the earlier days, people were able to drop their lust at the age of 40. They never had such complicated images in them. They related directly with their husband or wife. That is why they flowered out of it at an early age. They were able to move deeper into lust and come out of it. Lust simply dropped from them. *They* did not have to drop lust.

In Indian marriages, there is a beautiful verse which the priests make the couple recite. The wife tells the husband, 'Let you be my 11th son,' and the husband tells the wife, 'Let you be my 11th daughter.' It means, in the 11th year of marriage, they will look upon each other as a son or a daughter. The relationship would have undergone that much of a transformation by then.

When you see your children, you are engulfed with so much joy, are you not? Your relationship with your wife or husband would have undergone so much of a transformation that you will experience that same joy when you see him or her. The husband will become a son to the woman and the wife will become a daughter to the man.

When you don't have a clear understanding of your imagination, you suffer. Understanding is the key to get out of this. If you know how to live without suffering, you are leading a spiritual life. If you don't know how to avoid suffering, you are living a material life. There are only 2 kinds of life – life with understanding and life without understanding. Buddha life and *buddhu* life!

You are confused about your desires and fantasies and that is why you are not happy anywhere you are. When you sit on the floor on a mat, you are not happy because you are thinking of a chair. When you get to a chair, you are thinking of a throne. When you get to the throne, you are unable to enjoy it!

If your lust is pure without any feelings of guilt or desire, you will go deeply into it without any sort of guilt or imagination and flower out of it. It is only when your cerebral layer starts to function that you start bringing in your collected imagination and fantasy and fail to flower out of lust.

Drop your cerebral layer and start feeling love towards your own body as well as the other's body. Bliss is happening continuously inside your body but you are not allowing it to surface because you are caught up in your imagination. When you drop your imagination about your body and the other's body, the impurity in your lust is removed and the first step in the alchemy process, that is removing the impurities, happens.

Every body is beautiful

When you feel comfortable with your body, a certain grace happens to you. Understand that skin diseases happen mostly because you have some hatred towards your body. They happen because you have low self-esteem and disrespect for your own body.

You don't understand this and instead go about finding a cure for the skin disease. The root of it lies in your own cerebral layer that you have built over the years. You always look at another person's body and want to have a body like that. When you love your body, when you feel comfortable with it, you will look and feel beautiful.

In *Ramayana*, the Indian epic written by Tulsidas, it is said that when Sita walked into the court of Janaka, everyone including the great sages and *Rishis* like Vasishta and Sita's own father, Janaka, stood up to pay respect to her. Such was the sublime grace that exuded from her.

In *Tantra* there is a technique wherein you wake up every morning and touch your body at every point with deep love, and allow the subtle body to settle down in the gross or physical body upon awakening.

Anyhow, the more images you have collected from outside, the thicker your cerebral layer is. In earlier days, people were not so complex and neurotic; they were simple. The cerebral layer did not exist or it was there as a very thin layer.

Add friendliness to relationships

Once you drop your imagination about your own body and the other's body, you will be able to start showing compassion and friendliness towards the other's body. Friendliness is the component you need to add in the alchemy process to transform lust to love.

Violence is not the way. We talk of violence in the society, state and country. What about in our own homes and inside our own bodies and minds? I tell you: violence starts at home.

You may say, 'Swamiji, but we are not violent in our day-to-day lives.' You only think you are not violent. Observe yourself closely. When you walk on the street or in your own garden, what do you do? You unconsciously pluck at trees, leaves, flowers; you kick stones around and pull at creepers and what not. These are all acts of violence!

Just for once, walk into your garden and look closely at a flower or a leaf with utmost awe and love in you. Feel the beauty of it in your heart and look at it lovingly. Feel that it is a living being. Connect to the wonders of Existence through it. Handle it like it was a new-born child. Feel the emotion swelling from deep inside you.

Now think of the number of times you have unconsciously plucked at the same flower or leaf while you were walking near it. Do you understand the difference between the two emotions, the two attitudes? Now tell me, are you really being friendly towards everything and everyone around you?

Look at everything with awareness. Now, you are functioning from your unconscious and so you are behaving in a violent fashion towards these things. If you look at them with awareness, you will see the immense beauty in them and treat them with love.

How much do you abuse your own body? You overeat and cause disturbance to the beautiful digestive system functioning inside you. You stay up late in the night and torture your body when it is crying for rest. You smoke and drink despite knowing that is it not good for your body? Are all these acts those of friendliness to your body? Some of you hate your body and therefore neglect it.

So it is time to start addressing the violence within you. Automatically the violence outside will stop. We are always ready to point outside of us. What about our own imperfections?

A man once visited me and told me about his family. He said that his wife was a lawyer. I asked, 'Oh, does she go to argue in the court?' He said, 'No Swamiji, she argues at home!'

We are all ready to point fingers at others and argue. Instead, let us start removing the impurities in us and then automatically, there will be no need to argue outside.

Carry with you words that heal yourself and others. Show friendliness towards the other's body, mind and being. This is what is 'applied spirituality'. Spirituality is not ringing the bell regularly in the *pooja* room and praying to the Goddess Lakshmi, for wealth. It is imbibing Goddess Lakshmi's qualities of grace and goodwill. Wealth will automatically happen.

We all think that we only need to do rituals and we will get the results. No. When you chant 'Ram Ram' a thousand times a day with no intention or inclination to transform yourself, it is as good as chanting 'coca-cola' a thousand times a day! The basic idea behind rituals is to understand and imbibe the spirit behind them so that you transform yourself and then the material results will happen seamlessly.

Once you are able to show friendliness to the other, have the patience and perseverance to process your transformed emotion. At the end, you will experience the supreme and mutual emotion that is love. The other will also reciprocate your transformed emotion and then you have arrived! Your being becomes bliss! Then, you have done your meditation properly!

The beauty of love

When love becomes the centre of your being, sex becomes a deep union of two beings. The problem is, true love is lost under the covers and lust has taken over. As a result, the beings never come together; only the bodies come together. The relationship remains at a very superficial level. Anything superficial can be shaken easily.

Also, lust always blinds you. It takes you into unconscious intoxication. Love also intoxicates you, but it takes you into deep awareness. Lust and love are two ends of the same spectrum. Anything that puts you into deep awareness is meditation. Anything that puts you in an unconscious state is not conducive. This is the scale to see if what you are experiencing is good for you or not.

Also, when you love deeply, there will be no room for jealousy. Jealousy is there because you are afraid that the shallow roots will give way. If the roots are deep, why would you be afraid? Why would you get jealous? The trust in your partner gets shaky because the relationship is superficial, it is a relationship based on fantasy and lust.

Romance is not real romance if you feel it towards only one person. Life itself is romance! Your very being has to exude romance - towards Existence. When your being expresses itself through your head, it is intelligence; when it expresses itself through the heart, it is compassion; when it expresses itself through the body, it is energy and when it does not express itself but just IS, it is bliss!

When you reach this stage, you will not be dependent on anyone outside for joy. You will simply resonate with joy all the time inside yourself. Of course, you will be able to multiply it by sharing it with others outside.

When you feel deeply connected to a person, there will be no need for physical proximity to that person. You will feel happy and satisfied with just the feeling of connection with him or her. You will feel complete unto yourself and not look for anything outside for fulfillment. This connection will not suffer separation or anything else.

A relationship is all about feeling connected to someone at a deep level, beyond all things. When you don't understand this, you bind yourself to people with many conditions and you call it a relationship. It becomes shaky and you work hard at maintaining it and conclude that relationships are a problem!

People tell me, 'Swamiji, I want to come and stay in the ashram. I am not happy staying at home.'

I always tell them that if they are not able to be happy with 4 people in their house, they cannot be happy with 100 people at the ashram! Do you think that the ashram is some escapist lodge?

Be very clear: home is not anything outside of you. Being blissful all the time irrespective of what goes on around you is what is 'being at home'. If you are not able to do this, you will not be at home anywhere.

When I stayed for months together in an 8 feet by 8 feet enclosure, I was as blissful as I am today sitting on this throne. Please try to understand this. The capacity lies in understanding that your happiness has nothing to do with the outer world objects.

Imagine that a dog is biting a bone and starts bleeding from the mouth. It thinks that the blood is coming from the bone and bites further into it and licks the blood. What will happen to the dog? Only pain will happen. In the same way, we also think that the pleasure or pain is to do with things outside of ourselves and indulge further and further in it and become miserable.

Q: How can we protect our children from developing these kinds of problems?

To be frank, you cannot fully control the process. You cannot control all of the child's interactions with society. But there are some things you can practice at home.

As I said earlier, don't suppress the child's other half. Let it freely express and experience itself in different ways. Don't teach it to be gender conscious.

Just allow the child to be its own natural self, giving it adequate opportunity to explore itself. Children when untouched by social conditioning are by nature so comfortable inside their own boundary.

You might have noticed babies playing with their genitals, or pulling their big toe to their mouth and doing similar other things. These things just show that they are so comfortable and loving inside their own boundary, exploring and enjoying. But we don't allow them to do these things. We immediately stop them and tell them that it is wrong. It is good to allow them to explore.

And when it comes to their clothing, it is always better to dress them in single-piece clothing instead of two-piece clothing. The latter gives them a sense of dividing their body into two and with time, they forget and become insensitive to the lower half of their body. It is almost a division in their consciousness. That is why today, if you are asked to visualize yourself, almost always, only your upper half will come to your mind. You simply neglect your lower half.

Just allow the child to be free in its ways, even if it means that you have to take certain risks. Children have with them a certain sense of intuition and instinct. So, you can take the necessary precautionary measures and allow them to explore.

Also, children are so total in their expressions. So don't suppress them. They don't know to bring in their mind and exhibit superficial or hypocritical behaviour. We have all mastered the art of hypocrisy by allowing our mind to exercise restraint. We never express totally.

241

Also, allow them to use both their hands freely. We all discourage them from using the left hand for various things. Why can't the child be ambidextrous? There is nothing wrong in it. Arjuna in the *Mahabharata*, the Indian epic, was ambidextrous. When we hear of these things, we listen with awe but fail to understand that we are also perfectly capable of these things, if only we give ourselves the chance!

Also, if you have noticed, all children enjoy whirling. Whirling is their way of allowing centering of their energy to happen. You can whirl freely only when your worry center is clear. Children are so innocent and worry-free and hence they are able to whirl effortlessly. But when we see them whirl, our head starts whirling and so we stop them! We tell them, 'Sit in one place! It's not good for health,' and what not. I tell you, just allow them to whirl. Place a blanket beneath them so that even if they fall, they will not get hurt.

Never instill fear in your child! Let him be free; let him climb and fall a few times. If you constantly discourage the child, it can lead to various phobias like height phobia, darkness phobia, which can later turn into fear of climbing, of making new decisions etc. Just follow these simple things, it is enough.

Q: *Swamiji*, you were talking about how there is no such thing as a perfect partner. Then what is the purpose of matching horoscopes before marriage?

Now if I start speaking on this subject, I will have to pull down the whole structure of astrology! Not astrology itself, but the way we follow it today is foolish and nonsensical.

Understand that it is *your* life. You are living it; you should know the pros and cons. But you don't know anything about your life, and so you go around asking others! Where is your intelligence?

To surrender your life to a stranger, to let him make your life's decisions, just shows that you no longer even know how to run your own life. You have to take responsibility for your own life.

When people come to me with questions about their future, I tell them: Don't approach me to predict your future. Approach me to design your future. All these predictions are only for the weak-minded, be very clear about that.

Ancient astrology was a pure science. There was truth in it.

Let me tell you how astrology evolved.

In the past, when a child was sent to the gurukul to the master to study, astrology was used to diagnose what kind of personality, what kind of attitudes and aptitudes he possessed. Accordingly, he was trained.

The master would see what his natural tendencies were. If he had *brahmin* tendencies where intelligence was the prime factor, he would be initiated into *Veda Vidya* - studying of the *vedic* scriptures. If his personality was that of a *kshatriya*, where bravery and strength were the most dominant, he would be trained in martial arts. If he showed *vaishya* tendencies, wherein he exhibited many skills, he would be taught business. If he seemed to possess *shudra* qualities, where he was happy giving his time to routine labour work, he would be initiated into service. All four roles had equal value and earned equal respect.

243

This was the purpose for which astrology was used. Incidentally it also helped predict certain major milestones in a person's life. It was a science mainly used for this kind of diagnosis. Look around you today. A person who is a doctor by nature has become an engineer and an engineer has become a serviceman and what not! That is why there is a sense of total chaos in society.

Q: So ancient astrology is a proven science?

This is what I was afraid of! The moment I say, 'Yes,' you will all start running behind astrology! Tomorrow morning I will see a long queue before me with each one carrying his horoscope and saying '*Swamiji*, please predict my future!'

Don't worry so much about astrology!

Vivekananda gave a befitting answer to someone who questioned him about astrology. He told him, 'Go, eat well, exercise well, sleep well. You will become strong, physically and mentally. Then you won't worry about all these things!'

Only a person who is mentally weak depends so much on astrology.

Q: Does that mean that all the people who follow astrology are weak-minded?

No, you can't say that. But the majority are weak-minded. Even people who are normally intelligent sometimes behave foolishly in these matters. They come and ask me, 'Swamiji, if I wear such and such a stone or gem, will it be lucky for me?' How can you depend on a stone! You are live consciousness. You are nothing but God! I can't imagine... I am teaching you the science by which you can harness this whole cosmic energy, and you ask me about stones!

You might have heard about Swami Yateeshwarananda. He was a great man, an enlightened person. When he traveled abroad for the first time, he started out during *rahukala* - an inauspicious hour of the day, calculated by using the positions of the planets.

Someone asked him, 'Swamiji, how can you start during *rahukala*?'

He answered, 'You fool! I am the energy that guides the planets! How can they control me?'

See the courage of the man! It is a courage that comes out of deep understanding.

I am teaching you the science by which you can control the planets! So why do you bother about where the planets are and how they will affect you? Pick up the science of meditation, that's enough. Then nothing can touch you.

Go by consciousness

All our values are nothing but a substitute for consciousness.

If you are conscious, aware of what you are doing, you don't need values to tell you what to do. You don't have to follow any rules. Rules will be following you! If you are conscious, all virtues and discipline and spirituality will happen to you and you will naturally flower into a state of spiritual elevation.

Somehow, whenever we hear words like consciousness or spiritual elevation, we always think, 'No, no, this is not for me!' Without even trying any meditation technique, any practical way of elevating the consciousness, we come to the conclusion that this is not for us. So we go in for a substitute, for pseudo-consciousness – which is called morality, conscience, values.

Values are fine when you are at the starting point – but not as the ending point!

Vivekananda says beautifully, 'It is good to be born in the church, but not to die there!'

We should first drop the idea that to be spiritual is very difficult and different.

There is a song by Bhagwan Ramana Maharishi, an enlightened master from India:

Ayyae, ati sulabham, atmavidyai, ayyae, ati sulabham!

It means, *'Oh, so easy, this spirituality; oh, so easy!'*

In a later stanza he says,

If you want money, you need to work hard.

If you're looking for name and fame, you need to work hard.

If you want self-realization, all you need to do is keep still!

If you can slip into deep laziness, you will fall into divinity! This laziness is not what we normally know as laziness. It is not physical laziness. It's a kind of... mental laziness! If you can

246

completely – I mean completely – calm yourself, you can verily be spiritual.

To be spiritual is neither easy nor difficult. It's just the idea that you have. If you think it's easy, it's easy. If you think it's difficult, it's difficult. To be as you are, what is needed? Is it difficult or easy?   *I AM ALREADY THAT*

You cannot even use the word easy! It is as you are, right? You are already that, then how can you say it is easy to become that?

Just look in. Turn inward. A little trust in spirituality and a little meditation; that is enough! When you drop the fear that to be spiritual is very difficult, you will get the confidence that, '*Yes, I can be spiritual. I can be conscious.*' Then the question of '*is it right to drop my values*', will not arise at all.

Right now you are afraid to drop your values because you have nothing else to hold on to! We know, once we drop our values, all the suppressed desires will jump as if the Pandora's Box has been opened! And we know, if the Pandora's Box opens, there will be only chaos! We are afraid of our subconscious.

If you continuously practice meditation, your subconscious will be cleared. Then you will see, even if you open the Pandora's Box, there is nothing in there to jump out. You will see your face reflected in it; you will see a clear mirror!

Now let us enter into a meditation technique called the *Dukkhaharana* Meditation that will act upon the *muladhara chakra* and awaken the energy in it.

You ARE SPIRIT PETE YOU'RE JUST LESS CONCIOUS OF ITS POWER o..

Emotion: Lust, desire, greed

Chakra: Muladhara chakra

Location: Base of the spine

In Sanskrit, *muladhara* means 'the root and basis of Existence'. Mula means root and adhara means basis.

This *chakra* is locked by fantasy and imagination and it flowers when you drop your fantasies and welcome reality!

Meditation Technique to transform lust to love: Dukkhaharana Meditation – a technique from Kulaarnava Tantra

The Dukkhaharana Meditation

(Total duration: 30 minutes. To be done on an empty stomach.)

This meditation technique is called *Dukkhaharana* and is taken from Kularnava Tantra. It will bring out all the suppressed emotions in you. Many masters have employed this technique. It takes a total 30 minutes.

Breathing is the bridge to the universe. It is the system with which you are living your mind. If your thinking is calm, your breath will be relaxed. If your thinking is aggressive, your breathing will also be aggressive. You first need to control your breathing in order to control your mind

Presently, in our repressed state, most of us are half-alive and half-dead. In the first part of this meditation, deep breathing is carried out in order to create a churning in your repressed system. Your mental system is made fully alive by the increased intake of oxygen; it becomes more vital. Your cells will get more energy and will create more bioelectricity or bio-energy. This energy will melt all the repressed emotions like melting ice. It is like fanning the *muladhara chakra*.

You may practice this technique on an empty stomach, preferably in the morning. 21 days of *Dukkhaharana* will transform your being and bring a glow to your face and body. This is like taking a psychological bath. You will be able to experience the silence in you. When you kill *dukkha* or sorrow, *ananda* or bliss flowers in you and sends forth a beautiful fragrance from you.

249

Stand with your eyes closed. Breathe deeply and rhythmically from the depths of your body, always through your nose with your mouth closed. Move your hands, flex your knees and bend to a semi-squatting position and then rise up. Move as if you are a bird in flight, up and down, knees moving up and down, arms moving up and down, all rhythmic, in line with your breathing.

Do the movements gently and synchronise your inhalation with upward movement and exhalation with downward movement. If you have a heart problem, do only as much as you can. Similarly, pregnant women and others with physical ailments do only as much as you can. Do this for 10 minutes.

For the next 10 minutes, keep your eyes closed and tense each part of your body, part by part, limb by limb, then let it relax; tense and relax one limb and then move to the next. Start with your feet; move to legs; then to thighs; next to the hips; then to stomach and lower back; than to chest and upper back; then to your arms from finger tips to shoulder; next to the neck and shoulders; next to your face, and finally to the top of the head. Relax each part of your entire body before you move to the next part. This is like an isometric exercise with each part of your body. *TENSE MEDITATION*

At the end of these 10 minutes, you will become vacant inside. You will become cool, calm and composed.

For the next 10 minutes, sit down keeping your eyes closed and chant the 'hoo' *kara* sound, just the word 'hoo'. There is no need

Hoo ...

to chant it deeply and loudly. Just chant it in a relaxed manner. As you chant, simply witness whatever happens inside or outside your being.

The first two parts of this technique are actually a preparation for this third part that is the actual meditation. When you come to the third part, you will see that the mind becomes silent effortlessly, by itself. Silence cannot be forced upon you; it can only happen by itself.

Remain in this relaxed state with a smiling face and blissful mood. During this time, there may be many experiences; just watch them as you would watch the television. Watch your mind thought by thought. Don't focus on the *muladhara* at any time during the meditation, as this will create fantasies, which you are trying to remove.

At the end of the 10 minutes, slowly, very slowly, open your eyes. Carry this energy and silence with you.

Thank you.

Chapter 6

Face the fear

hy should we understand death?

All our fears are actually fear of death but under various disguises. Every single fear is related to the fear of death, but in a roundabout way. Because it is roundabout, we don't see it as fear of death. Without fear, the word *death* itself loses the meaning that we have been associating with it.

So what is death?

You will tell me, 'Death is what happens at the end of our lives.' If death were nothing more than that, it would be so easy!

But death is not something that happens at the end of our lives. It is something which is happening every moment of our lives. Every act of ours is unconsciously related to our death, the fear of dying. Death changes the very quality of our life. It is not the end; it is the climax of our lives – towards which our whole life is oriented.

Why do I say that? Because our whole life is controlled by our concept of death. Even our social structure is dictated by our concept of death. In fact, all great religions and world philosophies have arisen out of trying to answer one question, *'What happens after death?'*

In trying to answer this one question, different life solutions have taken root.

The cultures which believe in a single life, with no concept of reincarnation, have poured all their energies into excelling in life. They have achieved the peak in terms of assimilation of information, gaining of knowledge and material comforts.

These cultures have given rise to science. Science helps us live life at its optimum and get the maximum out of this life.

The cultures which believe in reincarnation have turned the focus of their life inwards. Their search is different. They are not motivated to live life in a hurry, because eternity is granted to them.

You can see it clearly in the behaviour of the people. In India, if a program is scheduled to start at 6 o'clock, you can be sure that it won't start before 7.30, because people have eternity before them!

Our whole mental set-up, the course of our lives, our society, our culture, our religion – everything is based on our idea of death. We try our best not to think about death, but death pervades every moment of our life!

When we understand the depths, the secrets and mystery of death, we will understand the secrets of life. We need to solve death and see it as a mere continuity in a different form. Otherwise, we will miss life itself.

If we understand that death is nothing but continuity in another form, we will not fear death. And when we stop fearing death, we will know to what extent we have been missing life.

We take life for granted and we live so superficially that we miss many aspects of life. Death will simply teach us to look into life with more awareness. Death is the greatest guru ever.

When we want to bring in conviction about something, we can do it in two ways: We can either experiment and see for ourselves what the truth is or we can take reference from someone who has already undergone the experience of it. We will now understand a reference from the *Upanishads*, the *vedic* scriptures from ancient India.

Death is the greatest teacher

There is an *Upanishad* called Katopanishad, which is the wonderful dialogue that a child had with Lord Yama – the Lord of Death. In Hindu mythology, the presiding deity for death is Lord Yama.

> There was a famous King by the name of Uchaishravas. He was suddenly possessed by a desire to control the entire world and so he performed a *Vaajapeya yaga* – a fire offering that is done when one wants to rule the whole world.
>
> According to the rules of this offering, one has to give away as offering, all valuable things that are of great attachment to them. Only then, one can get the position of the lord of the world.

Kings are always good businessmen. They have to be, otherwise they cannot be kings and have control over such vast property. They will see what minimum they can give and what maximum they can get out of it.

This king started offerings things such as cows that were at the fag end of their lives, that had given all the possible milk they could give for a lifetime, and that had given birth to as many calves as possible in their lifetime and ready to die.

He was offering all such worthless things.

His son, Nachiketa, about 7 years of age, was watching what was happening.

Nachiketa is the hero of this story.

He knew that his father was not doing the right things but he did not know how to tell him.

You see, children are very sharp and intelligent. You can't cheat them. Society has not yet corrupted and conditioned them.

He was watching his father carefully. He finally went up to him and said, 'Father, you have to give away all your highly priced possessions. I am one of your highly priced possessions. To whom are you going to give me as an offering?'

The king understood that his son was digging at him for what he was doing; but his ego didn't allow him to give way.

He continued with his worthless offerings.

Once more, the boy asked him the same question and the king kept quiet.

The third time, the boy shook his father and asked him to whom he was planning to offer him.

The king got very angry and blurted out, 'I will give you to Lord Yama. You go to Yama.'

An ordinary boy would have said, 'Why should I go? You have lived a full life, so you go!'

But Nachiketa was a very sincere and committed boy.

Commitment and honesty possessed him like a ghost.

To respect his father's words, he decided to go and meet Lord Yama.

Remember that the first and the last person on planet Earth to go and meet Yama was Nachiketa. Normally only Yama comes to meet people, but for the first time, Nachiketa went to meet Yama.

He reached the abode of Yama, but Yama was not there! He had gone out.

For three days Nachiketa waited.

Understand one thing here: A great truth is established at this point of the story. When we go in search of death, or we have the courage to face death, death will not be there as we know it!

Anyhow, Yama returned after three days.

His servants told him about the young boy who was waiting for him.

Yama rushed to see Nachiketa.

He apologized for not being there to receive him.

He further told him, 'For having made you wait for three days, I grant you three boons. You may ask for any three boons, and I will grant them to you.'

For Nachiketa, death turned out to be a God that granted him boons!

He asked for three boons.

The first boon was, 'My father should not be angry any longer. He should recognize me and receive me with love when I return.' Nachiketa asked for this boon out of the deep love for his father so that he does not suffer from the consequences of consigning his son to death.

Yama granted him the boon.

The second boon was, 'Instruct me in the fire sacrifice that leads to heaven, for there is no fear in heaven, nor old age nor death.'

This boon was also granted and Yama led Nachiketa through the fire sacrifice, and then named it Nachiketa Agni. This was a fire which could raise one's consciousness to a heavenly experience; an experience of pleasure.

The third boon was, 'Please teach me the truth of Existence, of life and death. Do I exist after death or not. Please tell me this!'

Yama was shocked at Nachiketa's question.

He told him, 'Please do not ask me this question. You are asking the very secret of death which I cannot deliver to you. I will give you immeasurable wealth if you wish, but please don't ask me this question.'

But Nachiketa was insistent.

He said, 'Even if I take all this wealth from you, I will be a mere trustee to your wealth for about 100 years to 1000 years, that's all. I still have to come to your abode once that period is over! It is not going to be of any use to me. So please tell me the secret of death instead.'

Yama saw the maturity and commitment of the boy to know the truth.

He decided that he should give Nachiketa the truth. The experience he took the boy through became the experience of the soul for the boy and Nachiketa flowered and became enlightened.

This is a beautiful story from the *Upanishad*. Don't analyze whether this story is a fact or not. Don't start looking for dates and history. It conveys the truth – that is enough. Use it as a ladder to reach the truth, instead of clinging onto the ladder and missing the truth.

What is the difference between an ordinary person meeting Yama and Nachiketa meeting Yama?

When an ordinary person meets Yama, Yama takes away his family without his permission. Yama takes away all his pleasures. Finally he takes away his life itself. All the things he covets like family, pleasures and life he takes away suddenly without his consent. Also an ordinary person never goes to Yama. It is Yama who comes to him as an unwanted guest. But Nachiketa went to Yama and Yama gave him back his family in the first boon. Through the second boon, Yama gave him the experience of heavenly pleasures, and finally in the third boon, Yama gave him enlightenment.

Four things need to be understood from this wonderful story. The first thing is that when we go in search of death, when we face death, it will not be there as we thought it would be. This is symbolized by Yama being absent when Nachiketa goes to meet him. Secondly, even if death is there, it is not the terrifying thing that we think it is; it is loving and giving. This can be seen from the way Yama greeted and spoke to Nachiketa. The third thing is that death is our greatest teacher ever. That is why Yama taught Nachiketa many things. Lastly, death can give us the ultimate gift – enlightenment, which Yama did!

For most of us, life never goes beyond the fear of death. We live and die between desires and fear. We don't know any other way of life. Or we don't have the courage to take on any other way of life.

In earlier times, people lived without the life security that we have today. There was no vaccination available against fatal diseases. There was no satellite-based advance warning of natural calamities and there was no security against famine or floods. Therefore, people were always mentally prepared for struggle, even for death. Especially the warrior class had to be ever-ready for death.

The Samurai warriors of ancient Japan knew the way to face death calmly.

Conscious death experience

We all live in constant fear of death. We are ready to escape it at all cost. Death is seen upon as our greatest enemy.

A small story about Socrates, the Greek philosopher:

> Socrates was killed by being forced to drink the juice of the poisonous herb called hemlock.
>
> Just before he drank the poison, one of his disciples asked him, 'Master, are you not afraid of dying? You appear to be so calm.'
>
> Socrates replied, 'Why should I be? I know that only two things can happen after death. Either I will continue to exist, in some other form or name, or I will cease to exist after death. In the first case, there is nothing to worry about. In the second case, who will remain to worry? So either way, there is nothing to fear!'

Socrates was fearless of death purely because he had a clear understanding of death and its consequences. Death is always looked upon as a 'discontinuity' and that is why people suffer when they see death.

Death is never a discontinuity. It is either continuity in some other form, or simply liberation, that's all. When man understands this, he will realize how foolish it is to suffer on this account.

Man is very attached to the physical form and that is why he suffers so much. The body is a mere vehicle for the soul. This has to be understood very clearly.

Although the only certain thing on planet earth for man is death, he is always taken by surprise when it actually happens! This is the most surprising thing about man.

A small story:

> A lady was celebrating her 100th birthday.
>
> Her entire family was there for the occasion.
>
> They were opening all the gifts and reading all the cards that had been received from family and friends.
>
> They showed the lady one card that had been sent by her 94-year old friend.
>
> The lady shrieked, 'God! She is still alive!'

We are able to apply death to everyone else except us! Everything in life we are prepared for except our own death. The irony is, everything in life is so unpredictable except death. The only certain thing in life is death. But the last thing we would like to be told is that sooner or later we are going to die!

> Bhagwan Ramana Maharshi, the enlightened master from India, became enlightened through a conscious experience of death.
>
> When Ramana was a young boy, one day he was just lying on his bed in his uncle's house in Madurai in South India.
>
> Suddenly he got the feeling that he was going to die! He felt that death was coming upon him.
>
> He had two choices – either to resist the feeling, or to accept it and go through it.
>
> Usually people resist, so they pass into coma and leave the body in a state of unconsciousness.
>
> 99% of us leave the body in a state of unconsciousness.

Though we know from the moment of birth that our life will culminate in death, we never try to visualize it. We never try to actualize the possibility; we never try to welcome it.

At least once if you go through it with consciousness, you will lose your fear for it automatically.

Ramana was courageous enough to choose the second path. He co-operated with the feeling.

He allowed death to happen. He decided to see what would happen during death.

He saw clearly one by one, the parts of his body dying.

Slowly, his whole body was dead. He saw his body turn into ashes.

Suddenly he realized that something remained even after that; something which cannot be destroyed. He suddenly realized that he was pure consciousness, beyond the body and mind. He was simply a witness to his own death!

That knowledge was tremendous and it never left him and when he came back into his body, he was Bhagwan Ramana Maharshi – an enlightened master.

When you conquer the fear of death, you conquer death itself, because death is just one more imagination! Just like how our greed makes us imagine the world to be more beautiful than it actually is, here our fear makes us imagine death to be more frightening than it actually is.

We wear glasses of greed and fear, which do not allow us to see reality. When you experience death psychologically, you release the energy that has been locked in the fear energy center called the *swadhishtana chakra* in your body, which is located in the navel center. When this energy center is activated, the whole quality of your life changes.

Because of your capacity to accept death as just a continuity in another form, your capacity to enjoy life is transformed. Your whole body relaxes; your consciousness expands; your living capacity expands. By understanding death and fear of death, your life will turn out to be rich; not wealthy maybe, but rich. Richness is what is really important in life.

But if I tell you all this now, you will not believe me. You will think that I am talking about impractical things.

A small story:

> A man who had been born blind was promised a cure by a doctor.
> The doctor assured the man, 'After this operation, you will get your vision back! You won't need to use your stick anymore!'
> Hearing this, the blind man became afraid.
> He said, 'Doctor, I understand that I will get my vision back. But how can I possibly walk without my stick?'

The stick had become such an integral part of the blind man that he could not even understand that he would be able to walk without the stick! How can you explain to a blind man that once he gains his vision, he simply won't need the stick? Right now he is too afraid. So all you can do is, perform the operation, and let him see for himself, that's all. He will throw away the stick on his own!

In the same way, even if I tell you that all your fears are only the ultimate fear of death, and that your self is immortal, that it is only your body which perishes, you will still hold onto your own ideas of fear, because you haven't experienced it.

Unless death becomes a conscious experience, the fear will never leave you. But you can do one thing. Repeatedly listen to these words. Develop a conviction about them. Try to see how your minor and major fears are actually related to the fear of dying. Bring some clarity into all your day-to-day fears. See how interrelated all your fears are. Bring awareness into your fears. Then you will steadily evolve and come closer to the truth.

The five types of fear

We can categorize all our fears into five major categories:

The first is fear of losing our wealth, our comfort, name and fame, prestige, and other outer world things.

The second is the fear of losing our health and parts of our body through some accident or disease; the fears concerned with our physical health.

The third is the fear of losing our mental health, our mental stability.

The fourth is the fear of losing our loved ones, or their love.

The fifth is the fear of the unknown: fear of God, fear of ghosts and fear of death itself.

Actually, if you deeply analyze our fears, all the five categories of fear are related to the fear of death. They manifest themselves in different ways, that's all.

Live totally

The main reason why people fear death is, they have not lived their lives totally. They are afraid because they feel desperate that they have not lived life enough. They feel this way because throughout their lives they have lived in memories of the past, in the anxieties of the future, for the sake of others, never in the present. Every action of ours has been due to the pull and push of each others' ego, each others' desires, each others' emotions etc.

If you deeply analyze your own life, you will understand what I am trying to say. You start your life where your parents left it. You simply take over the crown of desires, guilt, fear etc. that was passed down for generations, live your life and pass it down to the next generation before leaving. You have never lived totally.

What do I mean by living totally? Try to live with more clarity, that's all. Make the other people see sense in whatever they try to impose upon you. With clarity, you will be able to identify what your own desires are, what others have imposed on you and what desires you have borrowed from others. The first set of desires alone need to be fulfilled without any harm to any person or property. The other two need to be dropped with the help of clarity.

If you live this way, you will no more be fulfilling others' desires and you will be no more living others' lives. You will live your own life, and experience fulfillment, and you will be ready to die when the time comes. You will have no lurking confusion and fear of death. I am not asking you to be selfish. I am only asking you to bring clarity into the whole thing.

A small story:

> Once a Zen monk was ordered by the king to be put to death. He was supposed to be killed the next day.
> The monk remained calm and silent.
> One of his disciples, shocked by the monk's calmness, asked him, 'Do you realize you have only 24 hours to live? Are you not afraid?'
> The monk replied calmly, 'I have lived, and therefore I have no fear of dying.'

He means to say, 'I have lived every moment of my life, moment to moment. Every single moment has been so much for me! Why should I be afraid?'

If you look deep inside, you will realize that most of us are not afraid of dying, but we are afraid that we haven't lived our lives enough. We are afraid that we have lived a pseudo life. We feel a deep unexplainable regret about the whole thing. We feel we have not lived as we wanted to live. We don't feel fulfilled – and there starts the fear of death.

Continuously compromising for the sake of others, trying to live out a life that is not natural to us, trying to fit ourselves into a mould that society has prepared for us; all these things lead to a lack of fulfillment. The fear of life is what is reflected in the fear of death.

When you have lived in the deepest possible way, to your full satisfaction, you will not be in fear of death. Live without fear.

Live with the deepest individuality that you can manage. Live to your complete satisfaction and you will lose your fear of death.

If you live totally, without any hangover of any feelings, when you live your emotions with great clarity and totality, you will never fear losing your family and relatives also.

Fear of loss of dear ones

You fear someone's loss only because you feel you have not justified the relationship in some way in your life. You feel you have not been in it in totality, so you are not ready to let go. Physical separation is only one aspect of the fear. The real reason is lack of fulfillment in the relationship.

The word 'justification' comes into relationships because you have always been taught to live for the sake of others, fulfilling their needs and desires. And if you don't do these things, you get into the cycle of guilt and fear. If you just live totally, with deep clarity of the whole play of society, you will never be gripped by such compulsions.

You can live with total fulfillment and still not lose out on any love in relationships. If you live totally, not with a transaction type of relationship but with just pure loving energy towards the other, there will be no room for guilt or fear. Even if the person passes away, you will continue to feel love towards him or her, never fear of any separation.

Most often, relationships suffer because of the lingering fear of losing one another. If you deeply analyze fear in any relationship, you will understand that because our relationships are just transactions of some sort, this fear is prevalent.

Between a husband and wife, there is fear that the other may start looking outside of marriage. Between mother and son, there is fear that the son may start paying more attention to the wife instead of the mother. Between father and son, there is the fear that the father may not pass on the inheritance to his son or the son may not keep up the family prestige.

Like this, in any relationship, there is a core expectation which needs to be satisfied and guarded, and *this* gives rise to fear. But you can never satisfy any relationship totally. Any one who has tried to please their whole family will only become a dropout!

Understand: Fear is always imprisoning, while love is always liberating. But unless society instills fear into you, you will not listen to it and so it instills fear in you through all possible means – through insecurity, rules, regulations, worship etc.

Fear is what takes the form of jealousy also in relationships. Fear is the basis for most of our actions and emotions. Jealousy, anger, greed – all these emotions are rooted in fear. But we are not aware of this. We don't know that fear is the causative factor for all these. That is the problem. That is why we continue to be in the dark as far as our behavioural patterns are concerned. That is why relationships turn out to be difficult.

Understand that fear and love can never co-exist. If there is pure love in a relationship, there can never be fear. If there is fear, there can never be pure love. There is some vested interest in the relationship. There is some purpose, some objective, some expectation of security or greed or returns in the relationship. That is why fear sets in.

We look for security in every relationship. We need some security to settle down comfortably. This is actually a kind of imprisonment that we enjoy. People talk of freedom, but I tell you, they are so afraid of it! They like only imprisonment. In the comfortable cushioning effect of imprisonment, they think they are free.

A small story:

> A small girl asked her father one day, 'Dad, what is the meaning of the word guaranteed?'
> The father replied, 'It means that something is made well and it will last for a long time.'
> That night before going to sleep, the girl called out, 'Good night guaranteed father!'

All of us look for security continuously in our lives. But we say that we are looking for freedom. If we are really looking for freedom, why are we looking for security? Why fear? As long as you have fear in you, you will look for security. Until then, you can only delude yourself by saying that you want freedom.

A master is one who will throw you upon the utter insecurity of life. He is the only one who gives you complete freedom. That is why with him, you feel insecure, you feel afraid. Freedom creates fear.

You will never feel utterly insecure in your other relationships because there is always some push and pull of greed, fear and anger that keeps you well-settled in the familiar patterns of relationships. But with a master, you are totally free. So you become afraid.

A small story:

> A man was in prison for 20 years.
> On the day of his release, he appeared very worried and tense.
> His friend in the prison asked him, 'What has happened to you? Why are you so worried?'
> The man replied, 'I am afraid. What will I do when I go out?'

The prison has created such a solid pattern of security for the man that he does not know what he will do when he goes outside! This is the danger of getting caught in patterns and security.

A master will never offer you the security you are looking for. He will never offer you the patterns you are looking for. When you don't get the security you are looking for, you will grow with deep centering within yourself. You will grow fearlessly because you know there is nothing to lose. And when you know there is nothing to lose, you have no fear.

To show you that there is nothing to lose, the master throws you upon utter insecurity. Out of his deep compassion for you, out of deep concern for your growth, he doesn't offer you security. When you don't find the mundane security, you will find God!

All your fears are because you don't clearly know that there is nothing to lose. Just one encounter with near death can show you that there is nothing to lose and that all your fears are baseless. The master simply makes you understand this in his own way.

So don't try to escape from the master. Understand that he is here only to show you what you actually are. Your inherent nature is fearlessness. Over years, you have been instilled with fear. The master tries to break the layers of conditioning that you have taken upon yourself. If you just allow him to work upon you, with trust and love, you will see yourself transform in front of your own eyes.

Let me tell you a small story about a *Swami* with whom I was acquainted:

> This *Swami* used to have a number of clocks in his room, and each of the clocks would show a different time!
> I asked him about it one day.

He replied, 'Time is not my master. I am the master! Whatever time I want it to be, I simply choose the time from that particular clock.'

This *Swami* had already predicted that he would be leaving his body on a particular day and time.

On the night before his death, the Swami asked all his disciples to gather around him and sing hymns.

One of the singers was somewhat arrogant about his musical abilities. He never sang on this occasion.

As was the custom, the *Swami* wrote something on a piece of paper and passed it on to him.

The disciple was flattered, thinking that it was a request for a particular song.

But when he opened the note, he saw that the Swami had written, 'Please don't sing after my death!'

Even on his deathbed he was in a humorous mood!

Later that night, he instructed his disciples to take good care of the orphans who lived in the ashram. He said, 'Especially tomorrow, you will all be busy with preparations for my cremation. Don't forget to arrange for food for those children!'

Till the last minute, his concern was for the people he was leaving behind.

The next morning, exactly at the time he had mentioned, he joined his hands in a *namaskar* to all and his hands dropped, simply like a drama.

What a beautiful, calm and courageous way to face death! That is the way we should all go to death and that is the way we should look upon death even when our own family and relatives pass away. When you understand this, your whole idea of fear will slowly dissolve, because as I said, the underlying basis of fear is death itself.

Q: *Swamiji*, is it that fear is normally associated more with women?

Men are mainly caught in the lust and women are mainly caught in fear. The fact is, they both know this and exploit each other appropriately!

The man knows where exactly to touch the woman's weak chord. He will play with her insecurity and fear and exploit her. Similarly, the woman knows where the key lies with the man! She will play the game appropriately and exploit him. This is what goes on all the time in marriages.

Actually, at the time of Hindu marriages, a vow is taken wherein the man and woman vow to each other that they will both work towards exhausting each others' *karma* – unfulfilled actions and desires - in a smooth way, without accumulating any more *karma* in this life.

But these days, people are not even aware that they have taken such a vow because they are not the ones who are getting married. The priests are the ones who utter all the chants and get married!

It is such a beautiful vow that they take. We have accumulated enough and more *karma* in our lives. The only concern for us should be to exhaust it all at least in this birth, and attain liberation.

If you watch the drama of marriage from outside, you will understand how the couple create *karma* for each other.

Only when you watch from outside you will understand what a foolish game is being played. I always tell people that for actors and actresses it would be so easy to watch life as a game because they are all the time assuming roles and enacting them. They are the closest to seeing life as a great drama. The rest of us are so caught up with our roles that it becomes a solid reality for us.

Fear of small things

First of all understand that all small fears are mere projections of the ultimate fear of death. Second, don't resist the fear in you. Just keep repeating to yourself that you are scared and go through it, that's all! You will soon find that the fear is no longer there because you saw it through. Start doing this every time you feel fear.

When you consciously work on this, you will understand that what you call fear is nothing but your response or reaction to an incident or thought. Depending on how you respond, you can claim that you did not have fear or had fear. And, with more and more awareness, you can respond towards fear without fear!

Remember one thing: No one can claim to be fearless. One can learn to handle fear without fear, that's all. If anyone professes to be fearless, be very clear that they have not analyzed deeply the subject of fear and human response to it. Don't start thinking that they are superhumans and you are a lesser human being.

(A young girl speaks) Swamiji, *I remember how you made me overcome my fear of spiders! While in our discussions one day, I jumped up when I saw a spider and you laughed at me for it. You told me to meditate on the spider every time I saw one. Every time I saw one, I looked at it with awareness and concentration. Slowly I started wondering why I was scared of it after all!*

Yes. It is only a question of bringing awareness into our fears. You will then wonder what it was that caused the fear in you!

You can even sit by yourself and imagine that your fears are happening to you. In your imagination, confront them with deep awareness and calmness. If you suffer in the process of visualization, it is alright. Don't suppress it or punish it. If your body shakes with fear, let it. Just co-operate with it. Anything when lived out completely will have no effect over you. All your fears are simply fear of your fears, that's all!

A small story:

> A disciple was caught in a river one day.
> He was terrified of losing his life and he shouted out to his master to save him from drowning.
> The master said, 'Stand up!'
> The disciple screamed out, 'How can I? I am drowning.'
> The master said, 'Have I not taught you to help yourself?

Now stand up!'

The disciple said, 'Master, you are preaching to me at this moment of my impending death. Why don't you just save me!'

The master persisted, 'I said, stand up.'

The disciple was enraged at the master's persistence.

He simply stood up. The water came up only to his knee!

All your fears are nothing but the fear of your fears. If you shake off your fears and allow your intelligence to surface, you will find that your fears are just shadows of objects that don't exist.

Live in the moment and leave!

If you deeply analyze the fear of death, you will come to know that people are afraid to die because unconsciously, they feel that they should have been somewhere higher up than where they are now. They feel they have not reached their actual place in life and so they are not ready to leave.

Some people feel that others have cast eyes on them and so they have not been able to progress! The truth is that you have not cast your own eyes properly on yourself. That is why, even in your last days, you prolong your death.

If you properly analyze and understand your desires, fear and other emotions, you will not blame anyone for anything.

People who live their lives without any of these convoluted fears, will be able to live their death also. As I told you earlier, there are so many stories of living masters who told their disciples exactly what time of what day they would die and they died that way.

Many of the disciples have learned from their masters' death what they failed to learn from their teachings when they were alive. When we say that they lived their death, we mean they were able to announce that they were going to die and they died consciously. In their case, their death is literally 'leaving their body', that's all.

We all leave our bodies unconsciously, with a lot of suffering – the pull and push of unfulfilled desires torture us on one side and the body tortures on the other, saying that it has had enough. The mismatch between the mind and the body tortures us while we are alive and at the time of death also. When we are alive, if we live inside our boundary, inside our body, we will also leave our body peacefully. The problem is, when we live, we are always outside our body, never inside.

Let me explain this to you. Just look deeply into your way of life. Early in the morning, when you brush your teeth, what are you doing? You are already thinking of going to work. When you are at work, you are thinking of catching the bus to go home. When you are at home, you are thinking of work next day! When you are on vacation, you think of your office and when you are at office, you think of going on vacation.

Wherever your body is, you can be sure that your mind is not! You have never lived any moment of your life with fullness. You have always lived either in the past or in the future. This is what is called 'not living inside your boundary'. This is why at the time of death, you feel so pre-occupied and unfulfilled and unwilling to go. This is why you fear death.

You may ask why you need to know about dying consciously. Only when you know about death, can you live with the right understanding of life. Otherwise, you will not live life the right way.

Stop procrastinating

In life, you keep postponing everything. You postpone your enjoyment, you postpone your work, you postpone everything for tomorrow. You have to understand that 'tomorrow' also comes in the form of 'today' only! When it comes as today, you say 'tomorrow' again! It is a game that you play with yourself.

Finally, when death comes, you are so unprepared! You feel there is so much to be done. You feel cheated by life itself. The truth is, you have been deceiving yourself all along. But you land up blaming life for everything. That is why a clear understanding of death is necessary for you to live. Then there will be no delusions and you will be ready to die any time.

Procrastination is the mentality by which we lose out on life itself. People ask me, 'Swamiji, how are you able to do so many things in such a short period of time?' It is amazing for them to see my calendar for the year! They are amazed to see the various things happening throughout the year across the world. I tell them, 'It is very simple – I live totally in the present. I don't procrastinate like you.'

In our meditation programs, we take people through a guided meditation wherein they are told to visualize that they are going to die in just 24 hours time and that they should complete all the things that they would like to complete before they die. It is a beautiful meditation technique. They are even made to visualize their own death ceremony.

Once after this meditation, a young girl shared her thoughts.

She said, '*Swamiji*, I saw a poster in a shop which said, 'When you plan, plan concretely taking into account the future years to come. When you execute, execute like you are going to die the very next minute. After doing this meditation, I understand what it really means!'

You see, when you plan, you have to have a futuristic plan, so that too many things don't have to be re-structured for at least a few years. But when you execute, you have to execute in such a way that every sub-task that you take up in the master plan is completed successfully without any loose ends.

Even if you are going to die then, up to the point of what has been executed, everything will be perfect and the master plan will still be there as a reference for people to follow or amend as the situation demands. This can be achieved only if you work without procrastination in every sub-task that you take up.

Often, procrastination is what takes you to poverty. Poverty is your own choice. When you defer decisions, you take steps towards being poor. But you are blissfully unaware of this. You feel you have not been treated rightly by God and that life has been too short for you to realize your dreams. If you had used all your energy in the proper channel and with clarity, you would not feel this way and you would be ever ready to die.

If you just look at the mirror everyday and tell yourself that today is the last day in your life, you will stop procrastinating. You need not tell yourself this all your life; just a month will do. Automatically, you will start living your life without procrastination. Not only that, your fears about losing your prestige, embarrassment, pride and expectations will all dissolve, because you will know that you have nothing to lose.

People who have had a near death experience in some way like a narrow escape from an accident or a cure from cancer or something like that, will be able to live more fearlessly because they will know that they have nothing to lose! They will also live their lives with greater clarity and more intelligence.

The first lesson that you need to learn from all your education is that you should do the right thing at the right time and move on. Somehow, this is the last lesson that we learn thoroughly! After having gone through all the other lessons, we learn this lesson!

Procrastination is something that you bring about yourself. But the rest of the fears, society instills in you. Society makes you afraid of your own self, of others and of God. It makes you afraid of yourself with simple things like morality, names and forms, prestige and what not.

In the name of morality, it makes you lose confidence in yourself and that is why you are so unsure of yourself when it comes to morality. When you start following morality out of fear, there will be no chance for your inner intelligence to guide you.

Morality always instills fear

In our lives, morality is nothing but a poor substitute for intelligence. When you act out of your own intelligence, you can be confident of yourself. But when you act out of rules and regulations, you can never be sure of yourself, because you are not yourself to start with! You are not centered in yourself; you are centered on the rules.

If you live out of intelligence, these types of fear will never grip you. People who preach morality are so deeply in fear. That is why they preach about it. They are afraid either because they are unsure of themselves or because they know to be moral only with fear. Moralists can become neurotic with their concept of morality and discipline.

A small story:

> Once there was a moralist who normally walked on the streets with carefully measured steps.
> One day it suddenly began raining very heavily.
> The moralist just followed the crowd and ran along.

After running for a while, he realized that he was careless about his manner.

He said to himself, 'What am I doing! Running is undignified. A gentleman must correct his mistakes regretfully if he has made any.'

So he returned in the rain to the place where he had begun running, and walked again, with measured steps.

Morality makes you totally dull and dead!

When I tell you this, I am not telling you that this is a free world and you can do anything you like. I am telling you that you have to develop your own intelligence and live so that rules will only be a confirmation of what you already know and feel. This is real intelligence. Any proper rule will only be a confirmation of what the rightly flowered intelligence feels. So drop your fears and try to find your inner intelligence, your inner master.

A small story:

A young *sannyasi* lived across the road from a beautiful courtesan.

The *sannyasi* was all the time trying to meditate.

The courtesan on the other hand, carried on with her way of earning money.

Many men came and went from her house.

The *sannyasi* used to try his best to concentrate on his meditation, but his attention was more on the young woman and he kept cursing her for the kind of immoral life that she was leading.

284

The courtesan on the other hand, was not even aware of the *sannyasi* staying across the street.

Despite her lifestyle of offering pleasure to men, the courtesan was immersed in her love for Lord Krishna and spent as much time as she could in praying to Him and playing with His image.

The *sannyasi* and the courtesan died on the same day and reached the gates of Lord Yama – the Lord of Death.

After their records were analysed, the courtesan was sent to heaven while the *sannyasi* was sent to hell.

The *sannyasi* expressed deep feelings about the injustice of Yama.

Yama calmly explained to the *sannyasi*, 'All your life, under the guise of meditating, you were harboring lust for the courtesan. She, on the other hand, despite whatever she was doing, was totally focused on the reality of God.'

Moralists live a superficial, fearing and shallow life. They don't live totally. They are in constant fear of stepping out of morality. Their true intentions are kept well covered under the guise of morality.

It is alright to lose prestige

Like morality, prestige also gives rise to fear. Prestige, name and fame, social status – all these give rise to fear. These fears are nothing but fear of hurting your own ego. What prestige are you trying to cover? Just live with inner fulfillment and dignity; that is enough. The people who guard their prestige tend to be hypocrites.

They are also the people who live in constant fear. Their so-called prestige is so much in control of them.

A small story:

> A man was fishing in the river one day.
> He was sitting for a long time without catching any fish.
> He dozed off with the fishing rod in his hand.
> Suddenly, a heavy fish caught the bait and tugged at it.
> The man just tumbled into the water before he could wake up.
> A boy was watching this from a distance. He asked his father, 'Dad, was he catching the fish or was the fish catching him?'

With prestige, you have to be very careful. When prestige becomes larger than life for you, it will start consuming you.

Prestige makes you feel that you are extra-ordinary. It gives you a solid identity in society. People with money and prestige do all sorts of nonsensical and immoral things and get away with it. People talk about them behind their backs and greet them to their face because of their power and prestige.

This is the kind of prestige they are trying to guard so carefully. Understand: Existence will never choose you if you are like this. In the material world, you may get what you want, you may appear successful, but in the eyes of Existence, you will remain poor. Existence has its own ways of choosing.

Understand that prestige, name, fame and power are all your own imagination. You give life to them. You create them and develop a fear about losing them.

Just live with infinite love for everyone and everything around you. Feel deep love for anyone and anything that comes your way. If you live this way, automatically prestige will come to you. People will respect you for your quality, not for your quantity. And with this kind of prestige, there is no fear of losing. You don't have to guard it all the time.

Fear of hurting your own ego

Even fears like fear of public speaking are fear of losing one's prestige in a way. When you are afraid of talking in front of a gathering, you are actually afraid of what they might say about you. You are afraid that your ego might suffer because of something that they might say about you. And so you get into stage fear. It is a passive form of guarding your ego. Fear is very much a manifestation of ego. Understand that.

So what if people don't approve of your talk? The moment you are afraid of what others will say, you are only guarding your ego.

Fear of the ego suffering is also the reason why people get afraid when they go into meditation. When you go into meditation, there is always the fear of losing yourself – to Existence, to the Existential energy that is surrounding you. So you hold on. You resist meditation. Instead, if I tell you to chant something, you will happily chant. There will be no fear.

Your ego is so afraid that it will dissolve. If it dissolves, all the labels with which you identify yourself will also dissolve. You become a nobody! So you resist and remain somebody at least to yourself. This resistance is purely the fear of the ego.

Fear of the unknown

Q: *Swamiji*, you spoke about fear of the unknown. Can you explain further about that?

Yes, I am coming to that.

Fear of the unknown is nothing but the fear that we have of darkness, of ghosts and spirits, of God and finally of our own death.

A small story:

> One man was traveling on a train.
> The ticket collector came to him and asked him for his ticket.
> He frantically started searching for the ticket in his wallet, in his luggage and in his pants pocket.
> The ticket collector was watching him and said, 'Sir, why don't you search in your coat pocket.'
> The man replied, 'Please don't ask me to look in it now. My only hope is that it will be there.'

We are so afraid to look! We are afraid to look at our fears; that is the whole problem. So we delude ourselves in comfort zones and keep carrying on.

288

Never fear to look. The moment you fear to look, you are only creating more fear because it becomes more unknown to you.

When we talk about fear of the unknown, fear of spirits and ghosts is very common. There is no need to fear them at all. Just understand that spirits and ghosts are much less powerful than we are. We give them much more power than they naturally would have and let them control our fears. There starts the problem.

Don't go too much into the subject of spirits and ghosts. It is of no use. If you are well-centered and clear about yourself, it is enough. Automatically, nothing can touch you and you will also not have fear of such things.

Fear of darkness is also fear of the unknown. Fear of darkness is nothing but the fear of death. The same garden in your house, which you walk in at daytime, will you walk in at nighttime? No! You are afraid! Why? You know the boundaries of your garden well, yet why are you afraid? You are afraid not because of your garden but because of the darkness.

You are afraid that something might happen to you in the dark. This is what I mean when I say that every fear of yours is in some way related to the ultimate fear of death. In the case of darkness, it is very obvious, but in the case of your other fears, it is very subtle, that's all.

Actually, darkness is beautiful! It is like your own mother's womb. When you were in your mother's womb, you were in complete darkness. But after you came to the world, you lost this connection with darkness. You started fearing it as something unknown. Tantric followers meditate upon darkness to feel the intensity of Existence.

There is no need to be afraid of darkness. Just once, if you can look into darkness with deep love, with the soothing feeling that it is your mother's womb, you will not be afraid of it anymore.

When a child gets scared of darkness, don't tell him, *'Be brave'!* If you tell him this, he will only become tense because he is not supposed to get afraid. He will not drop his fear for darkness. Just allow him to go through the fear of darkness. Let him tremble a little. At least he gets a chance to explore his fear. When he does this a few times, he will slowly lose his fear of darkness.

Now we come to the fear of God. God is also unknown to us and so we fear God. Understand that God is nothing but the name that we give to Existence, to the Cosmos, to Existential energy, to the Life Force that pervades this universe. This Existence, this Universal energy knows only to love. If you can understand this much, automatically all your fears will drop.

There is no need to fear God

People ask me, *'Swamiji*, people say that if we do good deeds or *punya* instead of doing bad deeds or *paapa*, we will go to heaven and not to hell. Is this true?'

First of all, understand that hell and heaven are not geographic. There is no heaven located above your head or hell beneath your feet. They are terms created just to instill fear and greed in you, that's all. Hell or heaven can be interpreted as having either a tumultuous death or a peaceful and conscious death, that's all.

Any moment in your life that you have spent in meditation is a moment of *punya* or good deed. When I say meditation, I don't mean closing your eyes and sitting. I mean, moments that you have been consciously in the present; when your consciousness has been with you.

Any moment that has not been spent in such states is *paapa*. All the moments of conscious states are like your bank balance. At the time of your death, it is these states that will surface and liberate you.

People think that if they offer pots of milk to the deity at the temple, their *punya* will increase and they will reach heaven! Let me tell you: by offering milk to the Lord, nothing is going to happen. When you feel a swelling gratitude towards Existence, you can express it by offering milk to the deity that you worship as Existence. That is perfectly alright. But please do not link it with *punya* etc.

Even a drop of milk offered with pure joy and gratitude is a moment of sincere meditation that will stand by you at the time of death. On the other hand, pots and pots of milk offered out of sheer fear of missing out on gathering *punya*, will not get returns. So, please increase your awareness and live consciously. Make every moment, whatever may be the thing you are doing, a meditation. That is enough. Then you can live without fear of sins.

Let me narrate to you one incident:

> I went to a Shiva temple in a remote village in India.
> At the entrance of the main deity, there was a tubelight burning.

The light was hardly visible because on it was written in black ink, Vishnunathan B.Sc.

I was wondering how Lord Shiva was called Vishnunathan. Then under that I saw in small font, Kailasanathan – the correct name for Shiva.

Vishnunathan was the name of the person who donated the tubelight!

We have been taught to collect good deeds in our lives. So we start creating bank balances of good deeds. And we don't stop at that. We inform God repeatedly about all the good things that we have done... so that he doesn't forget! We become materialistic even when it comes to God!

Understand: God is not running a resort in heaven where you can enter by doing these good things on Earth. Thinking this way is like building a house in your dream, painting it, decorating it and waking up to find out that the whole thing was a dream. Where is the house? Is it of any use to you after you wake up? No! In the same way, you are only deluding yourself by this 'good deeds' concept.

I have seen people who decide to visit a particular deity in a particular temple with an offering, every Saturday of the week. If they are not able to make it on a particular Saturday, they will send their driver with the offering to the deity!

God knows you better than you know yourself. So there is no reason to fear Him or please Him. Even better than your mother or father, God knows you. He knows you not only in this birth but in all the births that you have taken until now. You are an open book in front of Him. He can refer to any page at any time!

So drop your fear of God and look upon Him as a totality of Existence. Look upon Him as the ultimate friend. However hard society tries to make you afraid of God, don't listen to it. Develop your own relationship with God - a solid and trusting one; the only relationship that is required in your life.

When you start relating with Existence or God, you start relating with yourself much better than before. You will know what exactly is going on inside you. Your inner intelligence will grow. Your fears will drop. You will learn to look properly into anything before feeling fear about it. You will not feel any compulsion to do anything. Intelligence will replace fear. You will be more relaxed and joyful. You will feel liberated.

When you understand this about Existence, all the wars that go on in the name of religion will not be there. The people who are in fear of their religion, the people who fight for their religion are people who have not understood the loving Existence. They simply miss the whole thing. They are like blind people fighting with one another.

And most importantly, please don't pass on your ideas about God to your children and instill fear of God in them. Teach them to embrace God. Teach them that God is the all-pervading Existence. Teach them that God is pure love and nothing else. Help them to grow with a loving attitude towards God and Existence as a whole.

Q: We often wonder, whatever is happening to us, is it fate or is it our choice?

A very commonly asked question!

Your present moment is the totality of all your past decisions. Now you are here in this place. You decided to wake up early in the morning, take the proper route, come here, sit, and continue to sit, am I right?

Like this, all your past decisions form your present – like being here right now. Your future is going to be a result of all your present decisions. When we make our decisions unconsciously and don't expect some of the results that come our way, we call it fate.

When we make conscious decisions, we are aware of the side-effects and after-effects. When we are not aware of the side-effects and after-effects, we call it fate. Actually, life is pure choice. It is we who make the decisions; never somebody else for us. May be a few major things in your life is driven by fate. But even those can be changed. Attributing every small thing to fate is pure escapism.

God is so gracious, even though the world is His, He allows us to have our choice! The only way you can make the right decisions is by infusing awareness into your very breath so that every action of yours, every decision of yours, happens with awareness and you never slip into any subconscious or unconscious decision-making. Then you don't have to worry about fate and destiny.

Drop the fear of insecurity

Understand one more thing: No one is waiting to lay their hands on your wealth and cause you so-called ill-fate. Somehow, we live with the constant fear that people are waiting to rob us of our wealth. It is not true.

In this fear, we build many walls around us. Finally we find ourselves entrapped in our own cell. That is why I say, 'Open the door, let the breeze in.' Have faith that the life force will take care of you. I am not saying 'Don't lock your house!' You need to lock your house. But after locking, drop the obsession with the lock, that's all!

Just take for example, you are traveling in a train. As soon as you settle down in your compartment, what do you do? You start conversing with the person next to you. You ask them where they are from. You try to make out what religion they might believe in. You ask questions about their background etc. Why? Are you genuinely interested in their details? No! It is because you see them as unknown and if you know all these things about them, psychologically you feel comfortable traveling with them, that's all.

If you are a Hindu and they are also Hindu, you feel relaxed. If you are Hindu and you find out that they are Muslim, you start feeling uneasy and afraid; you start eyeing them suspiciously. You might even start thinking about changing your seat. This is how your fear works. You are always unconsciously in fear of losing something.

Sharada Devi, Ramakrishna Paramahamsa's divine consort says, 'Trust others even if you are exploited. The very quality of trusting the universe will make you live like God on Earth.'

When intellect sharpens, you will be able to understand like a scientist. When emotions sharpen, trust flowers. When feelings sharpen, enlightenment flowers! So drop your fears and allow understanding and trust to happen in you.

Drop your fears about your property. Everything belongs to Existence. You are a temporary possessor of it, that's all. If you relax into this understanding, it is enough.

Fear strokes

Q: *Swamiji*, when we have fear, you ask us to be more aware of it and look into it. But sometimes, the fear is so sudden That it comes and goes like a sudden shock. We won't have time to even look into it.

You are talking about what is called a fear stroke.

Fear strokes are short spikes of fear. They just come and go in a few micro seconds' time. For example, you may be walking on the road. Suddenly you see a rope and think it is a snake. You experience a sudden rise of fear, which subsides in just a few seconds because by that time, you realize it is only a rope. This is a fear stroke!

There is always a current of fear in us. At times, it rises to a peak, that's all. These fear strokes can happen with great intensity although they are for a very short duration of time. Fear strokes

296

weaken the immune system. They release depression-inducing chemicals and even accelerate our ageing process. They are believed to even cause a heart attack or make our hair turn white.

On an average, they say that every individual has about 6 fear strokes a day consciously or unconsciously. Examples of fear strokes would be the telephone ringing well past midnight, or just while in the car and a motorist suddenly swerves to your side, or when you are watching a horror movie and someone taps you on your shoulder... so many things like this.

You get fear strokes in your dreams also, but you forget them when you wake up. Fear strokes are like shaking the roots of the rose plant. It is very dangerous for the system.

As you said, at the time of the fear stroke, you will not have any time to go into awareness. You won't have time to chant any God's name and go through it. But after the fear stroke, you can very well analyze the stroke and get a deeper imprint of the understanding of your fears. This will help in dissolving the whole idea of fear.

The intensity and frequency of fear strokes can be greatly reduced by reducing the intensity and the depth of the regular fear that is in us. Only from this regular fear, the fear strokes arise. If deeper understanding and clarity can reduce the regular fear, the fear strokes will also reduce.

Fear in general, is so overpowering that it can completely throw you out of control.

A small story:

> A disciple kept bothering a Sufi master to give him an initiation.
>
> Finally the master told him that he would initiate him on the condition that he went into the nearest town and kissed a woman in *burkha* and proceeded to the forest beyond to beat a tiger with his stick.
>
> The other disciples protested saying that this was too simple.
>
> The master just smiled and asked them to wait.
>
> A week later the disciple returned. He was terribly wounded and bleeding.
>
> The master asked him what had happened.
>
> The disciple said, 'I don't know why, but I beat the woman and kissed the tiger!'

Fear can simply blind you! It can take away your thinking and intelligence altogether for a few moments. That is why you need to deeply understand fear and overcome it.

In so many cases, when there is some fire or some calamity happening, people will be running in all directions out of fear. They will be opening doors in the wrong direction. They will be running towards the wrong exit although they know that it is not the right exit. Fear is so blinding.

Just as lust can change to love through awareness, fear can change to fearlessness and intelligence out of pure awareness.

Anything suppressed only takes up another form. It doesn't get uprooted totally. So suppression is not the way to overcome fear.

298

Awareness is the way. In fact, if you suppress fear, you are missing the chance of overcoming it.

When you continuously look into your fears with awareness, even when death comes, you will look into it with awareness and allow it to happen to you. It is important to be able to do this because ultimately all your fears are nothing but the fear of death. When you work on your day-to-day fears, your fear of death unconsciously decreases, and when your fear of death decreases, your day-to-day fears decrease! It is a virtuous cycle.

We will now do a beautiful meditation called the *Nirbhaya Dhyana*, to work directly upon our fears.

Emotion: Fear

Chakra: Swadhishthana chakra

Location: 2 inches below the navel

In Sanskrit, *swadhishthana* means 'where your being is established' – from *swa* which means 'self' and adhishthana which means 'established'.

This *chakra* is locked by fear, especially the fear of death and it can be made to flower by facing fear; by facing death itself.

Meditation Technique to face the fear:
Nirbhaya Dhyana – a technique from Vedanta

The Darkness Meditation

(Total time duration: 30 minutes. One should not do this meditation without the presence of an ordained teacher of Life Bliss Foundation.)

The *Nirbhaya Dhyana* is a meditation technique taken from *Vedanta*. It is a darkness meditation. Darkness meditation stops the mind from thinking of anything known. When the mind stops thinking of the known things, thoughts automatically dissolve. This is the concept behind this meditation.

Sit comfortably on the floor. Those who cannot sit on the floor may sit on a chair. The head, neck and spine should all be in a straight line.

Close your eyes. Breathe deeply. Imagine that you are walking into a dense forest. You are walking into the densest part of the forest. You enter a deep, dark cave. You cannot see anything with your eyes. You sit down in the dark cave. You cannot see your own body. Except for your own feeling of being there, you have no other identification.

How ever much you try, you are not able to see anything. In the deep darkness, you can only sense by touch that you are there. (*1 minute*)

You are born from the darkness that was in your mother's womb and you dissolve into the same loving, compassionate darkness. (*1 minute*)

Breathe in deeply the utter darkness that surrounds you everywhere. Breathe in deeply the darkness that has made your identity disappear.

Slowly, very slowly, experience´your body merging with the darkness. (*5 minutes*)

Slowly, very slowly, experience your body becoming the darkness. (*5 minutes*)

With every cell of your body, breathe in and breathe out the darkness deeply. (*15 minutes*)

Begin to feel yourself. Start to feel your whole body with all your senses. Move your body very slowly in the sitting position. Get up and move out of the cave. Start walking out of the dense forest.

Return to the meditation hall...(*3 minutes*)

Just carry this silence with you.

Thank you.

Chapter 7

You are unique

Comparison is the seed, jealousy is the fruit!

We always compare ourselves with others, and more often than not we feel what others have or what they have achieved is more than what we have, and we start feeling jealous. When we are not able to bear others' excellence, we get jealous. Comparison is the *seed* and jealousy is the *fruit*!

Comparison and jealousy are both actually non-existent! We create them ourselves and talk endlessly on how to overcome them. Comparison is like a shadow without an object. There is no basis for the concept of comparison. It is purely a figment of our imagination.

A small story:

> One man was part of a music group that gave live shows all over the world.
>
> In one particular how, he decided to wear a black wig while singing a few songs and a red wig while singing the other songs.
>
> He alternated the wigs and finished the first half of the program.
>
> During the intermission, the show director came up to him in the dressing room and told him, 'Sir, we request you to

wear only the red wig for the remaining part of the show.'
The man was surprised and asked him why.
The director replied, 'The people like the red haired singer's voice a lot better than the black haired singer's!'

We are so busy comparing all the time that we never see things as they are! Our mind is so caught up in comparison that it misses what *actually* is. If we drop the comparing attitude, we will be able to see things as they are.

What is comparison?

What are the major areas where we normally compare?

Beauty Swamiji....

Wealth.....

Name and fame...

Power, prestige...

Knowledge...

Health...

Alright, these are the areas where we normally compare ourselves with others. We can group these under four major categories: money, knowledge, beauty which includes health, and status. All our problems, all our complexes can be covered under these four categories, am I right?

Now...let us say that you queue up all the people in the world in ascending order of money. You are also part of that queue. Where would you think you would be?

Somewhere in the middle Swamiji...

Exactly! You would be somewhere in the middle. You would not even be able to *count* the number of people on either side of you in the queue.

And the people might have to keep shifting their places also because the amount of money that they have keeps changing every minute! Now, you have to decide if you are going to look at the length of queue in front of you and feel jealous or look at the length of queue behind you and feel grateful! It is in your hands.

You very well know that nothing can be told about where you are in the queue, but the thought disturbs you all the time! We are haunted by a phenomenon that does not really exist! The comparison has a purely negative existence!

Let me explain to you what I mean by negative existence. Take this bell here that is beside me. If I want to remove this bell, I can simply take it and leave it outside the room and it will not be here any more, am I right? This bell has a positive existence and so it is possible for me to do this. Now, let us say there is darkness in this room. Is it possible for you to take the darkness and keep it out? No.

But if I bring light into this room, the darkness will disappear on its own, right? This is because darkness does not have a positive existence; it has a negative existence. Because it has a negative existence, we cannot remove it directly like the bell.

In the same way, comparison does not have a positive existence. It exists only in our minds. It happens only when we exercise a certain thought in our mind. Because comparison does not exist in reality, you cannot overcome it by simply asking it to go away. You can overcome it by bringing in an understanding about it, just like bringing in light to dispel the darkness.

In Sanskrit, the word illusion is translated as *maya*.

We say, *ya ma iti maya,* which means *that which does not exist is maya!*

That which does not exist, but which continuously disturbs! That is the property of illusion!

Comparison is pure illusion.

Stop borrowing desires!

When I tell people about the queue of people, they tell me, 'Swamiji, it is better not to look at any side of the queue.' I ask them, 'Why? Why should you fear to look?' The fact that you are afraid to look itself shows that you are running away from your own mind. If you can look, but not be affected by what you see – then you have found the right way!

When you are able to look at everything, what you have and what others have and feel fulfillment all the time, then you are fine with it.

I am deliberately not using the word 'contentment'. People often say, 'Learn to be contented.' You can never learn to be contented. Contentment will flower when you understand the negative existence of comparison and jealousy. It will flower when you feel a deep gratitude for whatever is being showered on you every minute. It cannot be imposed from outside.

When you are on your own at home, you will think that it is enough if you have a home and car for yourself. You will feel relaxed with this thought. You will feel moments of gratitude and fulfillment. After some time, when you step out of your house in your car, and stop by at a traffic light, what happens? A Mercedes Benz pulls up beside your car...and your mind flips over its thinking. It starts thinking that your car is just no good. It starts thinking that it is high time that you bought a new car, if not a Mercedes Benz.

Just a few minutes earlier you were happy with your own things, but now what happened? You are starting to work out a new desire, a 'borrowed desire'. Be very clear that this is not your own desire. It is the desire of the owner of the Benz car. This is how you start working out others' desires in your mind as a result of comparison and jealousy.

Take another example: You may never have felt the need for a refrigerator in your house, but if your neighbor buys a refrigerator, immediately you will feel that you cannot do without it! Immediately you will find all the reasons in the world why you need a refrigerator. All these days you were managing without a refrigerator! Nothing has changed, but what has happened? Your mind has stepped in with comparison.

Borrowed desires happen so subtly in our mind, that is why although they are continuously happening, we continue to say that we are not bothered about the others!

A small story:

> One man returned to his neighborhood after almost 10 years.
> He went around the neighborhood with his friend.
> He was surprised to see the many changes in the place.
> He commented to this friend, 'Prosperity has changed the face of this whole neighborhood!'
> The friend replied, 'No, not prosperity, just plain jealousy.'

We are all the time trying to beat the other. When you are after borrowed desires, you will never stop, because when you are on the verge of realizing any one of them, another borrowed desire will come up from somewhere and you will be on track once more!

You keep running because you are centered not within yourself but on something outside. Your center is on other people. And their center is elsewhere, not inside themselves! Imagine how much you have to run, how much you have to pull and push according to the mass sway of off-centric thoughts and emotions! You become a puppet.

I tell you: Every time you want something, sit by yourself and think if you really want it or you want it because someone else had it. Do an honest analysis of each of your desires when they surface. Drop all your prestige problems and do a self-analysis. If you can't drop your prestige when you are alone, how will you drop it when you are with people?

If you are able to live out only *your* desires, you will die a peaceful death, full of satisfaction even if it is on the platform. If you live your whole life with borrowed desires, you will never see real fulfillment and even if you are living in a marble house, you will have a prolonged death, pulling and pushing, unable to get liberated from your unfulfilled desires.

In Jainism, there is a belief that when you are born, the entire quantity of food and energy that you will need during your lifetime is sent along with you. This is a way of saying that whatever your true requirements in this birth are, Existence equips you with the energy to fulfill them before even sending you to planet Earth.

But when you start using this energy to realize borrowed desires, you start feeling that nothing has been given to you; that nothing is enough. You feel tired, exhausted and frustrated that nothing is happening.

There is a difference between *needs* and *wants*. Your needs are already taken care of in some way. It is possible to satisfy your *needs*, but it becomes impossible to satisfy your *wants* because they are changing all the time.

For example: Let us say that you go to the shop to buy a fan for your house. But on the way you meet some friends on the road, who tell you that they are going to buy some other things in other shops. Immediately, you are tempted to go with them to buy them and so you change your track and go and buy along with them. Then you find that you don't have enough money to buy your fan!

In some places in India there will be monkey trainers who make a living out of training monkeys.

They will carry a stick with them and use it to prod the monkey to do whatever they want it to do.

They will wave the stick and shout, 'Dance Rama! Dance!' and the monkey will dance!

Then they will say, 'Turn cart wheels Rama! Turn cartwheels!' And the monkey will turn cartwheels.

The monkey will simply dance to the tunes of the stick.

Like this, we allow a stick called *comparison* to run our lives. We dance to its tunes, doing things that are not our own but that are dictated by the stick.

We are constantly in the rat race. And the thing about being in the rat race is, *even if you win, you are only a rat!*

But somehow, late in life, at some point in time, you understand that even success in the rat race doesn't give you a sense of fulfillment. Even success leads to a deep sense of discontentment, because, while you may have fulfilled all the material desires in the outer world, you have ignored your being all the time.

The call of discontentment is from your being. When you understand that, you turn towards spirituality. But when you don't understand that, you turn towards depression, because you don't know where you are missing it. You don't know where the thread is. You don't know what went wrong.

What more do you want?

I can tell you from my experience: Existence is always showering upon us. There is such abundance! But we are so well trained in the discipline of discontentment that we have become insensitive to what we receive. We always want more.

A small story:

> One man was doing rigorous penance in the jungle for God to appear.
>
> God appeared before him. He told the man to ask what he wanted.
>
> The man was overjoyed and said that he was a landlord and had lost all his wealth and that he wished to become wealthy again.
>
> God took pity on him and said that the following day, if the man ran from dawn to dusk, all the area covered by him would be his.
>
> The man was extremely happy.
>
> The next day he started running even before dawn.
>
> He ran as fast as he could.
>
> Close to noon, hunger beckoned but he didn't pay heed and kept running.
>
> Early in the evening, thirst and fatigue gripped him but he was goaded on by the thought of the neighboring landlord who owned many acres of land. Pictures of all his wealthy contemporaries came to him and he ran on.
>
> A little before sunset, he felt giddy and weak but managed a few more steps.
>
> At twilight, he faltered...and fell dead.

This is how we all live our lives. We run the race without even stopping to think why we are running! We run because everyone else is running! Shankaracharya beautifully describes this as *'thatha kim, thatha kim.'* meaning 'what next, what next.' We are all the time thinking 'what next'.

Another small story:

> One man was found crying at the doorstep of his house.
> His friend asked him what the matter was.
> He said, 'My grand aunt has died leaving all her wealth to me.'
> The friend was puzzled and said, 'But she was really old and besides she has left all her wealth to you. Why are you crying?'
> The man replied, 'You don't know... the week before that, my uncle died and left all his wealth to me.'
> The friend was puzzled and asked, 'Why are you crying then?'
> The man continued, 'And the week before that, my aunt passed away and left all her wealth to me.'
> The friend could not understand why all this was causing him to cry.
> He asked, 'Please tell me why you are crying for all this?'
> The man said, 'There are no more relatives who will die and leave me wealth!'

Of course, this is an exaggerated story, but we are like this. We don't feel happy with all the things that we have.

For just 24 hours, from morning till night, just imagine that you have lost your eyesight. Try going about your work keeping your eyes closed. In just a few minutes, you will understand the difficulty. It will be such a relief to open your eyes and see the world again. You will probably then thank God for your eyesight!

Do you ever compare yourself with people who don't have eyesight and thank God that you have been given eyesight? No! Why not? Because whatever has been given to you is *always* taken for granted. That is the reason. You think, 'It is anywhere there, let us go to *what next.*'

Doing, having, being

We all function around these three axes: *doing, having* and *being*. *Doing* for *having*, without enjoying *being*, is the sole cause of all our misery. *Doing* never catches up with *having*. Every time we work hard and fulfill one desire, there are more desires to make us run.

Never think, *'Let me work now, I can enjoy later.'* Don't think you can come back later and enjoy! I tell you, it will never happen. Every tomorrow comes in the form of today. *Doing* should lead to *being* every moment, only then you are on the right track.

Don't postpone living. Celebrate! Enjoy life – it is now or never. We all run throughout our lives thinking that we can enjoy later, but we land up finally running into the graveyard. When you get onto the running track, you lose your real capacity to enjoy. You forget how to enjoy.

As they say, *'There is more pleasure in the pursuit than in the attainment!'* Always, as long as you are chasing something, it seems that it is worth the whole world, but after you get it, somehow it loses its importance! If you become aware of yourself and understand what exactly you want, and try to do *that* alone, you will never find yourself in this kind of a self-contradictory and fragmented situation.

Ramana Maharshi beautifully says:

Adaivadar mun kadugey aanaalum malayaay kaatti
Adainda pin malayey aanaalum kadugai kaattum maya manam

It means, 'Mind is that illusion which shows a tiny mustard seed to be a huge mountain until it is attained, and a mountain to be as insignificant as a mustard seed once it has been attained!'

People ask me, 'Swamiji, unless we compare, how will we know where we stand?'

In the whole world, someone is sure to be better than you at whatever you do. There is a 99.99% chance that you are not the world's best engineer, the fastest runner or the most talented painter. Does that mean that you enjoy these things any less? Only when you think that you might be enjoying less than someone else, you start enjoying less! The moment the thought that 'someone else might be enjoying more than you' comes in, your whole flavor changes. You become uneasy and jealous.

It is like this: Poverty *itself* doesn't trouble us. The *thought* that we are poor troubles us! We might be leading a peaceful life as we are, but when the *thought* that we are poor enters us, we suffer. And how does this thought come? By seeing others and comparing. We feel this way because this thought directly hits our ego and we shrink - like a mango.

A small story:

> There were two shops opposite each other across the street, selling the same kind of things.
> There was always a stiff competition between them.
> The shopkeeper of one of the shops came out one day and put up a signboard outside his shop: *Established in the year 1929.*
> The shopkeeper of the shop across the street was watching this from inside his shop.
> The next day, he came out and put up a signboard in front of his shop: *All fresh stock. No old goods.*

You are unique

When you don't understand the potential you have been blessed with, when you have not discovered that you are enough unto yourself, you automatically don't feel confident about the stuff inside you, and you start following others.

Buddha says, 'Nothing exists except in relationship.' Suppose you were the only person on a new planet, would you call yourself tall or short? Ugly or beautiful? Rich or poor? Tell me! You can't call yourself anything, am I right? You will simply be *you*! That's all! Understand that this is the truth even when you are on *this* planet.

Each individual is unique. Can you compare a lion and a horse? Do we ever compare ourselves to flowers or birds or mountains? We simply enjoy their beauty. In the same way, why can't you see and enjoy other human beings also?

Although human beings appear to be the same, each one is unique and traveling on a different path. As long as you travel on your path with full concentration, you will experience fulfillment every minute. You won't even know what it means to look at another person's track.

A small story:

> One man was driving along a dark village road where there were no streetlights.
> He decided to follow the car in front of him to play it safe. They went on for some distance and suddenly the lead car stopped.
> The man went and crashed into it.
> 'Why didn't you signal that you were going to stop?' he screamed out.
> The driver put his head out and asked, 'Inside my own garage?'

If you concentrate on your own track, you will be continuously progressing and expanding your own capacity. You need to compare yourself with only yourself, never with others. You need to win yourself only by yourself, not by others. Every minute of comparison with others is a waste of time in *your own progress*.

Another small story:

> A man was running in a 1000-metre race.
> After running 200 metres, he looked back and saw that the rest of the runners were after him. Happily he ran on.
> After 500 metres, he looked back again and was happy that he was still leading and ran on.
> Every few meters, he did the same thing and finally won the race.

If the man had not looked back and instead concentrated only on running faster, he would have won the race in a much shorter span of time. He would have probably set a new record! In the same way, in our lives also, if our concentration is always fully on our own progress instead of on others, we can actualize our entire potential.

We are all the time talking about conserving petrol, water and electricity. What about conserving our own energy? What about using our own energy in a proper way? If we used all our energy for our own expansion, just imagine how much we could achieve.

See, the thing about comparison is, you always measure yourself with the weakest link in yourself or your performance. That is the trouble. Never measure yourself with the weakest link. You don't have to be egoistic and claim yourself to be something great. But you can have some self-respect and realise that you are unique unto yourself. Then you won't measure yourself in this way.

When you have self-respect, you will appreciate that each one is unique and understand that there is no scope for comparison. This is also the first step towards feeling grateful for just being!

A small story:

A king once went to a master to attain some magical powers, so that he could become more powerful than his neighboring kings.

He sat in front of the master and started telling him the purpose of his visit.

The master listened patiently to the king.

He then told him to go into his garden, where a rose bush and a cactus plant were growing side by side. He told him, 'They are your teachers. They can teach you what you need to learn.'

The king went into the garden, saw the two plants and could not understand what he was meant to learn from them.

He came back to the master and asked, 'What do you mean, master? I am not able to understand how they will teach me.'

The master took him to the plants and explained, 'This cactus plant has been next to the rose plant for many years. Never once has it even aspired to become a rose plant. Similarly, the rose plant has never ever aspired to become a cactus plant. They just attend to their own duties of growing and blossoming every day. If man had been the cactus, he would have compared himself with the rose and felt jealous at the attention that the rose plant was getting from people.

Or if he were the rose, he would have looked at the cactus enviously thinking how peaceful the latter was without the torture of getting plucked by people all day!'

The master said, 'This is the most powerful magical power you can attain!'

The two plants prospered because they used all their energy for their own growth. Not even an iota of energy was wasted on analyzing the other's growth.

It is time for self inquiry

In this world, people respect you only if you have achieved something tangible in the outer world. Educational degrees, beauty titles, company designations, published papers, bank balances, are all scales that society uses to grade you.

See, first of all, you don't need to be graded by anyone. Place trust in your own intelligence and grade yourself.

But understand that there is a lot to be achieved in the inner world too. The outer world achievements are all incidental. They will get you instant name and fame and money. The real achievement is in the inner world.

Center yourself well with acute awareness and simply take part in the outer world activities like a lotus untouched in a pond. Let the work in the periphery go on undisturbed, but center yourself in your being. You will then be able to perform much better in the outer world, because your inner intelligence will be growing and guiding.

Then automatically, you will stop swaying in accordance with the outer world achievements and feel stability and joy in the center of your own being. Finding your center is the only way out of this whole cycle of comparison and jealousy.

How many successful businessmen today are facing what is known as *depression of success*? They have achieved everything they wanted. They have realized their own dreams, borrowed dreams, everything. But they don't feel fulfilled. There is still a void in them.

They start wondering why they ran so much. This is because they ran without awareness, without stopping to give an appointment to themselves, without any self-inquiry. As a result, when they stop running or when suddenly they can't run anymore, they fall back into themselves and find that they are out of synch or dis-eased with their own being, and this is what becomes 'depression' or 'disease'.

When you fall into depression of success, you can resort to three ways. One is, resorting to drugs – addiction that will lead to further depression. The second way out is suicide – which is escapism. The third way out is meditation – looking inward for the solution. The intelligent ones take the third way out.

Self-inquiry is the way to bail you out of this depression. The problem is inside, while you search for a solution outside. You have neglected your being for such a long time and the depression that you feel is actually the call of your being. That is why again and again, masters have given ever so many techniques to center yourself in your inner core and merely function in your periphery.

When this same thing is told to you when you are at the peak of your career, you will not be willing to pay attention, because you have enough energy. Once your energy starts waning, you will feel that something is wrong somewhere. *That something* is what masters try to tell you again and again.

> Albert Einstein, the great physicist was on his deathbed.
> There were some close people sitting around him.
> One of them asked him what he would like to be reborn as if ever he was reborn.
> Everyone expected him to say that he would like to be reborn as an even greater scientist or something to that effect.
> Einstein replied, 'If ever I would be reborn, I would like to be reborn as a plumber.'

He felt that he had achieved all that was to be achieved, but *what for* he achieved, he had not achieved. He gave the world great truths but felt that his whole life had become a lie.

You see, in this whole process of comparing and running, you actually become a machine. Much of your daily activities becomes unconscious. You are able to drive a car without even being aware that you are driving it. You become a machine just like the car.

Right from brushing your teeth early in the morning to going to bed, you work like a programmed robot, with absolutely no awareness of your Self. You become efficient in all that you do no doubt, but you have lost the humanness in you! You have gone so far away from the purpose of taking birth on planet Earth. You become disconnected from your being!

When you are in continuous awareness, you will not only be able to do things efficiently but you will also do things with totality, with a sense of fulfillment, because *you* – the microcosm - will be in tune with Existence - the macrocosm - and you will fly with roots on planet Earth. When you fly without roots, you are forever in the danger of hurting yourself any moment. So understand, working with awareness not only increases your efficiency but also ensures that you don't stray from the purpose of your being.

Jealousy about another's body

Alright, now…let us talk some more on jealousy! Jealousy as you all know, arises out of comparison. When we are unable to bear the excellence of others in any aspect, we start feeling jealous. There are ever so many reasons why we get jealous.

For example, the moment you see that another person is more beautiful than you, you are unable to bear it. You start feeling terrible inside yourself.

First of all understand that God is an artist, not an engineer. If he was an engineer, he would have made every woman or every man with the same mould. He would have probably made every woman with the mould of a Miss World and every man in the mould of a Mr.Universe!

But God is not an engineer. He is an artist. He has made everyone in a unique way.

With what scale are you measuring beauty? There *is* no scale. It is all your own ideas and concepts. Even if a cinema star is beautiful, can you enjoy a single cup of tea through his or her form?

When you start longing for other people's bodies, you create a wedge inside yourself. You create a split personality inside yourself. Slowly, you start hating yourself.

Do you know, the eyes that don't linger on another's body have a certain beauty and innocence in them? Have faith in what God has done to you. It is only when you don't have that faith, you try to update yourself by indulging in all sorts of methods. When you accept yourself completely, a certain grace comes to you. This grace is far more superior to mere physical beauty.

Physical beauty is one thing while grace is another. Physical beauty can be achieved by any means. These days, you have ever so many methods of achieving physical beauty. There are beauty packs, plastic surgeries and various other methods. But grace is something that comes when there is tremendous confidence and calmness in you, when there is no craving in you, when you are completely at ease with your body.

When I went to America for the first time, the officers at the airport asked me how people would listen to me if I spoke wearing this saffron robe! I told them, 'Give me one week and I will make this a fashion in America!' A leader is one who has totally accepted himself. When you accept yourself, you become a unique flower, and tremendous freedom and confidence will happen in you.

It is very important that you learn to live with your own body. The moment you think that another's body or another's dimensions are more attractive, you create a gap between yourself and your body. I have seen people who have photographs of male or female models in the walls of their rooms and do physical exercises to attain the body structure of the model. When you think that another's body is more beautiful, you create a distance between you and you.

None of us deeply love our body. We carry it only like a load. We are never inside our body because we hate it. We are everywhere else except in our bodies. We therefore have a continuous uneasiness in us and are ready to burst at any time.

For example, if your driver does something minor, you explode effortlessly. At work, you are continuously in an irritable mood. Don't think the reasons for these lie with the people around you. People tell me, 'Swamiji, all my workers are so inefficient and that is why I get irritated.' Please understand that this is not the reason for your irritability. You are not at ease with your body and that is what causes the uneasiness and irritation in your system. It is a very subtle reason and that is why it is difficult to perceive it.

Q: Your face appears to be changing every time to me. Is it my imagination or is it true?

An enlightened being is like liquid – slowing without any ego. That is the reason why they appear to be changing all the time!

You will understand how an egoless state expresses, when we discuss about ego.

Drop possessiveness

Q: How do we get over possessiveness and jealousy?

Yes, how do we get over it? The fact that you have asked this question shows that you are ready for better understanding.

Human beings can never be possessed. When you try to possess a person, you actually reduce him or her to an object. You make the person a dead thing. Only dead things can be possessed. If you understand this, you will be free from possessiveness and the jealousy that arises out of it.

Can you try to possess a river? If you try to grasp the water in your hand, you will be doing a foolish thing, will you not? In the same way, don't try to possess people; just enjoy them for what they are and you will be free from the grips of jealousy.

When you try to possess a person, it becomes difficult for that person also. You will start projecting all your ideas on him. He will have to act so as to gel with your projected ideas. He will feel caged. He cannot be his natural self with you. Then it cannot be called a relationship anymore!

Also if you really love a person, liberate him! Don't try to possess him. Just love him with no strings attached.

I am reminded of a story:

> In a remote village in South India, where people did not know that civilization existed, there was an old couple.
>
> One day, for the first time ever, there was a fair in the village.
>
> The man went to the fair and saw all the items on show.
>
> He picked up a mirror and was awestruck by what he saw!
>
> He had never seen a mirror in all his life before.
>
> He took it home with him.
>
> Now and then he would take out the mirror, glance at it and put it back before his wife could see it.
>
> The wife however noticed it and when he was out one day, she picked it up and looked into it.
>
> She exclaimed, 'Another woman! Just as I had thought!'

There is no end to our imagination because of our possessiveness and jealousy!

Of course, you might say, 'Swamiji, how can I keep quiet if my husband or wife is eyeing someone else.' If your husband or wife is really eyeing another person, just look into the matter consciously, with awareness, and sort out the matter with your husband. This is different from possessiveness.

How to overcome jealousy?

By telling yourself not to feel jealous, you can never come out of jealousy. Only if you bring awareness into the whole thing and understand deeply, it will help.

To overcome jealousy, just see how the jealousy came into your system. Just analyze the sequence of thoughts and emotions that led to jealousy.

Soon you will understand that jealousy is there like a shadow without an object, tormenting you. Getting liberation from jealousy is a great liberation in one's life.

Second thins, don't condemn the object of your jealousy. Just by condemning the object of jealousy, you will not be liberated from jealousy itself.

By condemning the object of jealousy, you might be liberated from that particular object of jealousy, but you will get fixed onto another object of jealousy, that's all! It is like saying 'sour grapes' and moving on to another vineyard! So, trying to overcome the object of jealousy is not the solution. You need to work on the subject that is *you*.

If you feel that you are holding an emotion that you wish to get rid of, something that you feel is not conducive to your growth, don't resist that emotion. When you resist it, you will only be empowering it more. When you say, 'I should not get jealous,' you will be giving the same power to the word 'jealous' as you give to the words 'I should not'.

Instead, say to yourself, 'Let me be always compassionate towards everyone.' Don't use the word 'jealous' at all. Say something totally positive in the same context, that's all.

Also, instead of avoiding or running away from jealousy, live it through with total awareness. When you try to avoid it, it will

328

confront you at some other time with more intensity than before. Just remember that jealousy is not your true nature. Society taught you to be jealous.

Jealousy is not the real you. When this clicks in you, you will laugh at it instead of being involved in it. When you are able to laugh at it, it means you have started witnessing it instead of being a part of it. The moment you become a witness, it becomes easy to go beyond anything.

Also, if you see that the whole of Existence is nothing but a divine play, you will be able to see the jealous feeling also as a divine play.

If you understand that you are unique and there is no one in this world like you, the comparing nature in you will become meaningless and you will automatically stop feeling jealous. Always remember: Existence loves everyone and everything equally.

Make the most of the masters' messages

Q: Masters time and again try to inspire in us traits like love free from jealousy, better understanding and non-judgmental attitudes. Why is the understanding not happening in us?

You see, there are two things in this: When we catch the masters' messages and make a sincere effort in transforming ourselves, we have caught the right thread and we enter into bliss! But what we start giving importance to the master's personality instead, there starts the problem.

If you follow the master's teachings, you will become a spiritual fruit. If you cling on to his personality, you will remain a religious nut. Religious nuts are the ones who create confusion and conflict in society.

Whether it is Krishna's message in the Bhagavad Gita or Mohammed's message in the Holy Koran or Christ's message in the Holy Bible, the message remains the same, just the expressions vary. Whichever master you have the fortune of following, follow. But when you follow Krishna, if Krishna becomes more significant to you than the Bhagavad Gita, you are creating trouble for yourself and for others.

When Krishna and Christ meet, they will surely embrace each other. But when Krishna's cows and Christ's sheep meet, there is bound to be a fight!

Each one tries to spread peace claiming that his master's philosophy is the best. What happens? Instead of spreading peace, we become pieces ourselves!

Masters keep happening on planet Earth out of sheer compassion towards humanity. But man somehow manages to survive them!

The other way to transform quickly is, instead of pointing fingers at others or instead of waiting for a good time to start practicing, if each of us starts practicing from the very moment of hearing the messasge, things will automatically start happening around us.

For example, I tell you to start loving plants, animals, trees and humans alike. Instead of waiting for an auspicious time to start practicing it and eventually forgetting all about it, you can start start practicing it right now.

The simplest way to start might be to avoid abusing nature while you are walking on the road or inside your own home. When walking, some of us have the habit of breaking twigs off trees and plucking flowers. You could consciously stop doing these things and look at these things with more awareness and love.

These are the ways not to miss the masters' teachings.

But what do you do? You listen to the masters' talks or read some of their books, and say, 'What a great orator he is,' and forget all about it. Or, you advise some of your friends to listen to the speeches, and you simply go back to your old ways of doing things. What can be done then?

Please understand: I don't want you to just preach my teachings; I want you to practice them also.

Listen to this small story:

A man went to Africa for a holiday.
He was walking in his backyard one day when he was confronted by a lion that leapt on him.
He quickly ducked and the lion landed in the bush nearby.
The next day, the man went walking again and the lion appeared and attacked him once more, but again he ducked and it landed further away in the bush nearby.
The next day, the man stood inside his house and looked outside to see if the lion could be seen anywhere.

He spotted the lion behind a bush.

To his amazement, he saw the lion practicing low jumps!

See, when you apply the knowledge that you gain, you can grow in life. When you simply want to collect knowledge, it is of no use. If you are going to only collect knowledge, only your memory will grow, not your being.

Masters talk the ultimate truth that no one else can express.

It is like this: There is a vast and dense forest and you are trying to explore it with a small lamp, that is your mind.

With the light of the small lamp, you see a few feet ahead and put down what you see as the truth.

This is what scientists do. They see a few feet ahead and come out with one theory today.

After some time, they go a few feet further ahead with that light and see a few feet further and see something more.

They then discard the truth they declared today and bring in a new truth.

Be very clear that what was truth today but untruth tomorrow could not have been truth even today.

Anyhow, this is how they are trying to explore a dense forest with their mind.

But imagine now that there is a flash of lightning and the whole forest becomes visible in that one flash!

Then you know the whole forest and you can go about explaining things as and when needed.

This is what enlightenment is all about! It is seeing the whole forest in a single flash of lightning. So enlightened masters know the ultimate truth.

In most of the teashops in remote villages in India, you can see a familiar scene. There will be some standard visitors for the shop everyday who discuss all the great philosophies of the world. The heads of all the great Gods, masters and politicians will be properly chewed and digested by these people.

All the atrocities being committed in town will be discussed without exception. The whole world will be brought under scrutiny for lack of order and discipline. Finally, the man who spoke all this will finish his tea and leave saying that he will pay for his tea the following day!

The man who could not even pay for his tea will sit on the teashop bench and read the newspaper from the first page to the last and pass judgment on everything that he has read. Even the editor would not have read the paper so thoroughly!

So, start practicing. Sage Patanjali from ancient India says, 'If you can bend 5 inches today, try to bend a half-inch more tomorrow.' Like this, you should work steadily towards experiencing the truth that I am giving you. Otherwise, you will be no more than the people in the teashops. They cause depressions in the benches there while you cause holes in the mats here, that's all!

The problem is, most often, when we hear words of wisdom spoken, we always feel that it is exactly applicable to our friend or relative who is also listening to the lecture! We secretly hope that they got the message. But we miss the message ourselves! Remember: Even if there are a thousand people in the hall, I am talking to *you*.

Every word of mine is pregnant with the energy that is meant for you. So please don't listen with such ideas in your mind. Especially when husbands and wives come to listen to the lectures, when I say a few things pertaining to their practical lives, the husband will think, *she should hear this* and the wife will think to herself that the husband should hear it! At the end, both will miss it.

Man's inherent nature is to accumulate money and material things. At some point in time, he realizes that there are things that money can't get him. His pace in gathering wealth automatically decreases. He then starts gathering words or intellectual knowledge. This process somehow never stops. He becomes greedy for more and more words.

One who has stopped gathering wealth *and* words will find true knowledge. Often, we ask questions not because we really want to know the answer but simply because we are greedy for more words or because we want to show that we know something.

If you look deep inside, only one question will arise and that is the only original question for yourself. If that question is answered, you will become enlightened!

One man asked me, 'Swamiji, What is God?'

I slowly changed the subject and enquired about his family and his business.

We spoke for nearly two hours. In those two hours, never once did he get back to his initial question.

At the end of it I told him, '*Ayyah*, you asked me a question as soon as you came in. I did not answer it because it was not a question from deep inside you.'

If the question arises from deep inside us, we will never forget it or rest until we are satisfied with the answer. Some people ask questions, give the answer themselves and then ask me for an answer!

Q: If we should stop comparing, does it mean we should renounce everything and become a spiritualist?

Most people think that the moment I say you should stop comparing, stop running etc., I am asking them to escape from the worldly matters and become a spiritualist.

Spirituality, or for that matter *sannyas,* is not about renouncing at all. It is about having deep awareness, which will automatically shrink your mad desires to basic needs and give you the energy to fulfill them.

Whatever needs to be done in the outer world needs to be done, no doubt. You have to earn a living; you have to keep the body alive etc. All I am saying is, bring awareness into all this so that all unnecessary occupations in the outer world automatically disappear and you live with a clear understanding of the purpose of your very birth and life.

All forms of illusion, all borrowed desires, all instilled fears, all forms of jealousy and comparison, passion and lust will then undergo a complete transformation and become blissful energy to you.

A small story:

> A master was walking with his disciple when they came to a river.
> The disciple was surprised and asked, 'Master, are we going to cross this river now?'
> The master calmly replied, 'Yes, we are. You have to be careful not to get your feet wet!'

The disciple could not understand what the master was saying! The master was trying to tell him that spirituality is all about crossing the ocean of life without getting your feet wet. It is all about being like a lotus in a pond – untouched by the water although deep inside it.

True spirituality

Spirituality is actually *Life Engineering*. In colleges, they teach you different types of engineering. Life engineering is what needs to be taught to each of us. Spirituality teaches you to live like a *Paramahamsa* or a realised one, in the material world, neck deep in water, yet untouched by it.

It teaches you to live an intense and fulfilling life without violating any person or property. It teaches you to disconnect from your intellect and see with wide-eyed innocence the wonders of Existence. It teaches you how to move synchronously with Existence and experience the power of coincidence, where things happen automatically in response to your inner joy.

It teaches you to be in an ever prayerful and grateful mood. It helps you enjoy every moment from your inner core, instead of being swayed by your emotions. It shows you how to celebrate life every moment.

It kindles your inner intelligence and accelerates your performance in the outer world. It awakens your awareness and takes you to deeper consciousness. It takes you from lust to love, from worrying to wondering, from false to truth, from pain to bliss, from jealousy to celebration.

People think that they need to allot a separate time for spirituality; not at all. You will know from what I have just said that this is not required. The people who claim that you need to allot separate time are not spiritual people; they are religious people.

Religion needs time because of rites and rituals. Spirituality has nothing to do with quantity or time. It has to do with the quality of your life. If you have the sincerity to seek the truth, it is enough. You can then devote all your time to doing everything as an earnest meditation and you will attain your goal. You will automatically shine at work, at home, and in interpersonal relationships, without energy blockages.

You will adapt yourself to any kind of surroundings easily. You will feel at home at any place and with any type of people. Home will not be just the place you live in but the whole of Existence. You will break free from mental and physical conditioning and rise to merge and become one with Existence.

The problem is, people are contented with just following rituals. There is a certain security they enjoy in it. The science behind the rituals is no more known to people but the rituals are ego-fulfilling to them. Rituals are complex and we always find it a challenge to do complex things.

People come to me with their problems and ask me for a solution. I tell them that I will take care and suggest to them to sit for a while under the banyan tree while they are in the ashram. The banyan tree in the ashram is an energy field. But they are not happy with that answer. They ask me what rituals they should do to make things better.

If I tell them that they should go 108 times around the banyan tree, they will be very happy doing it! You see, when you go 108 times around the banyan tree, it becomes ego-fulfilling for you. You then feel that you have worked hard and that you deserve to get the benefit out of it.

Even in religion and rituals, I have seen people compete with each other! If your neighbour has done a particular offering in a particular temple, next you go and do the same offering in that temple. What is the focus on? The deity or the neighbour?

People feel proud in saying that they have visited so many holy shrines all over the world. Immediately, the people who listen to these stories make an effort in surpassing these achievements.

After visiting all these holy shrines, your *chakras* are still locked! Have you ever thought about that? All these things are done only to progress in the inner world, to be free from comparison, jealousy and similar things, but here also you miss the point. You do things for the sake of the outer world.

I have seen people reading recitations in front of the deity. They will read a few lines and then call out to the maid to find out if she has finished the job she was asked to do. Or, they will read a few lines and see how many more pages there are to finish! This is how they relate with God and they feel satisfied at having read the recitation.

And on top of it, they will repeat such recitations for 21 days because they have taken a vow to do so. Then they will proudly go and tell their neighbor or relative that they fulfilled such an arduous vow!

Everything that we do is mostly just to tell people that we did it and sow a seed of comparison in them. If you decide to follow rituals, do it with utmost sincerity, with a feeling of deep connection with Existence. When you do it this way, you won't even talk about it outside.

Rituals, meditation and courage

Q: While we are on the topic of rituals, can you please tell us something about the path of rituals and the path of meditation?

When you decide to follow the ritualistic path, commitment and sincerity must become your master keys. So do it with utmost sincerity. Then that too becomes spirituality. Today, there are hundreds of ways to do ritualistic worship. You don't have to get confused as to which to follow. Just decide to follow any one way and do it with commitment. It is the commitment that gets you the benefit, not the ritual itself.

Also, don't look for instant results. Today, everyone wants instant results like instant tea and coffee. Most of us feel that others' prayers are getting answered quicker than ours and so we should shift from our type of worship to theirs'. So much of comparison even in worship! Do what you are doing with commitment and faith, and leave the rest open. Things will happen automatically.

The ultimate goal of any religion or ritual is to tune in with Existence. Rituals are not a transaction to bribe the Gods.

I am reminded of a story:

> Three men started a business together.
> They decided to include God as a partner in it.
> They agreed that whatever profit they got, they would give away one percent of it to God.
> They started the business and made unexpectedly high profits.

Then came the problem: *How to give away so much to God?*

Each of them gave a suggestion.

The first man said, 'Alright, let's draw a circle and throw up all the money. Whatever falls inside the circle is God's and whatever falls outside is ours.'

The second man said, 'No. I have a better idea. We will draw a really big circle and throw all the money up. Whatever falls inside is ours and whatever falls outside is God's.'

The third man said, 'Look, anyway God is above us. Let us throw all the money up. Whatever he wants, let him take. Whatever comes down is ours!'

As long as we want something, we bribe God for it. As soon as we get it, we drop him until the next want arises! This is how we are taught to function.

Anyhow, coming back to the topic of rituals, there is something definite about them. It is structured and you know when exactly it is going to start, when it is going to finish, where you are going to do it, why you are doing it, etc. With rituals, you go into them, and come out as the same person. There is so much security in the whole process. That is why it has spread so much. Anything that is definite spreads.

But what happens in meditation? First of all, meditation seems too simple to produce any benefits when compared to rituals. People always ask me why I do rituals at the ashram. I tell them, 'If I tell people to simply come to the ashram and sit under the banyan tree and meditate, which is actually enough, they will not listen.'

If I did not have the temple, if they did not see the deities there, probably only I would be sitting under the banyan tree and meditating!

To make people take the first step towards their inner journey, I have to show them some of the things that exist in their minds. I have to talk in their language.

They will be very happy to see the *Dakshinamurthy* deity under the banyan tree, although they will be blissfully unaware of the energy field that is actually there around the banyan tree even in the absence of the *Dakshinamurthy* deity. This banyan tree is live energy. Its silence is a vibrating silence. It is enough if you just sit under it in meditation. You don't have to do anything complicated. Every leaf and twig here talks.

See, when you continue to worship idols, you have to become more and more aware of the tremendous presence of Existence that you are trying to connect with through the idol. Then you will automatically start seeing God everywhere. You will understand that it is not just the idol but the whole of creation that is pregnant with the presence of God. Then you can start relating with the whole of Existence.

In the case of meditation, if you go into it with sincerity, the outcome is not definite. A personality change may happen. You may emerge as a different person and this is seen as a great risk! It is like taking a gamble. Transformation starts happening. It is this transformation that you are actually seeking, but when it happens you are afraid.

You feel comfortable in the security of rituals. Rituals become a part of your every-day routine.

When you meditate, your awareness increases and when this happens, the fence that you have imagined around yourself, which actually society has put around you, slowly dissolves and you feel rebellious, not against society but against your own unconscious and ignorant state. This rebellion causes you to probe more into the cause of it and it opens out further avenues for you.

This is how you move deeper and deeper into a space that you have never entered before; a space which society does not even know; a space that has all along been inside you but locked; a space for which you have been unknowingly searching for a key to unlock. When you have found this space, you have arrived!

It is like this:

> A cow is tied to a rope and given a few meters of radius to move around.
> It moves around and becomes aware and mature through its intelligence.
> Then, the rope is loosened a little, giving it a few more meters of radius.
> It goes further around and becomes more intelligent and then it is given still more length of rope to wander.
> Depending on the cow's growing intelligence and consciousness, it can even be let free at some point in time!

The same thing happens in man. The more his consciousness grows, the greater freedom he enjoys and the cycle continues.

How does the master help

It is a question of how willing you are to allow the transformation of your energies.

But when this happens, society will tell you that you are moving away. You only have to have courage and faith in Existence and yourself and move on.

Here is where, more than any books or lectures, a master can serve as a *yoga danda* to you, a stick of support to help you stand up for yourself. Every time you feel beaten by society in your path of spirituality, when you feel you are against the majority, the master will pull you up in his own way and tell you to move on.

This does not mean that you are dependent on the master. It is like this: You are trying to find your way to a particular place. If left by yourself, you will ask for directions at several places. Sometimes you may be guided wrongly and so you may have to retrace your steps. After spending considerable amount of time, you will reach your destination. It may take you a long time to do so, but you will reach it. But what if you have a map or a guide? You will reach your destination without loss of time! Does it mean that you are dependent on the map or guide? No. It was just a quicker way of doing things, that's all. In the same way, a master is a guide who knows the way, who has already been to the place you are searching for and is available to guide you there.

With courage and conviction, it happens

When you have dedication alone, you will no doubt work hard towards reaching your goal, but when you have dedication with courage, you will take a leap towards your goal. This courage will come if you stop looking at others and look only into yourself, if you stop comparing yourself with others and watch yourself with awareness and make the necessary changes in you.

You need to stand up with courage of conviction on your own path. Courage of conviction will happen in you only when you are strongly centered in yourself without comparing yourself with others.

Society is waiting to pull you into the familiar patterns that it knows, into the miseries that it is familiar with and can handle; into the well-trodden and worn-out path. It is very easy and does not require courage to fall into this path. But to tread the lesser-trodden path of spirituality requires courage. When I say courage, I don't mean ordinary courage, I mean total courage.

To wear gypsy beads does not require courage, but to wear *rudraksh* beads requires courage! I give *rudraksh* beads to those who wish to wear them. The *rudraksh* beads are nothing but energy storehouses. They store the cosmic energy for you. They are like a battery house and recharge you when you get into a low. But society sees these beads as clear signs of *sannyas*! They see them as something worn by renunciates, without even understanding the meaning of renunciation.

They condemn people who stay in family life and wear *rudraksh*. But when they see the *rudraksh* beads on deities or *sannyasis*, they are happy and pray to them. So many of the younger ones come and tell me how their family reacts to them wearing the beads.

It is ironical. When people pray, they pray to the cosmic energy, but when the same energy is available to them in simpler forms, they are not ready to take it! They pray to it but run away from it!

If you deeply analyze this, it will seem so contradictory. They see themselves as so distinctly different from God; that is the problem. They are not ready to accept that they *are* God. Now I tell you: Whether you know it or not, whether you accept it or not, whether you like it or not, whether you believe it or not, you ARE God. This is the underlying basis of the *vishuddhi chakra* also – discovering your own unique self and infinite energy.

When your courage grows, society automatically fades into insignificance. When your courage is low, society automatically assumes power over you. It is all in your mind. How much power you give to society, that much power it will have over you. Never blame society for anything.

The choice has always been yours. Due to sheer lack of courage, you choose to go with what society says; you choose to pull and push by comparing and trying to beat one another, and then you blame society for it. It is not the right thing to do. Remember, the choice is always yours.

Just function with awareness, and infinity will simply open out. When it does, you will feel afraid because you are not used to

346

seeing such open space. You are used to seeing boundaries all the time. Now you are not able to see the fence anywhere. You start getting apprehensive.

You immediately think that you have entered the wrong space. Reality seems too much to digest. You start feeling insecure. You feel like going back to the warmth of your past beliefs and illusions. You feel you have made a mistake by not listening to society when it told you that you were going on the wrong path. You start doubting and then doubting the doubt as well. You feel like a lonely child left in the middle of a desert.

It is in times like these that you need to remember that Existence is always with you and that your courage needs only to mature and go hand in hand with faith upon Existence and then everything will be alright. Faith is the prodding stick for courage.

Unless a revolution happens inside you, you can never rupture and grow into a tree. Most of us remain a seed and die, because of lack of courage. We always try to dissect the seed to find the fruits and flowers. Will it ever help? No! The seed has to rupture to grow into fruits and flowers. Similarly, when a radical change happens, when a revolution is created in man, he will rupture and grow. All meditations are nothing but techniques to make the seed rupture.

When you start rupturing, all your priorities start changing. What was important before becomes less important now. Only the things that nurture your being will seem important. Your whole attitude will change. Your whole presence will change.

Your presence will automatically lure people to you although they might not approve of it! The radiance felt in your inner core will attract them with deep curiosity. While society will criticize you for your changed attitude, it will start finding your presence distinctly different.

When the transformation is happening, just utterly ignore anything from the past. The past will again and again try to pull you into familiar patterns and deep bondage. When you listen to it, you are allowing yourself to be in bondage. Just decide to hold on to the ecstasy and conviction of the transformation happening in you. This is your greatest test, the test of your perseverance to transform completely. Hold on until the transformation is complete and mature.

There is a cosmic energy that fills this universe and there is an energy that fills you. Spirituality is all about establishing a live connection between the Cosmic energy and the energy in you. When your individual consciousness merges with the Universal Consciousness, you become enlightened.

Just a desire to get enlightened will not do. It needs to be a conscious decision. See, ordinary desires are nothing but greed that don't really propel you towards your specific goal. A conscious decision is what will make you work towards achieving.

People don't understand these things properly and simply talk at a superficial level. When you don't understand, you misunderstand. But you think you have understood and there starts the problem.

Persist and it will happen

Spirituality is a science that gives a deep understanding of our body, mind and spirit. When you enter it with awareness, the outer world will slowly dissolve. When people see you from outside, they will think that you are renouncing. Only *you* will understand that you are not renouncing anything; the outer world things are simply dissolving on their own. The illusion disappears and you become de-hypnotized.

At one of our programs, I asked how many of the participants thought that I had hypnotized them. Out of a group of eighty, three of them lifted their hands. One of the ladies who was sitting next to the girl who had her hand raised laughed at her. I asked her why she was laughing. The girl was honest enough to lift her hand.

I am sure out of that group, many of them would have been tempted to lift their hands but didn't, fearing what I might say! Anyhow, three of them lifted their hands. I told them that I had not hypnotized them, but had actually de-hypnotized them.

They had started feeling the clearing of *maya* or illusion. But what happens is, you are so used to being in a state of illusion, that if it starts clearing, you think something has gone wrong! The problem is, when too much truth is told to people, a certain fear sets in. The comfort they were enjoying under the cover of ignorance suffers.

See, in whatever quantities your ignorance dissolves, in that much quantity you become possessed by God or Existence. Any effort that you put in your everyday life should be directed towards

349

emptying yourself so that you may be filled with Existence. Any other effort is just incidental and trivial in life. Remember this.

Every breath of yours should be towards increasing your awareness and consciousness. Only then have you really made a conscious decision to experience Existence or God. If this firm resolve is not happening in you, then you are still pretending to seek, that's all. You are simply cheating yourself. Don't for a moment think that you are cheating others. You are cheating yourself.

To turn your steps from outwards to inwards is the first step. That moment of taking the U-turn is the most significant moment. You will know when you have taken the U-turn. Until then, your mind will have been giving excuses and more excuses, citing people and situations and outer world circumstances as reasons for not being able to integrate yourself. Once you take the U-turn, all these thoughts will fade into insignificance. They will slowly lose their prominence. They will be there no doubt, but you will be steadily progressing, taking them in your stride. They will help you become a more effective watcher as they play their parts meticulously.

Taking the first step or the U-turn is what is the most difficult thing. When you take the U-turn, half the job is done. You then become more malleable to the ways of Existence.

When you take the U-turn, everything becomes meditation. Whether it is walking or talking or singing or dancing or simply putting your clothes on or taking them off, everything becomes a meditation and is done with increasing awareness.

You will simply watch yourself doing these things and slowly understand that the whole world is an illusion. When you take your first step inwards, you have in effect taken a leap because the first step is the real leap. Until then, you only philosophize, convince yourself and others that you are seeking and get more confused with less determination day by day.

When you take the first step, you are ready to win yourself. To win others is very easy. Just take a few weapons or use your tongue and simply destroy them, that's all. But to win yourself takes real courage. This *vishuddhi chakra* is all about winning yourself.

When you look inwards, you are ready to win yourself. Of course, when you are on the path inwards, there might not be anything tangible to the people around you in what you are doing. Only *you* will know that everything is happening inside and not outside. Only *you* will be aware of the revolution that is happening inside you. Only *you* will be able to tell the growing intelligence inside you.

People around you will not be able to understand the experiences you are enjoying. I tell you: never try to convince anyone that you are evolving inside. You may share your experiences with your spiritual friends who will be able to match your wavelength of thinking, but if you try to share these experiences with other people who are blissfully oblivious to the inner journey, you will only land up in deep misery.

Just allow the experiences to happen in you; neither hold on to them nor run behind them. Allow them to work like steam on you so that you may fully ripen. If you hold on to them, you will stagnate at some point and miss the whole thing.

Remember that all these experiences are tell-tale signs that you are well on your journey inwards. They are like signboards that you see on the road. Do you cling onto the signboards and say that the destination has been reached? No. Don't cling onto them. Move on to your destination.

A total commitment and determination is needed and this will come automatically to you when you are ready; when you are ready to drop your mind, that is society, and live with your heart; when you are ready to stop pointing fingers at others and point to yourself, come what may; when you understand experientially that your mind is societal and your heart is natural.

Also, when people ask you for proof of your experiences, just understand that there is no need to prove to them. Your experience is so intimate and personal to you that you will not be able to effectively share it with the other person. In fact if you share it, you will be bringing down the whole experience. Also, the other person may not be willing to believe what you are saying. They may tell you that you are deluding yourself. They may want you to explain the whole thing logically.

Logic cannot explain these experiences. God is beyond logic. If logic can explain God, then logic has to be superior to God and that can never be the case! So just relax and allow the experiences to happen to you. When anyone questions you, have the maturity to smile and move on. A smile can convey more effectively what you can't in so many words.

Great enlightened masters have experienced such tremendous joy in communion with Existence. People ask me to narrate my experiences but I tell you, it is all so personal and intimate that I cannot explain it to you in words. I can guide you; I can show you the way - the path for you to experience. The moment I start explaining, it will become mundane.

But I can give you the highest assurance that you will experience it, if you have the fire within you. The promise given by a master is enough energy for you to achieve it.

I am telling you all these things now in reply to your question about meditation and spirituality. You may think that we are moving away from the main subject. No! This *chakra*, this *vishuddhi chakra* is all about expanding yourself; about discovering your own unique self, with total awareness and understanding of the fact that there is no scope for comparison and jealousy in life. Just take in whatever I have told you and allow the energy behind it to transform you. I tell you, miracles can happen inside you! It will change the whole quality of your being.

The three layers of energy

Alright...Now, from all that we have discussed, you have understood that comparison and jealousy are non-entities and don't have any actual relevance to you at all. Now, let me try to explain some more on the *vishuddhi chakra* and the energy house that is in it.

We have three layers of energy in us. The first layer of energy is from our mind and it is this that we use for our day-to-day

353

activities from morning till night. Once this energy expends, we start feeling tired and irritated if we are given more work to do.

The second layer energy is the emergency layer. It is the energy that arises from our emotions. At the time of emergency, this energy opens out. Let us say you are really tired and walking back from work to your home. You feel you have enough energy only to enter your house and crash on your bed. At that time, suddenly if a dog starts chasing you, what do you do? You start running much faster than you have ever run before. Even if you are dead tired, even if you were earlier unable to move even a limb, suddenly you run with a different kind of energy! This is the emergency energy that arises out of emotion.

The third layer of energy is the being level energy. This is an infinite source of energy within you, which you don't use at all. This energy layer can be opened and experienced by deep meditation. Whether you accept it or not, you are in connection with all these three layers of energies. This *vishuddhi chakra* holds in it the key to these higher energy levels.

Let me narrate to you an incident that actually happened during my days of wandering:

> In a beautiful place called Almora in the Himalayas, there is a small ashram with a few huts for those who wish to meditate.
> The place is known to be frequented by tigers at night!
> I was there for a short while during my days of wandering.
> I used to meditate for long hours there.

They had a system wherein, when the head of the ashram senses the tigers coming, he would ring a bell and all the *sannyasis* would get into their respective huts and close the doors, until such time they were asked to come out.

On one occasion, at night time, while we were meditating, the bell rang and all of us got into our respective huts.

The next day, the head of the ashram came around to see if we were all alright.

He found that one of the huts was closed and the *sannyasi* inside was shouting through the window to open the door.

We all ran to the hut and tried opening the door but couldn't open it.

Finally, a few of us got in through the window and entered the hut.

To our surprise, we found that he had placed a big grinding stone against the door so that the tiger would not be able to push its way through.

We jointly moved the stone away to open the door.

It suddenly struck us how the man might have moved the stone single-handedly against the door in the first place! We asked him how he had moved it.

He replied, 'Moved it? I simply lifted it and placed it!'

When he heard the call of the tiger, he simply lifted the stone to place it against the door, that's all!

This is exactly what I mean by the emergency layer energy. Under normal circumstances, the same man would not have been able to lift that stone. Do you understand? Even after the incident,

355

once the emergency was over, he himself was not able to lift it away from the door in the story!

Out of fear or greed, the second level energy opens. For example, if there is an important meeting, do you feel tired? No! You will be alive and fresh. The desire or greed to attend the meeting will keep you in an energized condition.

The *vishuddhi chakra* is the door through which all these three layers of energy can be opened out, but you are not aware of it because you have not used these layers effectively in a long time.

It is like this: In all harbors, there is a place called a boat jetty where the boats are kept. It is commonly said that if the boat is kept in the jetty for long without sailing, it forgets that it can sail in the water!

In the same way, because you have not used the third layer of energy for a long time, you forget that you belong to it or it belongs to you. Meditation can open out this third level energy for you.

If you keep this *chakra* in a cleansed condition, you can scale great heights in the outer world and great depths in the inner world. When you have low self-esteem or jealousy, this *chakra* is locked. Low self-esteem is a passive manifestation of jealousy, that's all. Jealousy is active while low self-esteem is passive. Both are a result of comparison. With low self-esteem, you feel you are no good and resign yourself to it. In jealousy, you are unable to bear it and start reacting; that is the difference.

Understand that any self-esteem that you have that indicates to you that you are less than God is low self-esteem, because you ARE God. That is why I say there is no scope to compare yourself with anyone else.

You need to experience the second and third layers of energy hidden in this *chakra*, in order to understand the infinite potential that is lying hidden in you. This *chakra* is really the seat of energy for us. When we concentrate on it, we will be able to feel the energy radiating from it.

In the Himalayas, when I used to wander in my earlier days, so many miles I would cover by foot. I used to start walking at a slow pace, concentrating on my *vishuddhi chakra*. Slowly, I would pick up speed concentrating on the *chakra*. After a certain point, my body would start moving with a swinging pace and I would be just a watcher of it! I would cover many miles in this fashion.

All the food that you take or exercise that you do helps only the first layer of energy. Food is not the only source of energy. It is a common misconception that only food gives you energy. Food is one source of energy, that's all.

Yogis in Tibet do not eat at all. They simply drink water out of the shell of a *bilva* fruit. I lived like that for six months in the Himalayas. I got the energy from the sun, from the water while taking my bath, from the air while breathing. These are all *yogic* methods. *Tapasya* is the penance you do for enlightenment throughout your life. That alone vibrates in your being.

When you start competing with others, you forget your own self. You forget to strengthen your own being, which is your actual untapped source of energy. If you have physical strength and intellectual strength without the strength of the soul, it is of no use. It is only when you discover the strength of your soul, that you have touched your life source and energy.

Q: Once we are able to be without jealousy, have we completely gotten freedom in at least one aspect of our shortcomings?

Of course, if you are able to see a space where love can exist without passion or jealousy, you have definitely moved forward, but continue moving with complete awareness because you can very easily slip back into your old unconscious ways and find yourself going through all the old emotions once again.

Hold on to the newly discovered awareness and move with it. It can open up many more beautiful avenues for you to explore. Don't stagnate. The greatest danger is to cling on to a few experiences thinking that they are solid.

Masters never allow their disciples to stagnate in any experience. They always prod them on further so that the disciple may look deeper and deeper in his quest. People who have had visions of Gods and Goddesses most often tend to stagnate in their spiritual journey. They feel there is nothing more to be seen and therefore stay right there holding on to that experience. This should never be allowed to happen.

Until you have reached the state of eternal bliss, you can hit rock bottom at any time. So remember that and nurture your awareness continuously to take you to realms of deeper and deeper understanding.

Understand one thing: The work of a Mmaster is so delicate. He has to handle each and every one of you with utmost care and delicateness. He has to see in which way each of you will grow and make you flower in that way. Each of you has been through so many lives and accumulated so much ignorance. He has to work through all that and wake you up.

Life offers plenty of solutions, but there is always something that fits you the best. The intelligence lies in finding that out. When you apply your own intelligence and find it out, you will enjoy the benefits of it. Whereas, if you start looking at others and start applying their solutions to yourself, you will lose track of where you stand.

A small story:

> An old woman was going about dusting her old house in a remote village.
> Suddenly the door opened and a young sales man walked in.
> He spoke excitedly when he saw the woman dusting.
> He told her that he had many gadgets that would help her clean her house.
> The old woman said, 'But...'
> The man interrupted her and pulled out a lot of rubbish from a bag and put it on the floor.
> The old woman tried again, 'But...'
> The man told her to stand by and watch. He pulled out a device and explained, 'You see this machine? It will clean

any amount of dust in no time. It is so light in weight and therefore very easy for you to handle at this age. Let me demonstrate.'

The old lady tried, 'But...'

The man interrupted, 'Just show me the plug point.'

The lady finally said, 'But... electricity hasn't yet reached our village!'

In life, we need to be able to figure out what suits us the best! If we are clear about this, we will grow without a worry. But most of the time, we covet and apply others' solutions to ourselves, and then feel unhappy.

If we are clear about where we stand and what we need, we will grow steadily. Even setbacks in this way of living will only be ones that teach us how to function more intelligently. In this way, we at least function with our own intelligence and so it becomes an experiential understanding.

When you simply follow another's solution, there is nothing happening inside you; you are operating from your periphery. When nothing happens inside you, you cannot grow; remember that. When I say that you cannot grow, I mean you don't evolve from within. Material benefits may come, but you remain dead inside.

Remember that only when you grow from within, you are really growing. Don't get dangerously caught in outer world races. See them as mere play and play them well. Material benefits are needed for survival but all these should remain in the periphery. Your inner core should steadily grow. It is this that will guide you in your play outside.

The process of discovering your infinite intelligence is what life is all about. That is why I always say, 'Life is the path and not any goal.' As your intelligence grows, you will become more joyful and you will be able to play the game of life more effectively. So stop comparing and start discovering – the source of your real growth.

The *vishuddhi chakra* is the seat of higher creativity. When the energy of this *chakra* is unlocked, you will see that a tremendous flow of creativity becomes available to you.

When you change the quality of your *being*, naturally the quality of your *doing* also changes. Whatever you do, you do with greater efficiency, greater creativity. As a result, the quality of your *having* also changes. You will be happy with whatever comes your way and you will see that material wealth and success flow towards you naturally. So drop comparison and return to your being and discover eternal bliss, *nithyananda*.

Now let us enter into a meditation technique called the *Shakti Sagar*. It will make you understand experientially how you can harness the tremendous energy source that is available to you through your *vishuddhi chakra*.

Emotion: Comparison and jealousy

Chakra: Vishuddhi chakra

Location: Throat region

In Sanskrit, *vishuddh*i means 'beyond purity and impurity'. The name therefore means that this chakra can never get impure and hence never needs to be cleansed. That is why comparison, which locks this *chakra*, is like a shadow without an object. There is no basis for the concept of comparison. It is purely a figment of our imagination.

This *chakra* is locked by comparison and jealousy and it can be made to flower when we exhibit our individuality without worrying about others, and express fully our capacity, uniqueness and creativity.

Meditation Technique to realize one's uniqueness and energy reserve:
Shakti Sagar Meditation - a technique from Zen Buddhism.

WALKING MEDITATION

The Shakti Sagar Meditation

(Total duration: 30 minutes)

The *Shakti Sagar* meditation is taken from Zen Buddhism. The key to this meditation is to keep the mind fixed on the *vishuddhi* while the body moves.

Stand with your eyes closed and focus on your *vishuddhi chakra*. Stand behind a chair or some support and hold it (if required) and start walking slowly, very slowly in the same spot where you are standing.

Now start increasing your pace very gradually. Keep walking faster and faster in the same spot. Push your limits only to the extent that you can, with no discomfort. Don't over exert yourself at any time. At all times focus on the *vishuddhi*. You will be able to feel the energy coming from it. The important thing is never to slow down at any point in time. Try to jog faster than what you are jogging but never slower. Stop after 20 minutes.

For the next 10 minutes, just sit down quietly wherever you are. Keep your eyes closed and focus on the *vishuddhi*. You will absorb the energy that is generated during the movement. When you do this, the cosmic energy enters through the *vishuddhi chakra* and becomes a tremendous source of energy to you. While doing this meditation, you may wear your *mala* around your neck. It will serve to store the energy that you create during the meditation.

Thank you. We will meet for the next session.

Chapter 8

Drop the ego

MORNING AFTER
MEETING JUDS @ STARBUCKS
+ FINANCER:...

So Serious...

S eriousness is ego

What is seriousness?

Seriousness is nothing but paying undue importance to something, at the cost of everything else. It stems from the inability to see that all of life is just a drama that is unfolding every minute. Seriousness is the result of over-expectation from life.

A small story:

> Two boys were building sand castles on the beach.
> They suddenly had a quarrel and one of the boys got angry and kicked the sand castle.
> The other boy went and complained to the king about it.
> The king began to laugh at him for making so much out of just sand castles.
> But the king's advisor, a Zen monk, started laughing at the king.
> He asked, 'When you can fight battles and lose sleep over stone castles, why do you laugh at these boys for fighting over sand castles?'

If you really go to see, all our seriousness is just about sandcastles! For the child, at that young age, sand castles seem precious, whereas for us at our age, stone castles seem precious, that's all. Whether it is a sand castle or stone castle, the seriousness behind it is the same; just the object of seriousness is different. So don't laugh when children fight over sand castles.

Seriousness closes your mind to the openness and freedom of life. It makes you dull and dead. It curbs your thinking and makes you stick to the familiar patterns that you know all the time. It makes you egoistic.

> In a Zen monastery, there was a competition among disciples as to who had the best garden.
> One disciple was a very serious sort.
> He took the competition also very seriously.
> He kept his garden always neat and clean, and well-swept. All the grass was of the same height. All the bushes were neatly trimmed.
> He was sure that he would get the first prize.
> On the day of the competition, the master went around all the gardens.
> Then he came back and ranked the gardens.
> This disciple's garden got the lowest ranking.
> Everyone was shocked.
> The disciple went and questioned the master about it.
> He asked, 'Master, what is wrong with my garden? Why did you rank me the lowest?'
> The master looked at him and asked, 'Where are all the dead leaves?'

A garden maintained in such a way is no longer alive! It is dead.

Seriousness kills creativity. It destroys spontaneity.

Science has proved that when you perform a task in a relaxed and light manner, your thinking and decision-making capacity is automatically enhanced. The same task when performed in a serious manner dulls your mind.

All our seriousness is just sickness. When I say all, I mean ALL. And all our sickness originates from seriousness. Seriousness begets sickness and sickness begets seriousness.

One night, a man called me on the phone and started crying.

He said, 'I fall at your feet, Swamiji! Please help me. I'm so depressed! I am going to end my life!' and so on.

I tried to calm him down, and finally said, 'Why don't you come to the ashram tomorrow morning and spend a few days with me? Let us see what can be done.'

He replied, 'Tomorrow Swamiji? Oh... tomorrow I have to go to the office... shall I come next weekend?'

Most of us are like this: getting unnecessarily tense about our so-called problems. Just one jolt is enough and our seriousness will drop. When we wake up to reality, we see how insignificant our problems really are.

When you do something too seriously, when you are too concerned about the result, you are actually not allowing yourself to perform at the optimum level.

368

Of course, you need to make plans, you need to think ahead, but with sincerity, not with seriousness. Seriousness is not the same as sincerity. Sincerity is focusing on the task with enthusiasm and youthfulness. Sincerity is giving the task your best without worrying excessively about the result.

When you are serious, you don't enjoy; you don't laugh. How can you laugh when you are serious? Either you are serious or you are laughing. You can't be both at the same time because the very definition of seriousness is such.

But when you are sincere, you can be laughing and playful. You can continue to do in a playful and joyful way, and because you have finished the job, you have been sincere!

With sincerity, there is no worry, there is only enthusiasm.

When you are serious, you are egoistic, because you fail to see that the whole thing is only a cosmic drama. You feel that you are a separate entity... too much of 'I' and so you are serious. If you understand that the whole thing is only a drama, you can never be serious. When this understanding happens at a deep level, you will do things for the sheer joy of moving in tune with the cosmic drama or Existence.

Chronological planning Vs. psychological planning

You see, there are two types of planning: chronological planning and psychological planning.

Chronological planning is planning on a timescale. You decide that you will get up at such and such a time, finish your morning routine by a particular time, reach the office at a particular time, and get certain tasks done that day at the office. This is alright. It is a practical way to organize your work in order to get the best results. This kind of planning with sincere action will take you from happiness to more happiness.

Psychological planning on the other hand, is planning in your head with no relevance to time or space. It is just constant serious planning going on in your head, over and above the chronological planning. It is actually nothing but complex negativity being applied to the chronological planning that has already been done. It keeps you thinking that you are serious and dutiful. But you get into a dull state because all your energy is going into analyzing the plan again and again.

Psychological planning boosts your ego. It makes you feel great and worthy. It makes you feel that you are handling things of a great magnitude. It makes you feel that it is wholly in your hands to worry about it and make it happen. This is psychological planning.

This is actually a way of postponing happiness, postponing life, waiting for something particular to happen to start enjoying life.

We always think, *If I get married, my life will be settled. So let me work towards getting married.*

If I have two children, my life will be fulfilled.

Once I retire, I'll be peaceful.

It is the attitude of: *now I'll be serious; later I'll be happy!*

In the end, you will be happy neither now nor then. You will lose your capacity to be happy at any time.

Just live with simplicity, with spontaneity and with innocence; that will itself do the job.

Strive for totality not for perfection

Don't harp too much on perfectionism. I tell you: Perfectionism can make you neurotic. Whatever you do, do it wholly, totally. Then automatically, you will never worry about perfectionism.

Perfectionism is always something from your mind. It becomes a goal for you. You work towards it as a goal. And when you work towards it as a goal, it becomes dead and mundane. But when you are total, you are established in your heart, and it becomes a deep experience. The outcome then has to be beautiful and it will give you joy also. Then, whatever you do, you will be in tune with Existence.

Perfectionism never gives you joy; it only fulfills your ego. Even if you feel fulfilled at the end of it, it is only a fulfillment of your ego, never a fulfillment of your being. Be very clear that perfectionists are the biggest egoists. They miss the dimension of being total. Totality is possible when you enter into it deeply from your being. Perfectionism is never possible because it is in your mind and your mind keeps changing its definition of perfection.

Also, have the courage to make mistakes. Serious people are always afraid to make mistakes. They take themselves too seriously. They think too much about themselves. It is too much to make mistakes and have someone point it out to them. Actually I tell you, these people who are afraid of making small mistakes, end up making big blunders!

What is wrong in making mistakes? You will say, 'Swamiji, I can't afford to make mistakes in my work; that is why I am so serious.' What you say might be true; your work may not permit you to make mistakes, but that is not the point I am trying to make here. When you make a mistake, people will point it out and you will not be able to bear it. Your ego is bound to get hurt and you are very sensitive to this; you know this. So to avoid getting your ego hurt, you try your best not to make mistakes!

You plan so unconsciously and continuously to keep guarding your ego. But the reasons you give are all different. It is not that you are lying. It is just that you are not aware of the subtle way in which your system works. But if you deeply analyze and see, you will understand what I am saying.

There is nothing wrong in making mistakes. In fact, by making a few mistakes, you come to know clearly how to avoid making mistakes. The more you learn from mistakes, the more you know about how not to make mistakes.

Knowing how not to make mistakes is a very important thing. Only then you have seen both sides of it; only then you have explored the two sides experientially. Else, there is always the danger of falling into the unknown side at a critical time when you really can't afford to.

However, don't make the same mistakes again! Your mind always repeats patterns. Don't do it with mistakes also. Make new mistakes! And move on to better and better understanding!

I am not saying to deliberately make mistakes. That is foolishness again. I am only saying, do things to the best of your intelligence and enthusiasm but without worrying about whether it might be a mistake. The moment you are worried that it might be a mistake, you are worried about your ego getting hurt.

When you are not so concerned about your ego getting hurt, you will have the courage to take any jump. All your so-called worry is actually about your ego getting hurt. When you are free from it, you will act with more freedom and courage. You will be more willing to experiment.

A small story:

> In a clubhouse, one man had finished his round of playing cards and was leaving.
> He went to the coat stand and was putting on his coat, when suddenly a meek voice spoke behind him, 'Sir, are you Mr. Philippe?'
> The man turned around and replied, 'No, I am not.'
> The voice said, 'Thank God. I am Philippe and that coat is mine.'

We are so afraid that we might make a mistake and hurt our ego. So we move cautiously, with cordiality, just to be sure. These are nothing but passive forms of ego. You are so terrified of your ego getting hurt and so you behave in these ways. Drop all your guard of your ego and move about freely.

Move away from seriousness. Somehow, we always associate spirituality with seriousness. It is a big misconception. Seriousness can never be religion or spirituality.

Why do you think I keep telling you so many jokes and small stories? If I don't tell you all these things, you will start becoming very serious and when you become serious, you become dead and heavy. You will not be alive and light. I am not here to make you heavy.

I am here to unload you and make you light. I am here to show you that your seriousness is nothing but a form of your ego.

People who are loaded with the past and the future are always serious. They don't know how to laugh spontaneously. They feel that it is their duty to shoulder the past and future and be immersed in it in all seriousness. This is a very highly egoistic attitude. They feel that if they don't do it, there is no one to take care of it.

There is no need to shoulder the past and future. Just be in the present; that is enough. These people are completely missing the present. They are missing the laughter in their lives.

Laugh and let go your ego

Laughter is that which brings in a ray of energy from your being to your body. It totally rejuvenates your whole self. It can heal like nothing else can. It gives you such wonderful glimpses of the present, which you try to achieve through other difficult meditation techniques. Laughter is the most powerful meditation technique.

Laughter is the greatest spiritual quality. Sincerity and laughter always go together. As I said earlier, seriousness can never co-exist with laughter. Either you are serious or you are laughing. When you are sincere, you can laugh and do your duty sincerely.

How many of us can laugh with all our heart? Even in laughter we manage restrain! The so-called social etiquette has taught us to laugh in a polite way. When kids laugh, we condition them. We are a spray of cold water on their laughter. We tell them, 'Now that is enough!' We try to condition even their laughter.

I have heard mothers telling their daughters, 'Don't laugh like a man; laugh like a lady.' How can you culture laughter? Laughter is something that comes from your being. I tell you, all the conditioning of your children is just to make replicas of your own dull and dead self. Until you replicate yourself completely, you will not rest.

I spent some time with a few children during my visit to America this year. I spent about an hour interacting with them. I was so shocked when I saw that they simply did not laugh however much I tried joking with them. Children these days take on pseudo maturity and manage to exclude laughter from their system. If they cannot laugh as kids, what will they do when they grow up? It was too much for me to see them.

People tell me that my laughter is infectious. With those kids, for the first time, my laughter seemed non-infectious! They were just looking at me with the same mature look on their faces. I left them afraid that they may make *me* serious!

375

You see, maturity does not have anything to do with how you laugh. But somehow, we feel that when we are mature, we should automatically laugh less.

Laughter is such strength because it brings in energy from your core to your periphery. If you sit through my sessions, most of the time there will only be laughter. Some joke will be cracked or some story told and everyone will be laughing. I never allow seriousness to set in. Even with people who live in the ashram, I never allow seriousness to set in.

A small story:

> One very humorous speaker was invited to a town to deliver a speech.
> He came to the program with a big group of people.
> The organizers were surprised when they saw the number of people with the speaker.
> The speaker saw their surprised look and explained, 'It is becoming difficult to get people to laugh these days, so I carry my own audience.'

In the so-called elite circles, people will be laughing, but in a very cultured and well-mannered way! This is not real laughter; this is dead laughter. Laughter can never be conditioned. If it is conditioned, it is not laughter; it is not the meditative laughter that we are talking about. It is simply an expression of the ego inside, that's all.

If you analyze why you laugh when a joke is cracked, you will understand: A set of logically connected statements is first told to you. When you are clinging on to that built-up logic, the punch line is delivered and your logic is shattered! At the moment your logic is shattered, your mind is also shattered and you are in a state of no-mind or *satori*. You are Buddha!

When you are in no-mind, you are in the present. When you laugh, you are in the present because when you laugh you are in no-mind. When you are thoughtless, you are in the present. When you are with thoughts, you are either in the past or in the future.

Laughter is *total* and it can simply heal and transform you. It is the best and most easily available medicine for humanity.

Life is so precious that it is not worth spending it on dull and lethargic moments. Laugh and infuse your life with energy and bliss. Just decide to enjoy continuously, whatever the job may be that you are doing. Be sincere, not serious.

When you laugh, you radiate energy around you; it is infectious; you radiate a therapeutic bliss around you. This is also why, when a person in a bad mood walks in, he radiates the same mood around him and there is every chance that the people around him will be affected by it. I always tell doctors to do some kind of cleansing meditation because they are continuously in touch with patients who come to them with a lot of negative thoughts and diseases.

Q: But we need a reason to laugh. How can we simply decide to be humorous when we don't find anything humorous?

We always think that we need a comedian or a joke to make us laugh. When you start living in the present moment, your very existence will be beautiful and light. Your inhalation and exhalation of breath, the process of bread getting converted to blood in your body, the synchronous happenings of events in Existence; everything will be so beautiful. You will feel so much bliss and you will be ever smiling and laughing. Your whole being will exude laughter and bliss.

Laughing at a joke is alright, but when you fall in tune with Existence, you simply enjoy the big cosmic drama that is happening and you laugh at everything. Then there is no place for seriousness, no place for ego. You are no more solid. You are porous and playful. You develop a deep understanding of the Existential game and so you laugh.

You are able to see that everyone is only a player who has become so serious with their role, and you laugh at that. You laugh at how each one is deceiving the other when playing the game. You laugh at the thought that you are playing a game! When you are able to laugh, you have become the watcher, and when you have become the watcher, you are separate from the 'I' and 'mine' - the ego.

A small story:

> Once there was a conference of Buddhist monks on the meaning of true spirituality.
> Each monk went onto the stage and gave a long speech.
> Finally, it was the turn of a Zen monk to speak.
> He went onto the stage and simply started laughing! He laughed and laughed...from his being.

The laughter just rose from his belly. He started shaking uncontrollably with laughter.

His laughter was so infectious that soon all the others in the room started laughing, without even knowing why!

The laughter of all the monks produced a huge wave of positive energy in the room.

The monks reached a state of tremendous elevation.

Their thinking was shattered and their being was filled with bliss.

The Zen monk finally spoke, 'This is true spirituality.'

Laughter is the highest spiritual quality. It can lead you to enlightenment! Laughing is a great healing energy. If you laugh at your sickness, you will become healthy. Laughter is a beautiful way of connecting with the energy of Existence, which is pure healing energy.

In our meditation programs, we always include laughter and dance. They are the easiest ways to becoming a Buddha! Dance can make you simple and light. Dance, like laughter, is another easy and enjoyable meditation. When you can dance without a care, you become the dance itself. Energy will then gush from you.

You can dance without a care only if you are free from all your pseudo identities. As long as you think you are someone, you can't dance in joy. Dance is an outward expression of inner joy. And I am not talking about programmed dance where you know which step is going to come next. I am talking about letting go of your so-called identities and feeling the oneness with Existence and dancing with that joy.

The self-conscious ones are the egoistic ones. They are so bothered about what others will say about their dance and so they sit quietly. Again, they are guarding their ego and they are missing the joy of life like anything.

Once in a while at least, in your home, play some music and dance. Simply decide to let go. It can become an intense meditation that can take you beyond your mind and transform you in a way that words cannot. Be natural. Be original. The people who comment on your dance are simply missing out on the joy of dance. Don't bother about them. Just dissolve and become the dance itself. Laughter and dance are the easiest techniques to shed your ego and merge with Existence.

Q: When do we know that our ego is no more?

Simply put, when you no longer feel yourself as a separate entity, ego has dissolved. When you become enlightened, your ego has ripened and ruptured. When your ego drops, the resistance you posed earlier will disappear and Existence will simply flow through you.

Whether you know it or not, accept it or not, like it or not, Existence is trying to flow through you every minute, but you are so full of ego that you are unable to allow it. You miss the miracles of Existence because of your ego. You are unable to connect to Existence and so you continue to live in ego, ignorance and misery.

380

You are so full of ego that you are living far away from your own being. There is so much of accumulated stuff inside you that you need to get rid of, the stuff that you have accumulated over many lives; not just this one life. There is no space for even yourself inside yourself! And because of this, you are operating from your periphery all the time instead of from your inner being.

When your ego dissolves, you cease to exist separately, and you simply merge with Existence! This is the state of enlightened masters. I often tell people, 'Destroy what you are not.' People look at me with shock. When I say this, what I mean is, you are your inner being. That being is now contaminated with all that it is not - the various active and passive forms of ego. These are what you need to destroy and that is what I mean when I say, 'Destroy what you are not and you have arrived!'

You are a part of Existence, and whatever causes you to think otherwise, is ego. A fish, whether it likes it or not, whether it accepts it or not, whether it believes it or not, is a part of the ocean. It has two choices. It either lives happily in the ocean, or fights with the ocean and still continues to live in it, making its life miserable.

If you flow with Existence, you will enjoy every moment of your life. You will become, sensitive, creative and fluid.

A small story:

> A teacher took her students out for a picnic.
> They played games, ate their snack and enjoyed themselves.

Suddenly, the teacher drew their attention to a beautiful rainbow that had formed in the sky.

The children looked up at it with awe.

The teacher watched them and said, 'Alright now, let us give a clap to the artist behind it!'

The students were for a moment confused, but quickly understood and broke into applause!

Children need to be taught to appreciate the Existential beauty surrounding them or else they will lose the connection with Existence very quickly and become egoistic. They should not be allowed to become mechanical and egoistic. They should be brought up to be porous and sensitive.

When you can appreciate Existence, you have come closer to it. The whole of Existence is creativity. A creative person is closer to his heart than his mind. When you create, you are close to God. God is the creator, the created and the creation. When you create, you express your being, the quality of Existence. When you create, you are showing your love and appreciation towards Existence; you are adding a little more beauty to Existence.

When you are full of wonder for Existence, you can create. On the other hand, when you are full of ego, you cannot create; and even if you create, your creation will be a dead creation. It will be like a plastic rose, which looks perfect but lacks the fragrance and life. When an artist creates out of love, he can give a special quality to the creation. If he creates out of ego, the creation is dead in a way.

When you are not in tune with Existence, you will miss the fragrance of Existence. It is as if, when a beautiful fragrance surrounds you, you are closing your nose with stinking fingers. This is ego. When you experience the fragrance of Existence, you will start experiencing the synchronicity in it also.

You will be able to resonate with the whole of Existence. You will be able to see that every single leaf and twig are orchestrations of Existence or God. When you are in this state, whatever you seek, you will find, because you are moving in tune with Existence. Life then becomes a miracle! This is what we call the synchronicity of Existence.

And understand one thing: When you are resonating with Existence, you will not seek greedily. Simply, Existence will keep giving you what you need for the moment – even before you seek it. This is what I mean when I say, 'Whatever you seek, you will find.'

The problem is, we have distanced ourselves very much from Existence, from our source, which lies deep within us. So we need constant reminders about it. You can start shedding your ego by first admiring and appreciating the beauty surrounding you. That itself will start sowing the seed of transformation in you. It will cause you to understand that there is a life force mightier than your ego, which is conducting this universe.

The more you lose yourself to Existence, the more egoless you become. The more egoless you become, the more you lose yourself to Existence!

Q: Although we know at the intellectual level, that we need to surrender our ego, we are unable to. Why?

You see, man never wants to let go in totality. He wants to cling on to something all the time and that something is his ego. Your ego is your very strength. You have guarded it so well over the years. It is the basis of your very existence.

You don't know that there is a world beyond your ego which is much more blissful than what you are feeling now. Your ego is a life-sustaining element for you. But the simple truth is – you have to let go of it!

It is like this: Imagine that there is a seed that is sown. The seed *has* to rupture for the tree to grow, is it not? If the seed thinks that it will wait for the tree to grow and then rupture, is it possible? No! Like this, man's ego *has* to rupture for him to blossom. The longer he guards his ego, the more he is postponing his own flowering.

Until man meets his master, he might not even know where his blockages are, where his ego is hindering. But once he meets his master, he will know! He can transform. The master's sole purpose is to remove the ego of each of his disciples.

The words and actions of a master will seem abrupt and inappropriate when you see it from your logic. But it is pregnant with the truth; it is pregnant with the single intention of destroying your ego. A master himself descends out of sheer compassion for mankind. He has no vested interest in anything or anybody. He is beyond the treacherous ocean of desire. He is here simply to lift you to the state he is in; the state of eternal bliss; the state where only consciousness exists without the 'I'.

In the *Chandi* recitation, which is a recitation of 700 Sanskrit verses on Devi, the female energy principle, it talks about how Chandi Devi kills the various evil demons. It is not that She killed real humans. If She had killed real humans, we would not be worshipping Her through the recital!

The demons symbolically represent the various kinds of evils or ego inside man and it is this ego that is slain by Devi to liberate man from them. We have to understand that. One of the demons is a buffalo-headed demon! This is to make us understand that some of us are so thick skinned that no matter how many times the master awakens us to his path, we firmly stick to our path! We are not sensitive to the master's call. Understand, arguing with the master is the greatest punishment that you give to yourself. I tell you honestly, when you are caught in arguing with the master, no one can do anything more to harm you. You harm yourself enough.

Anyway, the master knows how to make each one flower in his or her own way and the least that one can do is open up to him with faith and courage.

Q: Although I know that You are my master, I feel hesitant and scared in your presence.

The very fact that you have come out with this statement means that you want to overcome your fear. You have decided to take the leap.

Let me explain. Your being has clearly identified me; but your mind is fighting. If your being has not identified me, you would not keep coming to me again and again. You face a lot of trouble at home for coming here, do you not? The easiest thing for you to do is stay at home and do your work. That would have made your family happy.

Why is it that you again and again want to come to the ashram and see me? Why do you want to again and again face the arguments at home for coming here? Is it not easier to just stay at home and make the others happy? The reason is, the pull that you feel is at the being level. It will not allow you to go back, once it has recognized me. Try as you might, you can't escape!

Your being now knows me. But your mind seems to be the hindrance. Remember to always follow your heart. That is exactly what you need to do here. When you follow your heart, you will reach me. When you follow your mind, you will keep missing me.

You are so afraid of losing yourself to me. That is your problem. Your ego comes under threat. You feel insecure about losing your identity. You start wondering where you are heading without an identity for yourself. Your ego faces a grave crisis when you come near me.

The ego immediately demands its food and the only way to provide it, is by running away from me. Your mind sways like the elephant's trunk, from one side of intense love for me to the other side of intense fear.

Remember, love is from your heart while fear is from your mind. Always, always, follow your heart. Love is natural; fear is societal. Fear and doubt are deeply related and are mere conditionings that have gone into you.

Understand very clearly that there is nothing wrong in doubting either. Doubt is your torch to enlightenment. It is very difficult for your mind to proceed without doubts. But your doubts should be ultimately transformed to trust. Only then you are progressing. As you move inwards, this will happen.

Q: What do we need to do *Swamiji*?

Just fall totally in love, that's all! Falling totally in love is falling totally into the egoless state. That is why a master who is in the egoless state is capable of only love and compassion. All other emotions like anger, irritation etc. are pseudo manifestations of his infinite love. He pretends to be angry and irritated. He comes down to your level, emotes at your level, and takes you through one more phase of understanding, that's all. He talks in your language until you understand his language - the language of Existence!

Q: But how do we start falling in love totally? It seems like it is easier said than done!

The first thing is to flood awareness into every action of yours. Become the watcher. You will start feeling that the whole thing is a drama and you are only watching it while playing a role yourself incidentally. The second thing is to stop being judgmental about everything that you see. When you stop being judgmental, you will simply love everyone and everything with total innocence.

When you are judgmental, you don't see what IS, you see what you want to see. Most of us have already formed our judgments in advance. They are the foundation stones for us. Then, we simply act using them as a base. Anything we see, the first thing we do is, view it through these judgments.

If we act in this fashion, how will we see things as they are? How will we ever fall in love? You can fall in love only if you welcome everything with freshness, with innocence. But what do you do? You start analyzing the pros and cons for even loving. When you start analyzing, you miss it. When you finally decide to do it, it may be too late.

See, the master-disciple relationship is there only for you to lose your ego. When you are alone, you cannot lose your ego. The master becomes the device, the support, for you to lose your ego. The more you dissolve into him, the more you will be ready to open up and lose your ego. When do you know that your ego is dissolving? When you start experiencing a certain joy that you have not experienced before.

You will start feeling joy for no reason at all. Just existing will make you happy. Of course, with the master, you are always undergoing a surgery of your ego and there will be moments of suffering as your ego is getting slashed. But when you emerge out of those moments, you would have taken many steps forward in your growth and you will feel boundless joy for no reason at all.

Just look at young children. They are so enthusiastic towards life. They are so loving. Have you ever wondered why you are not as enthusiastic as them? You were like them once upon a time, were you not? Then, where have we lost this enthusiasm and innocence?

(one participant ventures) We have grown up and become more mature Swamiji. *We are more experienced than them.*

Experienced at what? Boredom? Be very clear: We all think that we are more mature than children and that we have the right attitude towards life while children need to go through life and acquire this maturity.

The truth is, we have become so intellectual, that we have lost our connection with our heart. We operate purely from our minds. Even our emotions are dictated by our minds. We have stopped emoting from our being. We have lost touch with our core.

When we arrived in this world, we were in a state of celebration and spontaneity. Over years, society conditioned us and created the mind for us. The mind then solidified itself and started dictating terms to us. The spontaneity in us got lost.

Let me tell you, in this whole process of shedding our ego, we are trying to rediscover the child in us. When we were young, we were closer to realizing God. As we grew and became so-called mature, our social conditionings marred the child in us.

So many people ask me, '*Swamiji*, how is it that although you speak about the ultimate truth, you appear to be so childlike?' Now you tell me, am I childlike because I have not grown up and become mature? No! You simply interpret things in your own convenient ways, in your own philosophical ways; that is the problem.

But for societal conditioning, we have the ability to swim and fly without any training. It may sound absurd to you, but it is true. We have these abilities in us. We can swim and fly, until people start telling us that we are not capable of swimming and flying. If you place a new-born baby in a swimming pool, it will stay afloat without drowning.

The ego manifests itself in so many ways and we live according to it every minute of our lives. We all actually use masks in our day-to-day lives. We use one mask when we deal with our mother; we use a different mask when we deal with our father; we use a different one for our boss and so on. As long as we use the right masks with the right people, it is alright. The moment we use the wrong mask with a person, it means the ego has stepped in. All you have to do is switch masks efficiently and enjoy the show. Then you are a watcher and not involved in the game as a solid entity.

You can enjoy only when you know that you are something beyond the mask. Otherwise, you will get carried away by the mask and lose the whole charm of living. When you know that you are only using masks, your desires will drop.

It is like this: When you grow up, you automatically drop your toys. The toys don't interest you any more. In the same way, when you look at these masks intelligently, you don't have any desire for them; you simply use them and keep moving.

The ego manifests itself in many cunning ways. That is why all these explanations are needed about it. All these will help you see where you are standing as a blockage in your own journey inwards.

The fewer blockages you have inside you, the more fluid and flowing you become. When you have fewer blocks, you are more porous and vulnerable. When you have many blocks, you are solid and difficult to penetrate. Your ego poses such a solid barrier to everything.

DEFENSIVE RESISTANCE

For example, whenever someone says something to you, what is your first reaction to it? Your first reaction is a certain resistance, a 'No'. When you say 'No', it is so ego fulfilling. You feel solid and firm inside yourself. When you say 'Yes', you feel liquid and vulnerable. Your ego feels submissive. So you say 'No'.

Key

This is also why you feel good when you break rules at home or school or workplace or anywhere. Actually, the moment you defy a rule, you will have a great feeling about yourself. School and college students feel good when they cut classes. Why? Because they feel good in breaking the rule. With small children, the moment you say they are not meant to have certain things, they will ask only for that. Grown ups also enjoy defying each other in so many ways.

Husband and wife rarely concur in the first instance about any suggestion! Take for example our own devotees. If the husband gets attached to me first, the wife's first reaction will be only resistance to me. She might even read my books secretly and like them, but in front of the husband, she will not be willing to embrace me. The same holds good for the wives who get attached to me first. Their husbands will do all that they can to make it difficult for them, before finally falling in tune with me.

Such is the play of ego. Saying 'Yes' keeps you flowing naturally in a liquid state with no blocks. This does not mean that you should blindly say 'Yes' to everything. No! It means, make a decision trusting your spontaneity without the influence of your ego, that's all. Automatically, you will fall in tune with the right things.

Understand that saying 'No' is not a cautious move or any protective force that is going to be your guardian angel. Just be open without resistance and preconceptions; that is enough.

Comment: But Swamiji, *I was thinking until now that claiming self-importance is the only manifestation of ego!*

No! Ego comes in various forms: active and passive, which we have been discussing until now. That is why it is such a tricky element to discern.

Active ego and passive ego

The active ego is easy to recognize. People with active ego will behave in a highhanded fashion; they will claim self-importance openly; they will not bend down to people; they will be haughty. This ego is actually easy to deal with, for a master. He just needs to bang on it a few times and it will break!

A small story:

> A man lost all his wealth in gambling and got reduced to almost a pauper.
>
> One day, he went to a roadside hotel and sat at the table for breakfast.
>
> The waiter came to take orders.
>
> The man was surprised. The waiter was his old friend who had been as rich as he had been earlier.
>
> He looked at him and said, 'You serve as a waiter in this sort of a hotel!'
>
> The man replied, 'I'm only a waiter. I don't eat here.'

Active ego is very easy to recognize! A person with an active ego will not be willing to let go of it even if all his other defenses like money, wealth etc. are taken away from him. Active ego can be easily pruned.

But passive ego is very subtle and cunning. People who have passive ego will pose to be very humble, lacking courage to face people, shying away from taking credit etc. The worst part of this is, they think they are like this because they are not egoistic! The truth is, they are more egoistic than the other lot! They are so carefully guarding their ego from getting hurt by doing all these humble things.

When you are in deep awareness and understanding, you will be a mere watcher of your ego and in this state, you will automatically be neither humble nor egoistic; you will neither take credit nor shy away from it. And you will not even think or claim that you are neither of these; you simply will *be*, that's all. When anyone appreciates you or gives you credit, you will simply resonate with Existence and leave it at that, that's all. And there will be no need for any comparison or claim.

So be very clear: Most often, people think that active ego is the only kind of ego ever present. No. There is something called passive ego, which is more difficult to deal with.

People with active ego are like a dried and hard twig. If you bang, they will break. People with passive ego are like a fresh and green twig. Each time their ego is hit, they will bend but they will not break! Their ego is so well safeguarded that it becomes difficult to deal with it. Actually, they work very hard to safeguard it, but in a sweet and passive way. Passive ego is more dangerous than active ego.

For example, you are now with me in this class. So many questions must be arising in you. But do you spontaneously voice all of them? No. You manipulate them inside yourself and finally repress them. You manipulate because you are afraid you will look foolish. You don't want to appear foolish and so you don't ask. You are shielding your ego. If your questions dissolve in my presence, it is a different matter. But here, you are suppressing your questions.

You care so much for other's reactions and opinions about you. This ego is your very anchor point. If it is jolted, you will feel anchorless. So under the pretext of being submissive, you keep quiet. You miss one more opportunity of exposing your ego in the master's presence. You miss one more opportunity in taking a step towards flowering.

Let me tell you one thing: All questions are foolish at the end of the day. Don't for a moment think that some questions and therefore some questioners are wiser than the rest. When deep understanding happens, the questions will dissolve on their own. This is real wisdom. Anyhow, we all play so cautiously to safeguard our ego.

Social ego

There is another, one more play of ego which we all nurture well – what is called social ego.

What is this social ego?

You feel that your life is highly private to yourself and that no one should be exposed to it. Also, there is a social image that you have created for yourself which you safeguard.

For example, people come to me to discuss their child's erratic ways. But they are not comfortable when there are others around. You don't want others to know about these things because you have this built up 'image' in the eyes of society for yourself and your family members. If you let people in on your family matters, you feel like you are exposing your whole self to them. You are afraid that your image might come crashing down and there will be nothing to prop you up in society. This is social ego.

The image that you have so painstakingly built, the image which has become the identity with which you identify yourself in society,

395

is at stake. It is more of an identity for yourself than for others! If you can show yourself and your family just as you are, you will be more relaxed because then there will be no pressure to cover up anything.

Of course, you might say, '*Swamiji*, the only reason we want to keep these things a secret is, we don't want people to start gossiping about it.' Let me tell you: No one is qualified to talk about another. If they talk, they are fools. Remember this and automatically the power you give to them and their talk will simply disappear. It is you who have given them the power to affect you, is it not? Now, that power will disappear.

Just decide and live like an open book, that's all. By seeing your courage and body language, people will automatically understand that it is not going to help gossiping about you! Drop your social ego and live without any privacy. Is a great liberation.

Because of our social ego, we are all the time so self-conscious also. We are self-conscious because we think that people are looking and talking about us all the time. Be very clear: When you are self-conscious, you are very egoistic. You think that you are a big entity and that everyone's eyes are on you all the time. People actually have better things to do!

If you thought that you were a 'nobody', would you be self-conscious? Only because you think you are a 'somebody' you are self-conscious. And on top of it, you think that you are exhibiting humility by being self-conscious. That is the danger!

When you become self-conscious, you are living and yet not living. It is like a barrier to your beauty and grace. Your beauty does not come forth freely because of this. Look at animals and nature. They flow so beautifully and freely. Why is it so? Because they are not self-conscious. They are simply happy just being one with Existence. The moment you start thinking that people are watching you, ego has stepped in and you lose your natural beauty.

Children are not as self conscious as adults are. If you watch them play, you will see: There will be so much beauty and innocence in the whole thing. Even when you take pictures of yourself, you will notice that pictures taken without you being aware that you are being photographed look much better than the ones taken asking you to pose for the camera!

The moment you are asked to pose, you become self-conscious. Your ego is afraid as to how the picture might come out. The self-conscious ego is all the time calculating the pros and cons in everything. It is all the time weighing others' eyes and opinions and losing out on its own freedom.

Even in our meditation classes, if you see, I tell you to tie your eyes with the eye bands given to you before starting the meditation techniques. But what do you do first? You first see if the other person is tying his eyes properly! Some of you don't do the meditation properly because you are self-conscious of the volunteers and me who have our eyes open! You do the meditation in a restrained fashion and end up losing the very purpose of coming to the meditation camp.

When you stop calculating and start being innocent and open, you will be filled with wonder and freshness all the time. Life will never become dull and restrained for you.

Also, the innocent person never does any harm to anyone because to do harm, they need to calculate. Even if they do harm unknowingly, people will not get hurt because they know that they didn't really mean it. Their very body language will speak out their innocence and stand by them.

The ego of knowledge

Let us move to another important form of ego – the ego that comes with knowledge.

As you grow, you collect judgments and data about several things by reading books and talking to people. These two together make up your knowledge, your whole mental set-up. Anything that you see, you see through this mental set-up.

Anything that you see becomes merely a support to your already formed conclusions. There is no scope for any growth. You are all the time looking through a glass of a particular colour – a colour that *you* have painted! You miss a lot in this wonder filled world because of this.

A small story:

> A man was telling his friend, 'Do you know, I really made a fool of myself.'
> The friend asked, 'Why, what happened?'

The man said, 'I replaced ten cracked windows in my house and then discovered that I had a crack in my glasses!'

If we just look inward for one moment, we will understand that *we are* the common factor in all that we see. But somehow, we never look in. We never doubt our own mind. We feel we know everything; there starts the problem. Our mundane knowledge doesn't give us a chance to evolve.

The most dangerous thing in this is, you feel you are solidified with just your knowledge. You feel you have become a solid character by virtue of your knowledge. Little do you know that you have only become a burden on your being.

Your being is a river and you have made it stagnate with the so-called knowledge. Real knowledge is in knowing how to drop the knowledge that comes your way and live like a child, flowing with spontaneity. You need to move from ego to spontaneity.

We are ready to categorize and label all that we see in our lives. In the event, we simply rob life of its beauty. We categorize people, places, situations, everything that comes our way.

A small story:

A man once went to a movie theatre to watch a film.
The film started with the caption of a famous international studio, which had produced that film.
The man said to himself, 'Oh! I've seen this movie before!' and got up and walked away.

Every movie of that production comes with the stamp of that particular studio and the man concluded that he had seen the movie before! He missed it, that's all.

This is how we all are; grown-ups especially. Children are not like that. They see everything with freshness. They are so full of life; they are not dead like us.

When you go to the beach, just watch the children, how excited they are. Whereas when you go to the beach, you feel you know the beach already. The incomparable freshness and beauty of nature comes through your tinted eyeglass. The beach simply becomes yet another place. Understand, if at all you feel you are not enjoying life, it is because of your mind, because of your solid ego; not because life is not beautiful.

> A man went to Switzerland for a holiday and returned after a month.
> He met his friend one evening and decided to go out for a meal.
> The friend asked him, 'So did you enjoy the beautiful scenery in Switzerland?'
> The man replied, 'Yes, kind of. But the mountains kept coming in the way.'

We are so insensitive to Nature! And we complain that there is nothing to enjoy.

The capacity to enjoy is within you. As a child, you enjoyed everything around you. What happened after that? You became serious and forgot how to enjoy. You got dulled by your so-called knowledge.

As I told you earlier, people often ask me, '*Swamiji*, how is it that with all your knowledge you seem like a child. Every time you crack a joke, you laugh so spontaneously and we look at you with awe! When you start telling a joke, sometimes we've heard you say it before and so we don't laugh, but you enjoy it so much as if someone else were telling you the joke for the first time!'

You see, this is exactly what I mean when I say you've lost your spontaneity and capacity to enjoy. You acquire a 'know-all' attitude with your knowledge.

Now that I have told you this, let me tell you a story that I repeat very often in my talks and which makes me laugh every time I narrate it!

In my native place Tiruvannamalai in South India, during the yearly temple festivals, there will be a temporary stage constructed in the open, where famous drama troupes will enact plays, mostly scenes from the great Hindu epics like the Mahabharata and the Ramayana.
I used to go and watch those plays.
On one such occasion, they were enacting the scene from Mahabharata where Dusshasana attempts to disrobe Draupadi and she is ultimately saved by Lord Krishna.
The Draupadi character was played by a man dressed in a *saree,* an Indian costume.
As per their plan, he would wear seven *sarees*, one on top of the other and Dusshasana would pull them out one after the other keeping a count.

When the seventh *saree* was reached, Draupadi would scream to Lord Krishna for help and Krishna would appear. Somehow...the Draupadi character missed out one *saree* while getting dressed, and wore only 6 sarees.

On stage, Dusshasana started pulling and suddenly when the 6th *saree* was being pulled, Draupadi realized the mistake! He started screaming, 'Hey leave it! Hey leave it!'

Dusshasana thought that Draupadi was playing her role so beautifully and continued to pull!

Finally, Draupadi was standing on the stage with just half trousers and a blouse, with make-up of a woman!

But he had good presence of mind, and he screamed, 'Oh Krishna! How gracious you are; you changed my gender to save me from shame!'

Even now if I think of that scene, I can't stop laughing!

So understand that having knowledge is alright, but don't use it to solidify yourself. Just encounter every moment with openness. Don't have any preconceived notions. If you live with this openness, nothing will be mundane to you. You will then see that even your own wife with whom you have been living every day is fresh and enjoyable!

When this becomes your attitude, there is every possibility that the other person feels the openness in you and he or she also opens out to you in more enjoyable ways. It then becomes a positive cycle where you move from freshness to freshness every moment. Then there is only freshness everywhere; nothing is stale!

Ego is living without paraphernalia

When you live with ego, you need some paraphernalia, some support, some people around you all the time. This support is what gives you your identity. Without that, you are nobody. A king is a king only when he has his kingdom. On the other hand, a *Paramahamsa*, an egoless being, is a king unto himself. He needs no kingdom! He sleeps when he stretches his leg and eats when he stretches his hand! He simply follows the flow of Existence. He is a realized soul.

But when you become a *Paramahamsa*, a great kingdom will automatically form around you, and you will be neither touched nor tainted by it. Only the weak ones create a kingdom for themselves and derive their support and strength from it. Only the weak need the *status* to support them, their ego to support them. For a *Paramahamsa*, his 'state' will do everything for him; he will be untouched by the status that surrounds him.

You search for paraphernalia because you feel life is too empty and mundane otherwise. And you feel life is mundane because you are searching for miracles all the time. The greatest miracles of Existence are happening every moment in front of your eyes. But you are so pre-occupied with your ego that you are missing it!

Your own body is a miracle. It is greater than any supercomputer that can ever be invented. The millions of cells and the thousands of synchronized activities that happen in your body is the greatest miracle on planet earth. If you know how to drop your mind and live in tune with Existence, you will understand that what you search for in the name of miracles is nothing but the natural synchronous events that happen in Existence. Your ego simply makes these things look ordinary, that's all. Your knowledge reduces it to mundane logic.

Q: Why is it that we know, but we still decide to suffer?

This is a nice question! When we have the choice to live happily, why do we choose suffering?

You see, you don't know your Self, your being, which is actually your real identity. Over time, you start relating with the outer world and create a pseudo identity for yourself. With this pseudo identity, you can relate with the outer world. This pseudo identity is your ego. It is purely made up of the labels that others paste on you. You don't know who you really are.

Suppose I ask you who you are, what will you say? You will say, 'I am the father of so and so,' or 'I am the sister of so and so,' or 'I am a doctor,' or something else similar. But what are all these identities? They are only your relationships and professions. You are daughter to your father, wife to your husband, mother to your children. But what are you to yourself?

You currently exist only in relationships and professions. Your ego is built up on this. Your identity is only through this. That is why there is always a danger of losing your identity. It is a man-made fragile thing and so it may break at any time. That is why you need to work so hard in maintaining it.

Your inherent nature is actually 'being alone'. When you were in your mother's womb, you were alone. You are actually enough unto yourself. This is your individuality. Over time, this individuality is taken over by what you call personality. Individuality is natural; personality is societal.

It is like this: A parcel moves from one place to another and at every place, it starts getting stamped with various details. The parcel is actually not these stamps but the stuff inside it, is it not? In the same way, you are not the stamps that people put on you; you are the stuff inside yourself.

With time, your ego is built on these stamps and you need more and more people to feed it. That is why you will observe that you are totally unable to be alone, with yourself. When you are with yourself, you don't hear the voices of the others feeding your ego. Your ego goes unfed. So what do you do? You at least turn on the television and watch!

A small story:

Be Alone More
Be Still + Quiet

> A man belonging to a long-standing political party was dying.
> His friends came to know that he had switched his loyalties to the opposition party at the time of his impending death.
> They were astonished and asked him why he did that.
> The man replied, 'Oh! I'd rather one of *them* die!'

So strong is our pseudo-identification! It has become such a solid reality to us that it blinds us from seeing anything else. Even at the time of death, we find it difficult to drop our prestige! We live *and* die unconsciously.

The fear of losing your personality, which is your only anchor point, causes you to behave in the ways that you behave. That is why we say *your ego is playing up*. The whole of spirituality is all about losing this personality, this pseudo identification.

This can happen when you start watching. When you start watching, you will understand that you are the stuff inside the parcel and not the labels on it. When this awareness happens, you need no lecture, no sermon, no teaching or preaching.

MORE AWARENESS... WHAT DOE PETE WANT

Q: If we surrender to you, our master, will our ego be taken care of?

First of all, if you really surrender, you will become enlightened. There is no question of 'when I surrender' etc. But for argument sake, if you decide to allow me to work on you, I will prune your ego and keep it like a bonsai tree until such time you totally lose it and become enlightened. *CAUSE LESS HARM*

You will have enough ego to run your business, and do your daily activities, not to hurt other people and yourself. Your ego will be like roasted seeds that do not grow any more.

Understand that a man who is not yet enlightened has ego in him in some form or the other. But whether you have active ego or passive ego, the more you start being the observer, the more your ego will dissolve. That's enough understanding for now.

With ordinary people, you can easily shield your ego and get away with it. With a master, you can never deceive him. You can only deceive yourself into thinking that you have deceived him. However deeply hidden and well covered you keep your ego and cunningness, they will be simply bare under the master's gaze. While you struggle to shield it, the master tries to heal it. Only he knows what a cancerous disease ego is.

Let me tell you a few things from the Bhagavad Gita. The Bhagavad Gita was Lord Krishna's teaching to the world.

When the Bhagavad Gita starts, Arjuna is confused.

He says, 'Oh Lord! I don't know what to do in life. Please guide me.'

Krishna explains to him the *Sankhya Yoga* – the way to reach the soul.

He then explains the *Karma Yoga*, then the *Bhakti Yoga*, then the *Karma Sannyasa Yoga*, then the *Gnana Karma Sannyasa Yoga*, then the *Raja Vidya Yoga* and so on.

He explains different meditation techniques through 700 verses in 18 chapters.

At the end of it Arjuna says, 'Krishna, I am more confused than what I was when you started explaining. Which technique do I follow? Which is the technique that is best and the quickest? Which is the shortcut method, the ultimate technique?'

Krishna replies to this in the concluding 18th chapter.

With any master, the words that he concludes with, are the final, firm and ultimate truth.

Krishna says, *Sarva dharman parithyajya mamekam sharanam vraja, aham thva sarvapapebhyo mokshayishyami ma suchaha.*

This line that he says is such that if we imagine all the religions, philosophies and spiritual books to be a pot of milk, this is the butter extracted from it all.

He says, 'I have explained all the forms of justice to you. Simply surrender everything to Me. Surrender to Me and I will take care of you. I will free you from all your sins and lift you to liberation.'

Krishna is actually making a beautiful promise in this stanza.

Through this stanza, Krishna shows the world that *surrender*, is the final, firm and ultimate technique – the shortcut to the egoless state, to liberation.

Another beautiful story about Krishna and Arjuna:

> One evening, Krishna and Arjuna were spending time together.
>
> Krishna suddenly pointed out to a crow and said, 'Arjuna, look at that green crow!'
>
> Arjuna looked in that direction and said, 'Yes Krishna, I see it!'
>
> A few minutes later, Krishna exclaimed, 'Arjuna, see that black crow!'
>
> Arjuna said, 'Yes Krishna, I see it!'
>
> Krishna asked just to test Arjuna, 'Arjuna, how idiotic you are! There is no green crow ever. How could you have seen it in the first place?'

Arjuna replied, 'Krishna, when you said it was a green crow, I *saw* it as a green crow.'

Arjuna's very *senses* had surrendered to Krishna. Surrendering the senses to the master is the most difficult surrender ever. The master is Existence itself; he is the formless in form. When your senses perceive only what the master says, you have reached the highest point in surrender.

What is surrender? The word surrender has a very deep meaning. If we don't understand it correctly, we will misunderstand it! We will be committing a grave mistake. We will be misunderstanding deep truths.

A small story:

> One night, 2 drunkards were walking down a street past a halogen lamp.
> One of them saw it and exclaimed, 'Look, the sun has come out for us!'
> The other replied, 'No, it is nighttime; it is the moon.'
> The first one continued, 'It is yellow in colour and therefore it is the sun.'
> A third man who was drunk, walked past them.
> They asked him, 'Sir, please tell us whether this is the sun or the moon.'
> The man replied, 'I am new to this neighborhood; I do not know.'

So, when you ask someone who does not know, you will either not get an answer or you will get the wrong answer.

Only those who have experienced can explain clearly. If you ask the meaning of surrender to a person who has not experienced it, he will say, 'Just give everything to God, that's all.'

That is not surrender.

One man came to me and asked, 'If I surrender everything to God, will everything be alright?'

I replied, 'Yes, if you truly surrender everything to God, everything will be alright.'

He returned after 3 days and told me, '*Swamiji*, I have surrendered everything to God.'

I was happy and asked him, 'Where are you going now?'

He replied, 'To the bar.'

He continued, 'Whatever I do, God is only responsible from now on.'

This is actually a method of fooling oneself. If he has really surrendered, he would have surrendered the drinking habit also. He would not have even been able to drink any further.

Ramakrishna Paramahamsa, the enlightened master from India beautifully says, 'When real surrender comes from your heart, God will guide you in every step of your life and you can never do wrong.' When surrender does not blossom from inside you and is only at the lip level, you will fool yourself and others.

Surrender will keep you thinking of Existence all the time. You will slowly lose your own identity, your own ego. In the Bhagavatam, an ancient Hindu epic, there is a verse wherein a *Gopi* (name given to a group of ardent female devotees of Krishna) says, 'I am not able to think of anything other than Krishna. I have surrendered my mind to Him. If I have to think of anything else, I will have to take back my mind from Him. How can I?'

Ramakrishna Paramahamsa suffered from cancer during his last days.

He had healed many people of many diseases.

Someone asked him, 'Why can't you keep your mind on your own disease for a moment and heal it?'

He replied, 'I have surrendered my mind to the infinite energy. How can I take it back to keep it on my disease!'

This is true surrender.

The cosmic energy will take care of us. You might ask, 'Will this cosmic energy take care of all my problems if I surrender?' In the Bhagavad Gita, Krishna beautifully answers or rather promises, 'Without any other thought, when a man thinks only of Me, I will take care of his gifts as well as retention or enjoying of them. For those who surrender with commitment to Me, I will take care of their income as well as their prosperity. Their problems will dissolve.'

IS IT MY EGO THAT WOULD LIKE THIS

Commitment and maturity of mind are needed for real surrender to happen. You need not surrender to God or any master. You can

OR MY HEART.

411

surrender to anything. Surrender *itself* is a virtue and has a great power in itself. When you surrender, you are acknowledging that there is a life force greater than your ego, that's all.

Actually, God is only an excuse for you to surrender. The *act* of surrendering is what is important. God is not the goal; surrender is the real goal. When you surrender or when you lose your ego, you are no longer a separate entity from Existence; you merge with Existence or God. You will then understand that there is no God sitting above. There is only Existence that fills everything in this universe including you!

A small story:

> A man decided that he was going to surrender but did not know to whom to surrender.
> He decided that he would go to the forest and surrender to the first person who came his way.
> He went and waited in the forest.
> The first person to appear was a burglar who was escaping from policemen.
> The man caught his feet and declared that the burglar was his guru and that he had surrendered to him.
> The burglar was perplexed and did not know what to do.
> He replied hastily, 'Alright, if it is so, then close your eyes and remain here until I come back,' and he ran away.
> The man was a very committed person and remained there without food or sleep for a very long time.
> The story goes that just by seeing his commitment, the Lord appeared before him and gave him liberation!

412

It is not important to whom you surrender; it is the thought of total surrender that has the power to change your life into a blissful one. When you surrender, you become a possessor of the inexhaustible energy that is Existence, and you handle anything that comes your way.

You become strong and unshakeable, come what may. People around you will find you to be a pillar of strength. They will be able to feel the invisible hand of Existence through you.

If you have not surrendered, it means that your ego is still holding you back from merging into the infinite and you automatically become finite in your resources and energy.

A master is a device to help you surrender. Surrender does not mean that you are dependent on someone. It simply means that you are taking that person's help in dissolving your own ego, that's all.

Q: Can you please tell us more about meditation and how it can help in losing our ego.

Yes, but let me first tell you how and why meditation techniques came into being.

Man, ever since his creation, has wondered about and researched what it is that has created this beautiful universe; what it is that has created this beautiful earth and rolled it into space; what it is that makes the rivers flow and the mountains grow. He concluded that there is a force or energy that is conducting all this. He concluded that there was some tremendous energy that is running the whole show. He then started wondering about how to establish a connection with that energy.

The first people to come to this conclusion, and do research and establish a connection with this energy, were the *rishis* or realised souls or enlightened masters. Once they attained enlightenment, they created many ways for future generations also to realize this energy. The ways that each of them gave are the various meditation techniques and religions.

Each of them realized God through a different way, through a different technique, and recorded their way independently. This is just like how scientists create research reports on their discoveries and inventions. Each *rishi* gave a report on his enlightenment and this became a religion or a meditation technique.

These early realized souls formed different religions to establish these ideas on the life force that is conducting this world. We call this life force Jesus, Allah, Shiva and so on. You don't even have to believe in any God. Atheists don't believe in any God, but they have to believe in their own existence, is it not? If we believe in our own existence and search for an answer to the question 'Who am I?' that becomes a meditation technique, and we can realize God. Anyhow, these different ways or meditation techniques became different religions over time.

But what happened after that? People left this basic idea behind all the religions and started fighting in the name of religion.

THE ORIGINS OF CONFLICT & WARS

A small story:

> A Tamilian, an Englishman, a North Indian and a Bengali were traveling together.
> They saw a lake from a distance.
> The Tamilian saw it from the south and called it *thanneer*, which is the Tamil word for water.
> The Englishman saw it from the west and called it 'water'.
> The North Indian saw it from the north and called it '*paani*'.
> The Bengali saw it from the east and called it '*jal*'.
> All four of them were referring to the same thing, 'water'.
> But they started fighting over it saying that what each of them was saying was the correct thing.
> None of the four people attempted to get into the lake and see for themselves what water exactly is. The Tamilian was holding on to what his grandfather told him; the Englishman claimed that his grandfather told him it was 'water'; the North Indian and the Bengali were also clinging onto what their respective grandfathers had told them.
> They landed up fighting without even attempting to drink a mouthful and see.

This is exactly what we are doing also. People who fight over religion are doing the same thing. They have to understand that from whatever angle the early-realized souls saw, from that angle they named it; but everything is one – Existence or God. Krishna and Christ mean the same. People have seen them from different angles, that's all.

These four people, without getting into the lake, are arguing about what their forefathers told them! What will happen? They will only fight because each of them thinks that what their forefathers said was right. If they decided to put aside what their grandfathers said and get into the lake and see for themselves, they would understand that all their grandfathers meant the same thing! Then there would be no fight.

Today, only those who have not got into the lake and had a mouthful of water are fighting. Those who are spreading terrorism in the name of religion are those who have not got into the lake called spirituality and tasted the truth. The four people who are fighting are simply standing on the shore and fighting. So understand that the truth is expressed in various forms, that's all.

Coming back to meditation, simply put, meditation is allowing your mind to relax, that's all. Meditation is not concentration. When you concentrate, you actually try to exclude everything from your mind, which is an impossible task.

Just sit for two minutes and try to exclude everything from your mind; you will go mad! Every single thing that you try to exclude will come back and torture you. So concentration is not meditation. Meditation is simply including everything and relaxing.

Whenever you find time, just relax and be aware of everything around you. Listen with your heart to all the sounds happening around you. It may be the sound of birds, the sound of the calendar in the breeze, the sound of the fan above you, the sound of people around you, or whatever. Just listen with an open heart. Mind you, they are all not distractions. You are flowing with them

416

and so they are not distractions. When you flow with them, they cease to be distractions.

As you do this, you will realize that there is a certain silence, a composite core inside, that is actually witnessing all this. You will become more and more aware of that silence inside you. You will get glimpses of that silence in you.

Slowly, you will lose consciousness of your body also. You will only have awareness. You will feel yourself only through your awareness, not through your body or through your mind.

Meditation will help you realize that you are only a watcher in life. It will help you center yourself well inside your being and carry on with your outer world tasks much more efficiently and blissfully because you will be carrying an inner silence in you that does not allow you to get distracted or perturbed by anything. If you continue doing this, you start leaving the 'I' and 'mine'. Your ego dissolves. Your ego is nothing but the strong feeling and identity that you have about your mind and body.

Why do you think we are trying to create a worldwide movement for meditation? Meditation is the only key to global peace. When you start looking inward, you are no more distracted by the outer world distractions like power, money, vengeance etc. All your base energies will get transformed into higher spiritual energies. The collective consciousness will undergo a shift and automatically peace will prevail.

That is why I am focusing on transformation of individuals. When a set of individuals gets transformed with an experiential understanding, they will in turn inspire others from their own experience and this will continue to create a positive new mental set-up in society.

Unless your understanding becomes an experience, transformation is not possible. Meditation can make your understanding an experience. Meditation is the only hope for transformation of the individual and therefore transformation of humanity.

When you meditate, your intelligence grows. You start getting clarity on all issues. You no more need to ask people for alternatives. You simply know, that's all. You know because you are so much in tune with your inner intelligence. You know that it cannot be wrong.

You will know from your being that you are on the right track. There may be moments when the going gets tough, because you are against the majority, but you will know that the outcome is going to be beautiful and liberating! All you need to do is persevere and have deep faith in your own intelligence.

When you nurture yourself with meditation, your capacity will expand and you will be able to do so many things in the outer world. There will be no limit to what you can do and express. You will find yourself growing in different dimensions.

Anything will come easily to you when you are functioning with your inner intelligence and not with your ego. When anything becomes tough for you, it is only because your ego is making you alienate yourself from that thing. When you lose yourself and start merging with Existence, nothing will be complicated; you will simply flow. Your intelligence will automatically work for you to harness the Existential energy in you.

You will start seeing yourself as a miracle person! Things which seemed beyond you will suddenly become seamless. You will move from ignorance to deep awareness.

Q: When we are in deep dreamless sleep and when we are in real meditation, are we in the same no-mind state?

No. In deep sleep, you go to the level of the seed and come back to the state you were in before going to sleep. No growth happens in you. When you are in real meditation, you go to the level of the seed, the seed ruptures and you move on to the next higher state. That is the difference. They are two extremes. Of course, when you look from outside, extremes always look alike. A madman looks like a mystic and a mystic looks like a madman! Both of them have lost their minds but in different directions.

Q: How is it that you are so beautiful always!

(Swamiji laughs!)

Yes, this is an interesting question! How do I appear beautiful always!

You see: If it was only this form of mine that you find beautiful, that you are being pulled to, the pull would waver with time. It would waver with situations, attire and what not. Just think: You see me in the same attire, listen to the same songs, hear the same voice everyday and yet you are here with as much eagerness as ever. Do you think you would be able to continue like this with anyone else in your life? Understand that it is not the *person*, it is the *presence* that radiates the beauty that you feel.

As far as you are concerned, you are a *person*. As far as I am concerned, I am simply a *presence*, that's all. The egoless presence is so powerful that it simply lures you. There are so many male models and actors who are so good-looking with a much better personality, am I right? With all of them, you might be attracted, but not with a longing from deep within, like in this case, am I right?

Here, the longing is from your being, because your being sees the divinity behind the form. It is the only concern of your being. The egoless presence is ecstatic for your being. That is why you come here again and again!

You see: The longing to feel God is in the depths of every man, but it is not tangible! When you see me, you feel a pull and wonder what that pull is. That pull is the call of your being. But you immediately start thinking what it might be; you know only to apply your mind and reduce everything to logic. God is beyond logic. That is why you cannot explain with your logic why you feel a pull to come here.

All of you simply sit here gaping and wondering what it is that makes you look for hours, without batting an eyelid. When the longing within is deep, this will happen. The longing is the longing to reach home. For many lives you have tried to fulfill this longing but have been unsuccessful and so you come back again; you take another birth.

When you feel this longing, some of you pursue it and start your journey inwards while some of you get scared and escape! Or you linger in the outer circles and keep watching so that if anything happens, you can easily run away altogether! I have to then cheat you and teach you and show you that you have arrived and that there is nothing more to be done except letting go – of your ego!

You always operate from fear because you have been taught that way. Fear is a passive form of ego. You are so afraid that you might give in and so you maintain a distance under the guise of fear. Don't think that fear is something humbling. Fear is a very deceptive form of ego. You are so afraid to let go. You are so afraid that you might dissolve.

Understand that Existence is love. It is only love and nothing else. Also, Existence knows you because you are a part of it. If Existence doesn't know you then who does? So there is nothing to fear.

You don't have to put on any pretensions with Existence. You can just be your own ordinary self and Existence will continue to shower on you. Existence knows only to love and forgive. It does not know any other virtue. You judge Existence by your own egoistic and so-called moral standards; that is the problem,

When you know you are part of Existence, you will feel liberated. When you think that you are separate from Existence, you will fall into misery. You know, it is such a great feeling being a part of Existence! Because of your ego, you feel you are different from Existence.

When you turn your journey inwards, you will become increasingly aware that you are a part of Existence. Awareness will slowly replace ego. When awareness takes over, ego has to dissolve. There is no other way. Until awareness takes over, you will feel you are a solid entity and disconnect yourself completely from Existence.

Actually, the whole sky is there for you to see. But you see it through your window, just how much your ego allows you to see, and you think that the sky inside the frame is the real sky. All such games are nothing but games of the ego. Being aware of this is the first step towards getting out of it. Awareness is the master key with which you can open any lock inside yourself. That is why again and again I say, bring in awareness.

Q: *Swamiji*, how would you describe your concern for us?

My only concern for you is to help you to flower. That is the greatest thing that I can do for you and you can do for me! I want people to realize their innate bliss, their infinite potential energy. Right now, man thinks that he is a human being looking for spiritual experience. He needs to understand clearly that he is a spiritual being looking for human experience. I am working on teaching him that. *Concious Transformation*

And the only way he can learn it is by becoming aware of the forms of ego that are making him feel he is a human being instead of a spiritual being. When man moves from praying to becoming, he has found the key.

Become that!!

422

Q: How does the transformation happen when one meditates? And can you tell us more about the role of the master?

When a person meditates, all his base emotions like anger, lust, jealousy, over-attachment etc. get transformed into higher energy. This propels him into higher realms of consciousness and awareness. Then, he will not be restless like before. Transformation of energy can happen only through meditation.

When this transformation happens in every individual, the whole of society gets transformed. There will be less violence and more global harmony. The most practical way to global peace is through transformation of the individual.

With meditation and the master's guidance, transformation is a process that you go through to destroy all that is *not* you. It is a painful process that you go through with a master, because you have to let go of all the things that you held close to your heart; all the things that you thought was you.

The master will continuously show you what all you are not and everything will start dropping. He will create situations for your suppressed feelings to surface. You just need to allow him to work on you so that he removes all that you have accumulated over many lives.

I keep telling people: If you try to run away, you are missing the master one more time. Don't try to escape. I will place my hands exactly on the tumours that are hidden inside, the tumours that are your ego. Simply place your faith in me and have the courage to open up. I will then be able to heal all your tumours. Just by opening up to the master, half your ego has left you. The rest, he will take care of. You just need to put out your hand; he will lift you out, that's all.

When you are a sincere seeker, when you are ready for a transformation, you will open up to the master and things will happen automatically. If you are just a window shopper, then nothing much can happen; you will just move from one master to another and not learn anything from any of them.

When you meditate, meditate intensely. When intensity is there along with meditation, the transformation is bound to happen; the super consciousness is bound to happen. Normally, we are either intense and miss the meditation or meditate without intensity. We catch one and miss the other. We need to catch both in order to really flower.

It doesn't matter how long you meditate; how intensely you meditate is what matters. The quality of consciousness is what matters. When you make a conscious decision to turn inward, that itself will give you the intensity to meditate.

Q: We are always looking to achieve something in life. Is this also a play of our ego?

Yes, of course! You have come to the point. When you think that life has got a purpose and you run behind the purpose, you are being egoistic. When you realize the beauty of Existence and flow with it, you will understand that life *itself* is the purpose and all goals are just illusions. Then you have acquired awareness; then you are no more egoistic.

A master is the one who makes you understand the 'purposelessness' of life. When you search with a purpose, you miss reality, because when you run behind the purpose, you miss the present. You simply miss Existence.

When you realize the purposelessness of life, a new consciousness starts blossoming in you. You will then understand that the diamonds that you were protecting all along are mere stones. You will understand that the things that you thought were great, are mere toys. You will understand that money is not the real bliss that you are seeking. You are seeking beyond it.

You will start looking at life as a great divine play of Existence. You will enjoy the drama and play your role with utmost enjoyment and perfection. You will not live for goals; you will live for the sake of living and enjoying living.

Understand that I am not saying that you should stop earning money. Without money, there is nothing you can do in life. I am only saying, enjoy living every moment and make your goals just incidental. You must understand that the whole thing is just a drama and you are a player. When you get attached to goals, you miss this whole idea.

In a drama, does it make any sense to get attached to your role or to another character or to anything? No! It will straightaway seem ridiculous, will it not? In the same way, life is also a great drama; so don't get attached to it in any fashion. Just play your role and enjoy the whole show.

Understand that life is not the goal, but the path itself. When you have a goal, you will run. When you run, your feet will not touch the ground. When you don't touch the ground, you miss the beauty of Existence. When you run, you are literally missing the feel of Existence beneath you. When you drop the goal, the emphasis will automatically be on the path. The path is meant to be enjoyed; the goal will be taken care of automatically.

When you understand the purposelessness of life, you will understand the meaning of living. Until you understand this, you live your life in an unconscious fashion. You live without a proper consciousness. You live with a solid ego that sees only goals, and not the beauty of life itself.

Sacrificing your whole life for the sake of the goal is not the way to live. If you live this way, once every goal is reached, you will only repent at having wasted your whole life on insignificant things. Drop the goal and enjoy the path. Meditate on this teaching again and again. The truth will reveal itself to you.

One more thing: Don't exclude anything from your life and never think that you are missing something in your life. Spirituality is never excluding; it is always encompassing. When you exclude anything from your life, you are missing something. Instead, integrate and include everything. You will then become whole. When you become whole, you become holy!

Of course, if certain things don't interest you, then it is a different matter. You need not bother about including them in your life. Just function with awareness and keep flowing.

Understand that a scientist is a person who creates a formula to reproduce something that he has discovered in the outer world for others to experience.

A master is a person who creates a formula to reproduce something that he experienced in the inner world for others to experience. He creates a formula to reproduce the bliss that he experienced in his own consciousness, for others to experience.

I am now giving you a formula to realize the ultimate bliss or *nithyananda*.

Q: How should we go about destroying our ego?

First, understand clearly that you have ego in some form or the other – it may be active or passive. Then, understand the different ways in which ego manifests itself, the ways we have discussed till now. All your guilt, desires, fear, humbleness, self-importance etc. are all different forms of ego, which happen in you because you feel a solid 'I' and 'mine'. Once you have understood this, become the watcher so that you understand that the whole of life is a drama. By doing this, you will be able to feel your solid self dissolve, your ego dissolve.

When this starts happening, you will automatically resonate with Existence and see how things re-arrange themselves and make life beautiful for you. Then, live with the only aim of killing your ego. Don't guard it in any way. Be ever ready to kill your ego. When you are ready to kill your ego, you are ready to become liberated, that's all.

Q: You said that the *ajna chakra* is associated with innocence and intelligence. How would you explain innocence and intelligence?

When you break free from the rigid mechanism of the mind, you become fluid, flowing, like a river; then you are intelligent. When you are able to think laterally, you are intelligent. When you are spontaneous, you are intelligent. When it is difficult to challenge you, you are intelligent.

When you know that life is a drama, you are intelligent. When you understand that Existence is the ultimate life force, you are intelligent. When you are aware and conscious of your inner silence, you are intelligent.

When you can smile and laugh spontaneously without applying your mind to it, you are intelligent. When you radiate energy by your mere presence, you are intelligent. When you are not stuck anywhere for a long time, you are intelligent. When you can feel your ego consciously, you are intelligent. When you know that you are rich not because of your riches but because of your being, you are intelligent!

When you recognize a master, you are intelligent. When you are ready to let go your ego to the master, you are intelligent. When you play the game of life enjoying every moment of it, you are intelligent!

A small story:

> Three men were asked the same question, 'What would you do if you were told that you had only 10 more days to live?'

The first man said, 'I would put all my work in order, and tie all loose ends up so that my family does not suffer after I am gone.'

The second man said, 'I would enjoy life to the maximum doing all the things I have never done before.'

The third man said, 'I would consult another doctor!'

This is intelligence! When you can be spontaneous instead of getting caught in the familiar tracks of life, you are intelligent.

Another small story:

In a hospital, the telephone rang and the nurse answered it. A voice asked, 'May I know how Chanda Basu of Room no. 10 is doing please?'

The nurse replied, 'He is doing well and we are hoping to release him tomorrow evening. Who am I talking to?'

The voice replied, 'This is Chanda Basu. You never tell patients anything in this place.'

This is intelligence! When you are not stuck at a point for long, when you don't stay challenged for long, you are intelligent.

Now listen to this:

A man took his city friend to his farm.

He showed him around and later asked him, 'You must have found it amazing to see so many sheep! Did you attempt to count them?'

The friend replied, 'Oh yes. There were 300.'

The man was surprised and asked, 'How did you manage to count them?'

The friend replied, 'Oh, it was simple. I counted the number of legs and divided them by four.'

This is not intelligence! This is a way to show how we complicate simple things in life.

Next, coming to innocence: children are the best way to understand innocence. They just speak out without any editing. They don't calculate; they are so total in their behaviour, never cunning or hypocritical. This is innocence.

But what do we do to them? We try our best to teach them how to edit their words, how to manipulate. We teach them to move from their heart to their mind so that their pure innocence becomes contaminated by the mind.

A small story:

A boy was told that a wealthy aunt was coming to his home that day and that he had to be on his best behaviour.

The aunt arrived and a grand dinner was served for her.

The boy was watching her continuously throughout the dinner and finally asked, 'Auntie, when are you going to do your trick?'

The lady asked, 'What trick my dear?'

The boy replied, 'My dad said that you drink like a fish!'

Children simply say what they feel like! They express so freely. That is why they are so joyful to watch! Their innocence attracts us. But we don't understand this and we teach them to become cunning, to become manipulative.

> A small boy went up to his grandfather and asked, 'Grandpa, can you really imitate a frog?'
> The grandfather was surprised and asked, 'Why do you ask?'
> The child replied, 'I heard my parents saying that when you croak, we will have a small fortune left for ourselves.'

We are hypocrites most of the time. We never express ourselves freely. We are thinking something and saying something else. We have become so ugly because of this. We have simply lost our innocence.

Another small story:

> A mother was leaving her child with her friend for a day.
> She told her child to remember to thank the friend before coming away that evening.
> The child returned home that evening and the mother asked her if she had thanked the friend.
> The child replied, 'I didn't because when the other girl thanked her, she said, *don't mention it.*'

This is how children are! Of course, it is our duty to teach them basic things like gratitude etc., but I am trying to make you understand that we should not make children hypocrites. Let them understand the game and play it with awareness, with no ego, but only awareness. Give them the basic rules and intelligence to discriminate for themselves.

One thing to understand: The innocence of the child is due to its ignorance. This innocence is bound to be there in the child because it is yet to be influenced by societal conditioning. But once the conditioning starts happening and knowledge is gained, the child loses its innocence. But the child *can* reconnect back with the innocence that it loses over the years through deep awareness. This innocence regained is the real innocence, because this innocence is not out of ignorance now; it is out of a deep understanding.

That is the difference between the innocence of children and innocence of masters. Mundane knowledge squashes the innocence and nurtures ego. But intelligence and awareness can put knowledge aside and bring out the innocence once again. When this happens, you have found the way.

Q: How should we relate with God?

God is not any separate entity for you to relate with Him. Understand that first. He is not sitting above your heads in a place called heaven and waiting for you to relate with Him. He is there in each and every thing in this universe. Everything has been created by him.

He is the creator, creation and the created. He is the experiencer, the experienced and the experience. God is the name that we have given to Existence, that's all. When you understand this, you have started experiencing God; then there is no question of relating with God.

People ask me if I feel close to God. I tell them that I *am* God! I tell them that they are also God! But of course they are not willing to accept it. They want to know how to get close to God. Close itself means there is a small distance separating you and God. I am telling you that you *are* God! Then where is the question of close? Do you understand what I am trying to say? God is nothing but the name that you have given to Existence, and you are a part of Existence.

When you live in tune with Existence, when you have found your connection with Existence, you are God, that's all. When you live with a feeling of intimacy with anything and anyone that comes your way, you become pure consciousness. When you can feel the same love towards everyone around you irrespective of whether you know them or not, you are experiencing God in you. This is a simple scale to tell you how far away you are from God consciousness.

When you start falling in tune with Existence, you will start hearing the inner voice in you. Then no other guide is needed. You don't need people to tell you what to do and what not to do. You will simply know; your intelligence will keep guiding you. A master is the one who can awaken that inner voice in you. He works on you to awaken your intelligence.

Most of us can love only with a reason. This is how strong our ego is. When you are like this, be very clear, you are very far away from God! We claim that we shower love on our family and friends. Just look at all the masters who have happened on planet earth until now. What is the common quality that have drawn them to their mission? Pure love, that's all. If they experienced the ordinary love that we feel in your day-to-day lives, do you think they would have been able to set up their mission?

Is it possible to set up a worldwide mission with just ordinary love? How much drive would ordinary love give? It would in fact make you tired soon! If masters have time and again reached people across the world, transforming lives, it is because of the divine love and oneness that they feel with every single human being on planet earth.

In fact, if you read their biographies, you will see that almost all of them have put their family aside, have incurred the wrath of their family and have gone about reaching out to people. Family always resists in these cases. Of course, once maturity and awareness come in, they start accepting and following like the rest of the world.

Anything that makes you feel separate from God is ego. When there is ego, you cannot love consistently and with the same deep feeling all the time; your love will be highly subjective. It will keep moving between extremes.

Watch the body language of masters and you will know what resonating with divine love is. The easiest way to fall in tune with

Existence, is by watching the master's body language. A master is in tune with Existence all the time. He exudes love all the time, irrespective of who is in front of him. When you watch his body language, you will imbibe the qualities behind it.

If you watch the master over time, you will be able to perceive how he flows like a river, so beautifully, so poetically, so synchronously, in tune with Existence. Every action of his is in perfect synchronicity with Existence. That is why it is so beautiful to watch! Simply by watching the master, you can understand and feel the beauty and flow of Existence.

Because a master is ego-less, he flows without blockages. Because he does not have consciousness of 'I' and 'mine', he flows. Because he radiates nothing but love, he heals. Healing is nothing but concentrated love. That is why time and again, we have heard of the miraculous healing powers of masters. That is why masters are looked upon as God. Be very clear: Masters are the only living God. They are the supreme manifestation of the ultimate energy.

So, stop worrying about how to relate with God. Start falling in tune with Existence, and become God.

Remember: You cannot conquer Existence. You can only be conquered by Existence. When you lose your entire ego, you are conquered, that's all! When you become a conducive womb for God, He will reside in you. In the initial stages, you are a guest and he is a host. Ultimately, you have to become the host; you have to become a womb to receive Him. Becoming a womb means, melting and becoming vulnerable. Becoming vulnerable means, shedding your entire ego and dissolving into God or Existence. Then, life becomes music and an eternal celebration!

We will now do a beautiful and very effective meditation technique called the *Divya Netra* Meditation, for this *ajna chakra*.

Emotion: Ego

Chakra: Ajna chakra

Location: Between the eyebrows

In Sanskrit, *ajna* means 'will' or 'order'. The *ajna chakra* is known as the master *chakra*.

This *chakra* is locked by seriousness and ego and it can be made to flower by innocence, simplicity and intelligence, and by shedding all forms of ego.

Meditation Technique to be an innocent and egoless being:
Divya Netra Meditation - a Zoroastrian meditation technique

The Divya Netra Meditation

(Total duration: 30 minutes)

The *Divya Netra* meditation is done to awaken the higher intelligence in you. It works on the *ajna chakra* – the energy center located between your eyebrows – called the 'third eye', and connects you to the cosmic intelligence. The *ajna chakra* is known as the *chakra raj* – the master of all the *chakras*.

This is such a significant *chakra* that there is no religion that has not worked on activating it. When the *ajna* opens, the whole being enters into a different realm. A whole layer of faculties opens up. That is why all the oriental gods are represented with a third eye in their forehead. The third eye is a symbol for the awakened *ajna*.

There is an old saying, that if you die in Varanasi, a sacred city in India, you will automatically get liberated. Varanasi is not just the city as we know it. It is also the region where the *vaarana,* that is the eyebrows, meet the *naasi,* that is the nose, which is the exact location of the *ajna chakra*. It symbolically represents the death of ego in the liberated or enlightened state!

This meditation technique is taken from Zoroastrianism. This technique has two parts: One to cleanse the *ajna chakra* and the other to energize it. The *ajna chakra,* or the third eye, is known as the destroyer of illusion and lust. It helps open the super consciousness in you.

There is a lit prayer lamp in front of you. It has been lit using sesame oil or clarified butter from cow's milk. You may use a candle also, but ensure that it is made of vegetable fat. This is a guided meditation technique. Just follow my instructions closely.

Sit cross-legged on the floor with your eyes closed. Those who cannot sit on the floor may sit on a chair.

Focus on your *ajna chakra* as if to penetrate it. *(5 minutes)*

Open your eyes and look at the flame of the lamp through your third eye between your eyebrows. Your eyes may blink or burn or tears may flow; just allow it to happen. *(5 minutes)*

Close your eyes and again focus on your *ajna chakra*. Penetrate it deeply.
(5 minutes)

Open your eyes and look at the flame of the lamp through your third eye between your eyebrows. *(5 minutes)*

Close your eyes; do not focus on your *ajna chakra;* just relax.
(5 minutes)

Slowly, very slowly, open your eyes.

We will meet for the next session. Thank you.

Chapter 9

Flower in gratitude

P *ray out of gratitude not out of fear*

A man prays to God every day, 'O God, I don't have enough money. Please help me win a big lottery worth at least ten million rupees! If I win, I promise you, I will offer 20 percent of my winnings at your shrine. If you don't believe me, please deduct 2 million for yourself, and give me only the remaining 8 million.'

All our dealings are exactly like this – a mere business! It may not be so obvious in our lives, but if you deeply analyse your attitude of prayer, you will understand that you have a business deal with everyone, including God.

A small story:

> One day a poor man went to Emperor Akbar's palace.
> He wanted to request Akbar to give him some money for his son's studies.
> Akbar was known for not turning away anyone who asked for help.
> When the man reached the palace, he saw that Akbar was offering his prayers to God.
> He turned away without asking for anything.

But Akbar spotted him and called him back.

He asked him, 'Why are you leaving without asking for anything?'

The man replied, 'Your Majesty, I came to ask you for alms, but saw that you yourself were begging!'

If you observe our prayers, you will realize that we actually only beg. We simply ask, ask and ask. Our prayer is nothing but a begging bowl. We beg for material things, for smooth relationships, for power, for achieving our goals, for physical beauty, and what not.

We are asking for something or the other continuously in our minds. In fact we are so much in tune with asking, that it has become an unconscious process within us and we might not even accept that we are asking. We don't even see it as asking. It has become a natural way of life! We have become very involved in it and therefore unable to distance ourselves from it and see it with a fresh mind.

Understand that there are only two kinds of religion in the world; religions based on prayer, and religions based on gratitude.

The religion of prayer is all about asking God for something or other. It can be followed by the masses, because it is very much in tune with our asking attitude. It is in tune with the conditioning that has gone on inside us from a young age. Asking is the prayer that we have been taught since we were children. It seems like the most natural way to approach God or Existence.

On the other hand, the religion of gratitude is based on just an overwhelming gratitude from within, towards God or Existence. It is quite contrary to what is taught to us from childhood. We have always been taught to thank only for what we receive, that's all. We have been taught gratitude as social etiquette; nothing more than that!

How then can we be thankful all the time? It is too much to digest! That is why these religions of gratitude are followed only by a select few.

Only a few meditative religions, like Buddhism, Sufism, Hinduism and Jainism touch upon gratitude. These religions have very few followers, but the quality of the followers is high.

There is nothing wrong with prayer, but getting stuck in the act of asking while praying is where the trouble starts. Prayer should be used as a jumping board to enter into meditation; a meditation where gratitude becomes prayer and your being becomes bliss!

You might think, *'Giving your gratitude can be a social habit, but how can it be a meditation?'* You will understand what I mean when you actually *start* giving your gratitude. When you start giving your gratitude, you will understand the value of your life.

I tell you: You are only aware of the people who are directly responsible for providing and caring for you. But during all these times and thousands of other times that you are not even aware of, you are helped, protected, and cared for by Existence, by the cosmos, by the universal energy.

444

You always think that whatever was given to you was either because you deserved it or because it was an accident. When you start seeing and feeling the invisible hand of Existence taking care of you, you will understand that you are wanted here by Existence. Only then you will understand that you are being showered upon continuously by Existence.

The fact that you are *alive* is enough to show that Existence wants you here and cares for you. It is only when you don't understand this, you feel dull and depressed and keep asking as if you are the most deprived person in the world.

If you listen from your being to what is said here, you will be able to tune yourself and become sensitive to the wonderful giving ways of Existence!

God is loving, not terrifying

Most of us pray with fear to God. You can see mothers telling their children that if they don't do certain things, God will get angry with them. These statements take root in the child at a very young age, and give them a wrong concept of God. This is the conditioning that you give your child at an early age. When they grow up, they face serious dilemmas because of this. Instead of embracing Existence with love and gratitude, they stand apart from it with respect and fear.

Religion, if followed out of fear, will not take you anywhere; it will not pave the way for a transformation to happen in you. You might progress materially by the faith that you have in your asking, but you will remain where you are at the being level. The purpose or real fulfillment of life can never happen on the material path; it can happen only at the being level. People who undergo what is called depression of success will be able to relate to what I am saying in a better way. We have discussed depression of success in the earlier sessions.

Religion has to be followed out of deep love and gratitude for the divine or Existence. Although society teaches you to worship God in the name of fear, I tell you: never do it. Always pray with love and gratitude towards the divine.

A small story:

> A Sufi Master, Junnaid, used to pay his gratitude to God five times a day.
> One time, he and his followers were wandering through some villages where Sufism was not accepted as a religion. In the first village, people accused them of begging, and threw meagre alms at them.
> The next day, in the second village, the people refused to give them any alms.
> On the third day, the village they passed through was so hostile that the villagers drove them out with sticks and stones.
> That night as usual, Junnaid knelt down and offered his gratitude to God.
> His disciples were watching him. It was too much for them. They could not understand why Junnaid was thanking God. They were furious.
> They cried out, 'Master! For three days we have gone without food! Today we were even driven out of that village

like dogs! Is this what you are offering your gratitude for?'
Junnaid looked at them and said, 'You talk about three days
of hunger! Have you thanked God for the food you have
received for thirty years? And know one thing: my gratitude
is not for receiving or not receiving anything. It is simply an
expression of the deep joy and love in my being. It is a
choice-less and prayerful expression, that's all.'

When you live with overwhelming gratitude in you, you have found
a space wherein nothing else is needed. It means that you have
fallen into meditation. Then, you will not worry about anything
else. You are on the right track. Your mind is no longer a
hindrance to your growth; your mind has disappeared. The mind
cannot step in when you are brimming from your heart. When
there is no space for the mind, where will discontentment come
from? Discontentment cannot come from the heart. It is purely a
product of the mind.

Awaken to the beauty of Existence

Your mind always stands between you and Existence. It prevents
you from hearing, seeing, feeling and emoting with Existence.
Once you go beyond your mind and see the beauty of Existence,
gratitude will become your prayer and bliss your being! You will
then enjoy liberation and permanent joy!

When you drop the mundane logic of your mind, you will flow like
a river – choicelessly, effortlessly, joyfully with the flow of the
current. You will then play your role and enjoy every moment of

it. You will then understand that you are a part of a wonderful drama, where the more sensitive you are to the director, the more effectively you can play and enjoy your part!

When you go against the current, you need to put in effort and exercise choices. When you go with the current, you don't need to make any effort; you will not feel tired; you will not feel frustrated; you will only feel a flowing lightness! Everything will then appear beautiful.

A small story:

> A man was on a cross-country train.
> He spent all his time in the observation car, watching the passing scenery outside.
> An elderly lady was seated next to him and he told her that the best part of the journey was the breathtaking scenery outside.
> The lady shook her head, sat for a while looking out of the window, and left.
> A little later, the lady came back, sat for a short while looking out of the window, and then got up and went.
> After some time she came again and this time she sat behind him.
> After a few minutes, she tapped him on the back and asked, 'Excuse me, but do you see something that I don't?'

We simply miss the beauty of Existence! We are always looking for reasons to enjoy, reasons to celebrate, questioning what we enjoy, and what not! We have lost our connection with Existence altogether because of this.

Instead of feeling gratitude towards everything around us, we are *asking* and questioning all the time. We need to get back this connection with Existence again. Gratitude can help bring back this lost connection. It can help you find your roots once again. It can help you commune with nature, with Existence.

A small story:

> A man prayed very hard in a temple one day, 'Oh Lord! Please give me 1000 rupees for 15 days. I am very desperate to receive it. I will return the money to you on the 16th day from today when I get my first paycheck.'
> The temple priest was listening to his prayers.
> He felt very sorry to see the man in that state.
> He had with him 500 rupees. He put it in an envelope and gave it to the man saying that God had asked him to give him the money.
> The man was overjoyed. He took the envelope home and opened it.
> He counted the money and saw that there was only 500 rupees and not 1000 rupees.
> The next day he went to the temple and prayed, 'O God! Next time, please don't send the money through the priest; send it directly. He took half of it.'

We take everything for granted and remain discontented!

Don't take anything for granted

Remember that life *itself* is a gift to you! Have you worked hard to get it? Can any of you say that you have worked very hard to earn this life? No! That is why we don't realize its value! We simply take everything for granted – our bodies, our daily food, the beauty of Nature – everything is taken for granted. We ask God for diamond rings – but do we thank him for giving us fingers to wear them? With time, even the diamond ring will lose its value to us!

> One day, the Geography teacher in a school asked her students to write down the Seven Wonders of the World.
> All the kids listed the great wonders like the Great Wall of China, the Pyramids, the Eiffel Tower and so on.
> One girl was writing and she kept writing, shaking her head and continuing to write.
> The teacher came to her and asked, 'What happened; have you forgotten what you learned?'
> The little girl said, 'No. I am a bit confused. There are many more than seven.'
> The teacher was surprised and took her sheet and read it. She then read it aloud for the class to hear, 'The seven wonders of the world are: I can see; I can touch; I can smell; I can hear; I can taste; I can laugh; I can love...'
> The class was suddenly filled with penetrating silence.

These small things are forgotten because we think that they are small. Everything becomes small to us when it is easily available.

There are so many millions of people in this world who can't see, who can't hear, who can't talk, who can't taste. We never think of all these things. We are always thinking of what more, what better, what next, all the time.

A small story:

> A man was traveling on the highway to get to his village.
> After just one hour of travel, his car jerked and stopped.
> He was panic-stricken and saw that he had run out of fuel.
> He walked a few kilometers praying and sweating and panting and finally came to a town.
> He spotted a gas station and went in. He explained that he was penniless, but badly needed fuel to get to his village. They turned him away.
> He then spotted another station on the opposite side of the road and walked into it and explained his situation.
> The manager of the gas station took pity on him and agreed to give him a few litres free of cost.
> The man asked, 'Can you give me the money instead? The station across the road is cheaper.'

Until something comes to us, it seems very precious and we remain in a prayerful mood; the moment it comes, it loses its value and we move on...to another prayer!

We always live with a 'what next' attitude. We are unable to relate to gratitude because of this.

For example, if we go to a shop and see a new type of alarm clock with some new features, immediately we feel that our life will be much better with these new features. We will feel that the whole quality of our life will change if those new features become available to us. We will feel that we will become a lot more efficient with this clock in our lives. So we buy it and take it home.

After a few days, what happens? We won't even have the time to wipe the precious clock! The poor clock will be lying somewhere covered with dust and you will even get scolded for buying it and cluttering the house with one more item! And you will have also moved to some other gadget, some other desire!

We always feel that something that we don't have is as big as a mountain without which we cannot survive, but when we actually get it, somehow it becomes too small a thing. This is how we miss the wonderful attitude of gratitude in our lives. We keep running behind 'what next'.

Bhagavan Ramana Maharshi, enlightened master from India, tells God: 'I am so very intelligent. I gave you all that I had, all my life, full of suffering. You in your compassion gave me in return your presence of bliss!'

Bhagavan tells God that he is more intelligent than God Himself because of this intelligent exchange! Such is his adorable sense of gratitude towards Existence!

Another small story about Sri Ramakrishna Paramahamsa:

> It is said, that whenever Ramakrishna saw someone from Chaitanya Mahaprabhu's place, he would fall at his or her feet.

Chaitanya Mahaprabhu was a great enlightened master from India.

On one such occasion, when Ramakrishna fell at someone's feet, the people around him asked him why he fell at ordinary mortals' feet.

He replied, 'Whether they are ordinary or extraordinary, it does not matter. They are from Baanigaati – where Chaitanya did an important *sankeertan*. The moment I hear that they are from there, the very name creates memories of Chaitanya in me; that is enough. I pay my gratitude to them by falling at their feet for having brought Chaitanya to my mind. If I had not met them, in those moments, I might have been thinking of something else unworthy. They are therefore instruments through whom divine memories and ideas are kindled in me.'

That was Ramakrishna's reply!

For bringing thoughts about Chaitanya to him, Ramakrishna fell at their feet! Can we imagine this today? This is what I mean when I say, everything and everyone should be looked upon with gratitude for whatever they are doing. They are all part of Existence and they are all moving in some synchronicity, orchestrated by Existence. When we are sensitive to this happening, we will be able to feel gratitude for the way things are happening.

We need to imbibe this sense of gratitude from great masters. This is the only thing we need to imbibe from them; the rest will be taken care of automatically, because when you imbibe this, the power of coincidence will make things happen for you and Existence will simply shower upon you. But today, things are very different.

Listen to this small story:

> A beggar stopped a man on the road and asked him, 'Two years back, you used to give me 20 rupees. Last year fully, you gave me only 10 rupees and for the past few months, you have been giving me only 2 rupees. Why?'
> The man replied, 'First I was a bachelor, then I married and now I have a baby, that's why.'
> The beggar cried, 'What? You are using my money to run your family?'

The beggar says, 'You are using my money to run your family!' Actually, many of us think that it is our birthright to expect another person to keep providing for us and for our needs. And we simply take them for granted.

Understand: Even our own father or mother or husband or wife should not be taken for granted.

So understand: When you change your attitude from seeking discontentment, worries and depression, to seeking the present with gratitude, you will automatically be able to harness the energy of Existence better. You will then be able to appreciate Existence better and gratitude will then become your attitude.

A man went to the market to buy vegetables for his wife.
He bought ladies' finger, came home and showed them to
his wife.

The wife saw the ladies' finger and said, 'Oh! These are so
over grown. I will not be able to cook them.'

The man went the next day and bought some more ladies'
fingers, choosing carefully this time, and came home and
showed them to this wife.

The wife said, 'What have you bought? They are too tender
to make the dish I had in mind.'

The next day, the man went to the market, prayed to the
shopkeeper and said, 'Please give me some good ladies'
fingers that are neither too ripe nor too tender.'

The shopkeeper picked the best ladies' fingers himself and
the man took them home and showed them to his wife.

The wife saw them and said, 'What? You've bought ladies'
finger today also!'

When we take things for granted, appreciation will never come
spontaneously for us. We will never appreciate anything including
our relationships.

Another small story:

A man came home from work one day to find his wife in a
terrible mood.

She screamed at him, 'I finally managed to train the maid to
do all the work in the house and she has now quit!'

The man asked sympathetically, 'For what reason, dear?'

She replied, 'Well, you are the reason! She claims that you spoke so rudely to her over the telephone that she felt she needed to guard her self-respect and therefore quit.'

The man was baffled and blurted, 'But I thought I was talking to you!'

We always take relationships for granted. Learn to treat every individual as a part of the whole and feel gratitude towards him or her; then you will never take anyone for granted. You will then worship and respect everyone for being a part of Existence.

When you don't take things for granted, you will count your blessings. If you sit and analyse, you will realize that we always count what we have not received! However much we are showered, we are not happy because we are thinking about the things that have not yet reached us!

Imagine if you had to sit down and make a list of things that you feel you have been showered with in life. You can start the list with your own eyes. As I said earlier, do you know how many people have not been blessed with eyesight? Can you even imagine what will happen if you woke up one day and realized that you have turned blind? You will not even be able to get out of bed and go to the bathroom! Every task you performed thanklessly earlier will demand all your effort now.

Anyway, if you started writing a list of things that you have been given in life, it would be a long list. Once you finish this list, write down a list of the things that you feel you have not been given. This will also be a long list... a very long list actually! The list will probably start with a Benz car and end up being longer than the Benz itself! Both the lists are endless, infinite actually, if you write sincerely without missing a single thing.

Alright, now we have the two lists in front of us. It is now up to us to decide which of the lists we are going to focus on. Are we are going to look at the things not given to us and make our lives dull and dead, or look at the things that have been showered on us and enjoy, making our lives beautiful? It is purely our choice!

A person who takes everything for granted will look at the second list with greed and discontentment. When you are greedy, you will automatically feel only discontented, because there is no end to your greed and therefore contentment can never happen in you! Anyhow, this person totally misses out on the joy of life that is there in the first list.

Anything that comes his way, whether it is small or big, will seem ordinary to him and he will only wait for the next thing to arrive. And when the next thing arrives, that will also look ordinary to him because he is already thinking of the next thing!

Whereas, a person who is always in gratitude, will not even know that the second list exists! He only knows to feel and breathe gratitude every moment. Life is an eternal celebration for him. He will be so light and joyful. He will be a treat to watch. He will exude a beauty that is unique unto himself.

Just by being in gratitude all the time, every so-called mundane thing in life can become sacred and wonderful! I tell you that you think that life has become mundane *only* because of your attitude of taking things for granted. Life is not mundane as you think. Every small thing is beautiful. Your mind is what is mundane; your mind does not allow you to penetrate and see the beautiful way in which Existence is flowing.

Your mind has become a dead pattern that is constantly repeating, 'what next'.

When you are able to look at things with a wonder-filled attitude, with awe, it fills you with such gratitude and fulfillment because you are not questioning at that point in time. You are not allowing your mind to play at all. You are simply resonating with your heart. It is then that you become a child, and when you become a child, nothing is mundane; everything is wondrous!

Learn to look at everything with gratitude and awe. Take your own body for example. Just try this small exercise now. Sit down and close your eyes. Visualize that your little finger on the right hand has been cut in a minor accident. Imagine now that your little finger is only three fourths of its original size. There is no other deformity in your body that you know of. You have a perfect body. Suddenly, only your little finger is cut.

What will your reaction be? It will be very difficult for you to digest it. For every simple task that you use your hand for, the little finger has a role to play. What will happen to you? You might even become depressed.

Now just think, how many people are there in this world with so many deformities. There are so many people who don't have all five fingers even! From your head to your toe, even if there were a single handicap, you would miss enjoying some aspect of life.

Just try to spend a few minutes every day in your room by yourself, touching every part of your body with love, and thanking that part for enabling you to enjoy so many things in life.

Have you ever thought about your body in this fashion? How much you take your body for granted! How much you abuse your body. Some of us even hate our body because we feel it is not beautiful enough. I tell you, if you do this exercise every day and feel deep love and gratitude for every part of your body, you will see that your whole body and face glow with a new radiance altogether.

Your body responds to your mind. Never neglect it or take it for granted. After all, it is only with your body that you are able to enjoy so many things. Even for you to come here today and listen to this talk effortlessly, you need all the parts of your body to function properly.

What more do you want?

An important thing we need to understand is that desire and gratitude can never co-exist. When you feel one desire after another, it means that you are not living with gratitude. When you live with gratitude, you can never have any desires. When you live with gratitude, whatever is given to you will simply fulfill whatever you need at that moment, that's all. Even before you ask, you will be given, so there will be no question of asking!

Things are always perfect when you function with gratitude. Otherwise, things are always lacking and ugly. Man's greed is such that even if he is made king of the Earth, he will think, '*The seas don't obey me; the sun and stars don't obey my commands!'*

In the *Shiva Purana* (stories on Shiva), there is the story of Shiva and the *Brahma Kapaala*.

The *Brahma Kapaala* was a skull that Shiva used as a begging bowl, when he was wandering in the guise of a mendicant.

The strange thing about the *Brahma Kapaala* was that, whatever alms people put into it, it would promptly swallow!

No matter how hard Shiva tried to fill it, the bowl always remained empty.

This *Brahma Kapaala* is actually inside all of us. It is nothing but our own ego; the ego that swallows everything and asks for more! The ego that prevents us from enjoying what is being showered upon us.

Whether you want to base your life on *asking*, or on *gratitude*, is entirely up to you. Gratitude is not some kind of morality that can be imposed on you from outside. It is an attitude that has to flower from within, out of a deep understanding of Existence and its ways. When real gratitude happens, it can transform your whole perception of life and bring lasting peace and joy for you.

> Once a man went to Ramana Maharshi and said, 'Bhagavan, I want peace!'
> Ramana replied, 'From your own statement, just remove the word 'I', remove the word 'want' – and what remains is peace!'

The only way to have a live connection with reality, with Existence, is by dropping your conditioning, your ego and breaking the wall you have built around yourself; then you will be able to see that the connection was always there! You don't have to do anything special; you simply have to drop what is *not*, that's all!

When you are loving, flowing, and filled with gratitude, you will always feel the tremendous energy of Existence flowing through you and you will always be with a sense of fulfillment, not because of any gains but because it has become your very being! This fulfillment is the ultimate fulfillment that every man is seeking, although he is not aware of it. He searches for it again and again in all material things and keeps missing it.

Have faith in Existence

Whether you accept it or not, Existence is taking care of you and all you need to do is place your faith in it and do your duty with gratitude. You will then be showered upon by Existence.

But we don't have faith.

A small story:

> A man lived without any faith in God.
> Suddenly one day, he fell from a hilltop and found himself dangling from just the grip of a tree's root.
> He was filled with terror.
> He suddenly remembered people talking about God all the time.

He thought to himself, 'Why not try to ask God for help' and he cried out, 'Oh God! I have never had faith in you; are you really there? Can you save me now?'

The voice of God thundered back, 'Sure son, just let go of the root that you are holding and I will hold you from beneath.'

The man cried out again, 'Is there anyone else out there who can help me!'

We are simply not ready to place our trust on Existence! The very quality of trusting the universe in your being will make you live like God on Earth! You are missing out on this wonderful opportunity due to your own ignorance and ego.

If we consciously feel a sense of continued gratitude towards the cosmic energy, we will be able to feel ourselves being taken care of in its very lap. We will feel ourselves being cradled by this energy, like a child is by the mother and whether you accept it or not, this is the truth.

A man dreamt that he and God were walking on the beach through the journey of life.

He told God, 'Oh Lord! I dreamed that you and I were walking on the sands of the beach. When I looked back at the trails on the sand, I saw that at times when life was most testing, at times when I had the deepest troubles, there was only one line of footsteps; the other was missing. How could you move away from me during those times?'

God replied, 'Son! It was during those times that I carried you!'

Let me tell you from my own experience: In my days of wandering, I traveled several thousand kilometers by foot. I traveled with just two pieces of clothing and a vessel for begging food. I took a vow not to touch money, and not to save food for the next meal.

People ask me how it was possible. I tell you now: I simply placed trust in Existence and concentrated on my goal of enlightenment, and Existence took care of me; that is how it happened. *How Comforting*

When you hear me saying things like, *'Have faith in Existence,'* you may think that this concept is for yester-years of justice and saints. Not at all. I am talking from my own experience, from what has happened to *me* who is sitting right in front of *you now!* And I think I am the youngest in this gathering! So I am not talking of anything from long ago. Understand that.

Just try living with gratitude and watch the miracles happen. Existence gives, if you are ready to receive without a question, with just a brimming heart.

Thank for what you already have

A man dreamed that he went to heaven and that an angel was showing him around heaven.
He walked alongside the angel.
First, they entered a large workroom filled with many angels.
The room was bustling with activity.

The angel guide stopped and explained to the man, 'This is the Receiving Section. Here, all petitions to God that are received through prayer are sorted out.'

The man looked around and saw that it was terribly busy with many angels sorting out petitions written on different pieces of paper - long sheets, scrap sheets and what not. They were from people all over the world, in different languages.

Then they moved on and entered a second section.

This section was also filled with many busy angels and lots of packages and papers.

The guide angel explained, 'This is the Packaging and Delivery Section. Here, the grace and blessings that the people asked for, are processed and delivered to them on Earth below.'

They walked on and at the end of the long corridor they stopped at the door of a small room.

To the man's surprise, only one angel was seated there, bent over the desk.

The man asked the angel, 'How come this section is so quiet? Which section is this?'

The angel friend quietly replied, 'This is the Blessings Acknowledgment Section. The acknowledgements sent by the people for the blessings that they have received, are meant to be processed here.'

We all ask and ask, but how many of us thank for what we have received? How many of us include gratitude in our prayer along with our asking?

BE GRATEFUL ALL THE TIME

464

Try out this small exercise when you are by yourself:

For two hours, keep aside your worries and needs, and focus on all that Existence has already given you. You will immediately think, *'If I don't worry about my needs, how can I fulfill them? Who will take care of my family? What will happen to my business?'* Agreed, you have to think about all these things. But just for the next two hours, take all this load off your head and do what I am saying.

In any case, do you think your family or your business is running because of you? Let me tell you, things are running smoothly not because of us, but in spite of us! If Existence had to depend on our intelligence to sustain our families or our wealth, we would all be destitute by now! And be very clear: by simply worrying, nothing can be achieved. I think we spoke enough about worrying earlier!

So just for a few minutes, close your eyes and focus on what has already been showered on you, what you already have. Mentally go over everything – your body, your wealth, the people who support and help you, your house, your luxuries, your vacations, everything. Enjoy all of them in a relaxed and grateful way. Take as much time as possible.

Don't rush and go over it in a hurry. Just live all of it in your mind. Stay with that feeling. Stay with that wonderful feeling of fulfillment for a while. Feel yourself becoming filled with gratitude and overflowing with it. When you open your eyes, you will *see* that what you have is more than enough to run your life! And you will wonder what more you want!

Become gratitude and enjoy!

You have to just *become* gratitude! The best way to become gratitude is to learn to enjoy without a reason. Enjoy everything that you see, everything that you hear, and everything that you do, with the supreme confidence that Existence is taking care. Life will then simply transform in front of your eyes and you will be overflowing all the time because you are always enjoying it.

A small story:

> There was a man who was walking past a mango grove, which was overflowing with mangoes of different varieties.
> He entered the grove, looked around, studied it, took down some statistics and left half an hour later, with facts and figures.
> After a while, another man walked past the same grove.
> He entered it, plucked a few mangoes, ate them joyfully and left!

Now, please don't stop by at any mango grove and eat up the mangoes. You might get stoned for it! Try to understand what I am trying to say. Just learn to enjoy life without questioning, although I don't mean that you should drop all your work and only enjoy all the time.

You need to work, no doubt. No one is going to give you everything if you only enjoy. I am only saying, don't look for reasons to enjoy, that's all. Simply enjoy everything without questioning. Let enjoying become your very nature, then gratitude will become your very being.

Your profession may be anything, your social status may be anything, your economic status may be anything, but enjoying is something that every man can do irrespective of all this.

The problem is that you always feel that there should be a causative factor for everything *including* enjoyment. You have trained your mind with these kinds of thought patterns. This is also the reason why, you often feel, that others have been blessed with things that they don't deserve, while you have not been given enough for your efforts.

You always think that you need to work hard in order to enjoy. No! Working hard is alright, but it has nothing to do with the capacity to enjoy. Drop this idea. This is the only way you can stop complaining or feeling dissatisfied.

Existence showers. If you choose to enjoy it, you will. It is purely your choice. You choose wrongly and then complain or blame someone else. Remember, no one is responsible for anything that happens to you. Everything is a conscious choice that *you* make unconsciously. Because of lack of awareness in you, you make unconscious and monotonous decisions and land up complaining about life. *You ARE RESPONSIBLE FOR YOU*

Always remember that heaven and hell are not geographical locations in the outside world. *You* create them within yourself. The moment you lose trust over Existence, you alienate yourself from it and carry hell with you wherever you go.

A teacher once asked her students, 'Can anyone tell me where you think hell is?'

After a long silence, a girl stood up and replied, 'In my dad's study.'

The teacher was surprised and asked her why she had said that.

The child replied, 'Every time I go to my dad's study, he says, get the hell out of here!'

Be with gratitude, it is enough

Children are trained from a young age, to think of hell and heaven as entities outside of them. They are trained to think that God is sitting above, on a big throne, and watching every movement of ours, and noting down our sins and good deeds.

By thinking in this way, we start the cause and effect cycle of all our actions. We associate good deeds with heaven and bad deeds with hell. We start thinking of God and the whole of Existence as a transaction center. Each one of us becomes a businessman in our own way, whatever may be our real profession!

What do you do when you go to the temple? You purchase flowers, coconuts and fruit, and go to the deity inside and make an offering in your family's name to the deity. You tell the name, birthstar etc. of each and every member of your family and do the ritual.

The poor priest will hold one bowl in his hand and you will be telling him a long list of names with all the details of each of your family members. You are so afraid that God will send the blessings to the wrong person, to the wrong household! You give him the exact geographical location etc. and emphasize to him that it is *you* and no one else who has come with the offering. Only after doing this, you leave the temple. Am I right?

As if God does not know you if you don't tell him all this! As if you need to remind God of your existence so that he will shower on you.

All you need to do is feel continued gratitude towards Him, that's all. He is always showering on you.

It is not that he sees you in trouble and then decides to bail you out, or sees that you are alright and therefore ignores you. All this is our own conditioning that we project on God. All this is what society has taught us from a young age.

Simply enter into the temple with a feeling of gratitude; stand before every deity for a few minutes with deep thankfulness, and leave the temple in that same mood. That is enough. The rest will be taken care of. This is the ultimate prayer. Gratitude is the ultimate offering.

Use these few days you are going to be here effectively to experience what I am saying. Allow gratitude to take root in these few days, when you are away from the outer world. Open up and allow yourself to flower. This is a rare opportunity for you. This is a chance for you to transform. Don't miss it. Create that new inner space in you, which will go with you when you leave this place.

Gratitude happens from the heart

The problem is, we are always trying to reach God through our heads. You can never reach God through your head. If you simply drop your head, you will automatically function through your heart and discover that you need not even reach out to Him; He is already there in you!

With your head, you will always seek outside and you can never find God outside. Also, you will be looking for reasons to feel grateful. When you move from your head to your heart, a whole new space will open out for you, and you will realize that you always knew, and that it was your mind which was causing all the havoc and not letting you realize it.

When you operate from your heart, you are always in gratitude. Do we ever say 'mind-felt gratitude'? No! We always say 'heart-felt gratitude', do we not?

Next, you will ask, 'How do we move from our head to our heart Swamiji!' Just be aware of your head, that is enough! Only because you are unaware of your head, you allow it to function in an undisturbed fashion, in a mechanical fashion. Once you become aware of your head, you will be able to drop it.

Gratitude is not any virtue. It has to be your very attitude. When you feel *only* gratitude, you can tune yourself beautifully to Existence, and then Existence will reveal to you its magical splendour. All you need to do then is sit back and enjoy!

Let me explain what I mean by tuning. We all know how the radio works. The same radio, without any change in its physical form, can be connected to many radio stations airing different programs, can it not? While you are listening to a particular station, if there are any disturbances or cross-talk, what do you do? You fine-tune it. Now, just apply this same concept to tuning to Existence.

There are thousands of programs happening around us. Whatever we tune ourselves to, *that* we will experience. Now, tuning to any one program is purely our own choice. You have the freedom to choose the program you wish to listen to, right? In the same way, if you choose to tune yourself to discontentment and similar negative things, you will be caught in the never-ending whirlpool of worry, discontentment, dilemma and what not. Whereas, if you choose to tune yourself with the central chord that is running this whole show, you will catch the right thread in all the chaos that is around you and will be free from all these emotions. You will become a beautiful flower that blossoms with a fragrance.

The more you fine-tune yourself with Existence, the more ecstatic life will be.

Discontentment will pull you down, make you heavy and miserable. On the other hand, gratitude will make you light and blissful.

Feel causelessly grateful

A small story:

> In a Christian household, a girl was sitting at the dinner table with her mother.
> Food was served at the table and she started eating her food without saying grace.

The mother was shocked and asked her how she could do such a thing.

The girl promptly replied, 'There is nothing on this plate that I have not said thanks for at least once before.'

We know to feel grateful only with a strong reason.

One more small story:

A young girl asked her mother, 'Mom, how many more days remaining before Christmas?'

The mother asked, 'Why do you want to know?'

The girl replied, 'I was just wondering whether it was time for me to start being a good girl.'

This is how we train children to think and behave. We teach them how to do transactions. We teach them that everything is nothing but a transaction. We don't teach them to be spontaneous and flowing. We don't teach them to live without a purpose. We make everything goal-oriented for them.

Because of all these things that have been done to children, you have to work hard in undoing them first. Be very clear that all that I am doing with you is only undoing. I am continuously undoing. Imagine the amount of doing that has been done to you! Over generations, people have been passing on their ideas to you. I have to first undo all that and then create a space in you for you to flower.

When I tell people to feel a continued sense of gratitude in them, they come back later and tell me, 'Swamiji, these days I say thank you to the cab drivers and to the servants at home.' Be very clear: when gratitude becomes your being, you will not even report these kinds of things.

When you are grieving the loss of a dear one, do you verbalize your grief? Will you be able to verbalize your grief? No! It becomes such a deep-rooted emotion that it becomes the state of your being. You can only *feel* it; you can never *report* it.

In the same way, gratitude when it becomes your very being, will simply become your state; you will not be reporting it. You can never report it also. Of course, saying 'thank you' is alright for social reasons because unless you express it, it doesn't reach the ears of the other person.

But what I am trying to tell you here is, we need to move from gratitude of the mind to gratitude of the being. The gratitude that we are talking about, you will never be able to express, because it runs *so deep*.

Real gratitude runs very deep

People often say to me, 'Swamiji, we are so grateful to you for so many things that have happened in our lives after association with you.'

For reasons of social etiquette, you may thank a person for something, but gratitude is not something that you direct towards a person. When you feel gratitude towards a person for something you have received, it is simply gratitude of the mind. This is the kindergarten stage of gratitude.

Real gratitude is a deep overwhelming feeling inside yourself, not as a result of any gain but just at the thought of existing, at the thought of the compassionate life force that is Existence, that's all. This gratitude does not need any relationship; it is not dependent on anyone or anything; it is not under the sway of any emotions like lust, anger, hatred or love. It simply IS, that's all.

You express your gratitude with words because you are egoistic and you don't want people to think you lack courtesy. But the moment you express it, you belittle or falsify it.

Actually, your very *body language* can convey the state of gratitude in you. Your eyes can convey it; your smile can convey it; your warmth can convey it much better than words. Tears of gratitude express it better than anything else. When you are overwhelmed, when you are brimming, tears overflow.

I am not asking you to cry! I am only telling you that when you overflow, your body will show it, you cannot hide it, and that is the real indication of the state of your gratitude.

And remember, these tears don't belong to any caste or creed or religion. They cannot be classified as Hindu tears or Muslim tears; these tears don't belong to any religion. They belong to the being and the being is beyond all this. Gratitude is one thing that can dissolve all man-made barriers and conditioning; that is why it is the ultimate prayer.

Anything deep can never be expressed wholly. Poets may write poems to express it, painters may paint to express it, writers may write to express it, but there will remain a portion that can never be expressed through any of this. Existence can never be expressed by ordinary things. That is why it is so mystical and luring. That is why it is so exciting beyond what words can describe! That is why you can only feel it and not express it. That is why you come here again and again!

When you come here, you don't have to express any gratitude, because even without you expressing, I will know. When real gratitude is overwhelming in you, I will know it even before you do! I know the beat of your heart! I know it from the look in your eyes! In fact, when you express to me, you might be deceiving yourself because most of the time, you think and talk in contradicting ways. You might be thinking something inside, but you express something else outside.

Existence *knows* when a person is flowering from within. Just feel the deep gratitude towards Existence, that is enough. You don't have to express it, just *become* it, that's all.

In India, there is a tradition of touching the master's feet. When you are overflowing with gratitude to the master, there is no way to express it. You then simply touch his feet, feel the oneness and express the gratitude in you.

Many people come from many places to visit me. Some of them come and stand in front of me and don't say anything. Just tears of joy flow from their eyes. They don't feel compelled to say anything, because they cannot say anything more than what their tears are conveying. They are just emoting from their being.

When you are in the presence of the master, just be there with a deep sense of gratitude and love, with a feeling of gratitude at just being present near him. You will find that all your questions will dissolve and you are filled with a certain joy in no time. When you fill up easily, it means that you have caught the right thread.

Always be with the master with deep awareness; then you will not miss it. When you are in gratitude with the master, the master's energy will pour into your being and his experience will simply flood you.

And when you feel *only* gratitude towards the master, the need to be physically near him will also slowly dissolve. Gratitude helps you cut across space and time. It dissolves boundaries and makes you expand. When you expand, you feel one with everything. After some time, even gratitude will seem like a disturbance; just silence will prevail!

Even in relationships, if you feel that any relationship is coming to an end with no love lost, you can simply feel gratitude towards the other and depart, that's all. Just feel gratitude inside you for having been associated with the other person for that period of time, for all that you learned and enjoyed because of your association with him or her for that period of time, and depart. Then, even *that* becomes beautiful.

Feel grateful to your enemies too!

People ask me, 'Swamiji, how can we feel gratitude towards our enemies?'

FEB 19 - So Loud my He SpoAKS!

I ask you, *why not?* Your so-called enemies are responsible for making you stronger. They are a challenge to you; they make you grow. By hurting you, they show you a different perspective of life to deal with. Why not then feel gratitude towards them?

After all, you want to grow, do you not? Every moment, you want to become more intelligent, do you not? If these people did not open up opportunities for you, you would be living deluded by only friends surrounding you. That is not going to help much. You need to get roughed out; only then you will rupture and intelligence will flower.

The seed *has to* rupture for the tree to grow. If the seed is happy remaining a seed, it will simply disintegrate with time and die, that's all. No transformation will happen to it.

So So True.

When it comes to so-called enmity, an ordinary man will make it look ugly. He will take it to a point where everything becomes a vicious cycle, moving from hatred to hatred. In so many families, there are feuds. It becomes ugly and too much to deal with. Why? It is *you* who have allowed it to grow in that way. You did not function with deep awareness and intelligence. You were not functioning with fulfillment and so you allowed it to grow in an ugly fashion.

If you were functioning with fulfillment, you would not have been able to see any *space* for the enmity to grow. It will be an unknown language to you. Even if the other person wants to continue the enmity, you will not feel any hatred towards him. If he wants to end the relationship, you will end it only with gratitude again!

In so many families, people don't look each other in the eye or they actually even take pains to avoid each other in public places. Why all these unnecessary things? Why are you wasting your energy in these kinds of things? Never allow hatred to consume you. Look at it with deep awareness and intelligence. Hatred will disappear and only love and gratitude will remain.

Q: These days I feel only gratitude to you, and in a way, I don't have any wanting from you. But strangely, I want you to remember my name and call me by it now and then! Is this a kind of discontentment or craving from my side Swamiji?

This is a beautiful thing you have come up with. It goes to show that you have analyzed yourself very deeply. You see: When you seek attention from your mind, through jealousy or discontentment, it becomes unhealthy. But when you ask with love and gratitude, it is not a craving; it is simply a deep love for me, that's all.

When you pray with a wanting, it is simply ungratefulness and a play of ego. But when you ask out of deep love, it becomes a prayer, filled with gratitude and devotion. There is a difference between the two.

You are in awareness, so it cannot be called discontentment or craving. With time, this too will drop for you. And one more thing: You have had the courage to come up with this question! I am sure many others secretly feel the same way, but have not said it aloud! They may have consoled themselves by saying, 'What is there in a name,' or they may feel shy to come out with it! Of course, there is nothing in a name. But, you need to go beyond it with an experiential understanding, not delude yourself out of it. The fact that you have come up with the question shows that you are willing to courageously go through it.

Gratitude and the master

People ask me, 'Swamiji, what can we do for you in return to show our gratitude to you?'

I tell them, 'The best that you can do for me in return is flower!' That is the best that you can do for me and the best that I can do for you. Understand that. When you internalize these words and make gratitude your being, you have done a lot in return for me.

MEGAN

But, If you feel that you have to do something in return, do some service to society; help others. Help awaken others to the joy that you have discovered. Don't do it out of ego or superiority. Do it for the *love* of sharing, for the *joy* of sharing. Give your full energy and enjoy doing it. It will become a joyful meditation for you and an awakening for them.

Every time you feel deep gratitude, you are actually in meditation. So just imagine if you were in gratitude forever! You would be in meditation all the time.

SUCH REALIZATION FOR THE
GRATITUDE FOR MY ENEMIES... FOR 479
A MOMENT I THOT I WAS DISCONNECTED &
REMOVED FROM REALITY

Gratitude can never be taught. Of course, the idea of feeling grateful can be told to children when they are young so that they know about it. But it remains social conditioning just like other things, in the same way as you are taught to respect your elders, and to wish your teachers a good day in school. It is just a mechanism of the mind, not an actual feeling inside you.

Even now, be very clear: I am not teaching you to be grateful. I am only trying to create an *inner space* in you wherein you will *feel* what I am saying; wherein it will become your own experience. The energy behind my words can create that space in you, that's all.

Whenever you are given freedom, you become a better individual and you are ready to open up. When you are under psychological slavery, it becomes difficult for you to explore and find your inner space.

I always tell people that I am a *liberating* Guru! I give tremendous freedom when working on people. Only then it becomes easy for them to explore and evolve.

Of course, I am not telling parents that they should give their children complete freedom and watch them without interfering. I am only saying that psychological slavery should be avoided. Just create the conditions for children to evolve. Take the necessary precautions, no doubt, but allow them to experience the truth for themselves instead of stuffing it down their throats. Give them enough space to grow and experience their inner bliss.

Sometimes people ask me, 'Swamiji, how is it that you are so blissful all the time!'

Masters are always in an ecstatic state because of the deep state of gratitude that just continuously bubbles in them; because they are in communion with Existence all the time!

When you feel gratitude only towards me, or just towards anyone else, you miss the whole. Gratitude is not a beam that is directed in a controlled manner towards appropriate people. It is a fragrance. When you wear it, it simply radiates from you. That is why a master appears so blissful all the time. A master is like a fragrance that you can experience and enjoy! That is why you are drawn here again and again!

Understand that every moment is beautiful, if you are ready to receive and see it. It is not only when we are celebrating a function or we have seen success, or we have achieved something, that the moment is beautiful.

Every single moment is beautiful because Existence simply flows spontaneously and joyfully and all events happen in synchronicity all the time. When you understand this, nothing will ever seem 'wrong' to you. You will then wonder what people are complaining about all the time!

When you feel gratitude towards Existence, the whole of Existence becomes a temple to you. Then you are in a prayerful and meditative mood anywhere you are. You no longer need to go to temples and pray. You simply merge with the whole and feel blissful all the time.

When the whole of Existence becomes a temple, the trees, the sky, the earth, everything becomes one. When you bow down before it, what can you ask for? You will simply bow down with gratitude for being part of the profound Existence, that's all.

When this happens, you can relate to the trees, to the sky, to the earth and to everything else. You then move from communication, which is a language of the mind, to communion, which is the language of the heart. You then shift your center from your mind to your heart.

How God functions

For those of you who believe that God answers your prayers, let me tell you one thing: God is so compassionate that most often than not he leaves your prayers unanswered!

It is like this: When a child asks for an ice cream when he is suffering from a cold, do you give it to him? No, you don't give it to him.

Now, the child might feel ungrateful to you for it, but you know that you are doing your best for the child because he does not know that what he is asking for is not the right thing for him at that time.

In the same way, with your deep ignorance, you don't know what is best for you but keep asking God for various things. But out of pure compassion, God gently brushes aside your prayers and bestows you with the things that you actually need and prods you on towards better intelligence, which is his *only* concern for you.

482

Remember that the more your inner intelligence grows, the less you pray or ask.

What can you ask God for? The moment you ask, it means that you think that there are a few things that God does not know! It means that you feel that unless you ask, God will not know. It sounds ridiculous, does it not? Can there be anything that God does not know?

Understand that God gives you what you *need*, not what you *want*. If he starts giving all that you want, you will move from misery to misery! When he gives you what you *need*, you will move from intelligence to more intelligence and somewhere, the asking will drop and gratitude will happen.

God gives you the strength and courage that you need to overcome difficulties.

He gives you the wisdom to dissolve your so-called problems.

He gives you an invaluable resource that is your own updated intelligence, to bring you prosperity.

He gives opportunities for you to explore your own love and care.

He gives you the intelligence to understand that all that you have is all that you need.

He gives you the maturity to flower with a fragrance.

The basic problem with all of us is, we are all ready to believe that God has the *shakti* or power to give us what we want, but fail to understand that he also has the *buddhi* or intelligence to decide whether or not it is good for us! Simply because we believe that God has *only power*, we keep asking and asking.

We always feel that we know what is best for us and pray to God for that. We want to use *our* intelligence and *God's power* to get us what we want! We clearly tell him, 'This is what I want and this is how things should be, so please do this for me with your power!' We give all our wants with our preferences within brackets, as a prayer to God!

This is the attitude that gets us into complications. We have to understand that God not only has the power, but also the intelligence to decide what is good for you. When we understand this, we will stop our method of praying.

We think that the whole world is running because of our intelligence. Be very clear: the world is running in spite of our intelligence!

A small story:

> God and all the scientists of the world had a meeting and a competition.
> Whatever item that God made, the scientists reproduced it identically out of some material. The scientists were able to reproduce things with no problem.
> Finally, God made man out of dust and challenged the scientists.
> The scientists started to pick up dust...
> God said, 'Wait! Make it out of *your* dust, not *mine*!'

Man has to understand that Existence is the creator, the created and the creation. Only then can he simply start enjoying things without a care. Only then can he relinquish possession and doership.

We are so used to the concept of trading that it becomes difficult to understand that there can be someone who is not even our blood relative, who can care for us unconditionally, without expecting anything in return. It is too much to believe!

I tell you that Existence cares for you like no one else can. This truth I can tell you, but it is up to each one of you to realize this from within, from your own experience. Only then it will be first hand knowledge.

I always tell people, 'I cannot teach you spirituality, but you can learn!' I can tell you great truths so that you will at least know what you don't know. But making that truth into an understanding for yourself is up to you. I am ready to tell you how many ever times you want to hear the truth.

A small story:

> Once when Adi Shankaracharya, a saint from ancient India, was on a pilgrimage by foot with his disciples, at one place he felt very thirsty.
> They looked around but could not find anything to quench his thirst.
> There was only a palm grove, where they were producing country arrack.

Shankara entered the grove and asked the workers if they had anything to quench his thirst.

They said they had nothing except the country arrack.

Shankara asked for the country arrack and drank it.

The disciples saw Shankara drinking. Immediately, they also asked for the arrack and drank it!

The arrack did not affect Shankara because he is an enlightened being, having boundary-less consciousness!

He walked on steadily but his disciples were staggering behind him!

After a few days, again they were walking, but this time in a desert area.

They felt thirsty and this time they saw only an iron forgery.

Nothing else was available.

Shankara asked the worker attending if there was anything to drink.

The worker said there was nothing to drink.

But Shankara saw the molten iron, the liquid iron and asked the worker for it and drank it.

After drinking the liquid iron, he turned to his disciples and offered it to them!

The disciples were simply shocked.

Shankara wanted to make them understand that they should do what he *says* and not what he *does*. The arrack did not affect him because he was established in boundary-less consciousness. Unless you have experienced it, you will not know. So you cannot simply imitate from outside. It has to happen from inside for each of you, and then you will know.

How committed or how connected you want to feel with the truth, is your own decision. I can only help those who help themselves. I can give my hand to lift you up, only if you are willing to at least lift your hand to reach out to mine. If you really want to be lifted, you would at least put out your hand to me. Otherwise, I will allow you the freedom to simply be where you are, that's all. That is why they say, 'God gives you the freedom to be in bondage!'

Most of us think that we are not helped by God the way we should be. I tell you, God knows you better than you know yourself. This is the truth. You have to understand this, that's all. Just try to drop the doubt and have some faith; that is enough. The rest will be taken care of automatically.

A small story:

> Two goldfish were inside a fish tank.
> One of them asked the other, 'Do you really believe in the existence of God?'
> The other replied, 'What else do you think changes our water everyday?'

If you believe that Existence takes care of all your needs, you will be free from any kind of worry. But remember, as I told you, your needs are different from your wants. Your needs are few but your wants are many. Your needs are automatically fulfilled by Existence. When your wants increase, you lose faith in Existence because you don't see them being fulfilled.

You see, ordinary belief is just believing, that's all. Faith on the other hand, is belief plus energy to put it into action. You can start with belief but you have to end in faith. With belief, there will be a doubt; with faith there will be no doubt, because you would have experienced it. When you have experienced for yourself the wonders of gratitude, you will attract more and more fortune for yourself. I am declaring this from my own experience.

Gratitude brings more to you

A small story:

> A boy once visited a king's palace.
> He requested to allow him to stay for a night in the palace.
> The king agreed and the boy stayed.
> The next morning, the boy came up to the king and complained endlessly about the shortcomings of the accommodation provided to him.
> The king ordered the boy to be taken out saying that even a day's accommodation was too much for a person such as him.
> The boy felt very bad and went to a Sufi saint and narrated to him the happenings.
> The saint did not say anything. He simply asked the boy to become his disciple.
> A few months later, the saint told the boy that he was going to visit the king and asked him to accompany him.
> They went and asked to be allowed to stay for a few days in the palace.
> The king agreed.

The next morning, the king asked the saint if he was comfortable with the arrangements that had been made for him.

The saint expressed heart-felt gratitude towards the king for the comforts made for him.

The king was very happy and immediately ordered his men to pay more attention to the arrangements made for the saint.

The saint told the boy, 'Do you see now? This is the secret of life. Feel grateful and you will be showered.'

This is what happens when you thank Existence instead of finding fault with what has been given to you. By feeling gratitude, you send out positive vibrations that will automatically bring back more than you can imagine for yourself.

This does not mean that you have to praise people with your lips and cunningly deceive them to get more. No! When you are in a state of thankfulness all the time, irrespective of your state in the outer world, your gratitude will radiate from you. Then, things will simply start happening for you.

People ask me, 'Swamiji, there is so much suffering around us. Why is this so?' I tell you, this is all nonsense. First of all, there is not as much suffering as you make out to be. There is suffering alright, but it is magnified by your own mind. If you take proper statistics and see, you will understand how much your mind plays in these things. It has become casual social talk to say all these things and magnify the whole situation. Secondly, there is suffering because our faith has disappeared, that's all. We have become avaricious, driven by our unconscious ways.

Understand that Existence simply orchestrates the happenings in the universe. All the events are so synchronously conducted that the more *aware* you are, the more you can perceive the amazing order in what now seems to be chaotic to you. We just need to be aware of this and play our part accordingly; life will then flow like music.

When you become sensitive to this phenomenon, from small events to larger ones, you will start realizing how things are being re-arranged and made to happen with *you* being a simple instrument in the whole process. The power of coincidence will start revealing itself to you in its entire splendor. You will become aware that you are part of a macrocosmic orchestra wherein you just need to flow with the music and enjoy it! It is only when you fight the flow, when you try to go against it, that the problem starts.

Go with the flow

A small story:

> One day, people came rushing to a man and told him that his wife had fallen into the river and was being washed away by it.
> The man immediately ran to the river, took off his clothes and plunged into it and swam upstream.
> The people screamed, 'Why are you swimming upstream?

She would have obviously been washed away downstream.' The man screamed back, 'Only I know my wife. Even in the river, she would have gone only against the current, not with it!'

When we fight the flow, the problem starts, because it means that we have allowed our ego to step in between Existence and ourselves. On the other hand, if we understand the flow of Existence and go with it, we will be spontaneous; we will be able to take on everything that comes our way and we will expand with gratitude.

When you are spontaneous, it means you are ready to take on any responsibility. I always tell people that responsibility is the ability to respond spontaneously. Masters take up responsibility for the whole world! How? Because they are so spontaneous and moving with the flow of Existence all the time! They know that if they simply flow with Existence, Existence will make things happen in a natural fashion!

If you talk to the *ashramites* in our ashram, they will tell you about their experiences. It is very hard for them to know things before hand and keep pace, because events happen spontaneously! Over time, they first learn to drop their ideas of needing enough lead-time in order to function, and then slowly they learn to be ready for anything at any time!

An outsider will be amazed to perceive the orderly chaos that happens at the ashram. Be it worship or functions, I will tell them just a few hours ahead and things will get done.

If we learn to flow with Existence, we can live without any worry. But somehow, we all have mastered the art of fighting Existence. We then suffer. If you tune yourself with the flow of Existence, you will find that every moment, you are being watched over and given what you need for *that* moment.

When you tune in, you carry the radiance and energy of Existence with you. You will be able to see things getting re-arranged, things falling into place like a jigsaw puzzle so that things happen for you; you will be able to feel people receiving you with a strange spontaneity and enthusiasm wherever you go. People will look at you differently. They will experience an unexplainable pull towards you. Your life will become a song that is being played by an unseen musician, to which you are simply dancing. Life becomes just music and dance. It becomes a celebration!

Start seeing the real miracles!

Instead of celebrating, we are all the time searching for more, searching for miracles. We are all the time looking for miracles to occur and feel that they are not happening.

Miracles are never *done*; they simply happen continuously around you! It is your recognition that makes them miracles! Use gratitude to tune yourself with Existence and you will see the miracles that are happening! Gratitude will tune you to the miracles. Either you enjoy them or you miss them. It is your choice!

When you miss them, you will remain discontented. It is like this: the door is open but you are knocking continuously on it! I am telling you that all that you need is already there and you only have to receive it, but you are not ready to believe this. You don't see the miracles that are already happening around you and instead go in search of them.

Understand that turning water into wine is not a miracle. Turning man into God is the real miracle. PC Sarkar, the famous magician will do the former. It takes deep understanding to do the latter.

A small story, which Ramakrishna Paramahamsa used to tell often:

> Two brothers lived together.
> The older brother decided to pursue business while the younger one went on to become a *sannyasi*.
> After a few years, they met each other again.
> They asked each other what they had achieved in the previous few years.
> The older brother listed all the material things that he had achieved in the outer world. He explained about his business and how much wealth he had accumulated. He then asked the younger brother what he had achieved.
> The younger one simply took him to a river, crossed it seamlessly on foot and proudly declared, 'This is what I have achieved.'
> The older brother hired a boat and ferried to the other side of the river and said, 'What? What takes two pence to achieve, you have achieved in so many years!'

People think that if they can do miracles in the outer world, they have become spiritual and powerful. No! Understand: Spirituality is not a game of miracles in the outer world. It is a game in the inner world, to change your personality to individuality, which is the greatest miracle! Changing personality to individuality is the greatest miracle.

People time and again beg me to do miracles. I tell them that these so-called miracles are not a scale to measure my state. But they don't want to listen. Even if, just to demonstrate simple techniques like materializing etc., I do one or two things, people will start coming to me to watch these miracles, for the magic show; *not* for transformation! That is my worry.

One day, upon persistent begging from a few devotees, I teleported a Lakshmi idol and gave it to them. I explained to them that it was not a miracle. Just because you don't know the cause and effect relationship of what you see, you think it is a miracle.

What actually happens in teleporting is, just like the sound waves from your voice over the telephone get converted to electrical signals and transmitted over a medium and then get re-converted back to sound waves at the other end, I just convert matter into energy, move it across air and reconvert it back into matter, that's all. There is no miracle in this.

So stop searching for miracles. Live with a feeling of gratitude and love for Existence and automatically, you will see the real miracles happening to you. Your transformation is the greatest miracle that can happen through a Master! And remember, you don't need miracles from a Master; you only need intelligence.

When your intelligence grows, you will handle your day–to–day activities effortlessly and you will be in peace. For example, if you are a manager, you have many duties: you hire people, supervise their performance, fix their salaries etc. Are you able to do all these things without getting stressed? With intelligence, you will be able to handle them without getting stressed. You will be in peace. What you need is intelligence, not power. Remember that.

When you understand and experience that Existence is taking care, you will transform and move on to becoming an individual liberated from all these kinds of delusions. We always place our faith in people, astrologers, fortune-tellers, planets and stars and what not; never on Existence that is the very life source of the universe.

In India, there is a thrilling tradition wherein people ask about their future to a parrot!

On the pavements on the road, there will be a parrot in a cage with its owner beside it.

The people who go by will stop and pay the owner some money and faithfully ask for their future.

The owner will open up the cage and command the parrot to step out and pick a paper from a row of stacked papers.

The parrot will come out of the cage, pick out a paper with its beak, and hold it out to the owner.

The owner will read out what's written on it. That is the prediction of the person's future!

A man with 6 senses asks a parrot with 4 senses to predict his future! How is it possible? Just leave all these foolish things and start falling in tune; catch the central chord that is gratitude, and move in tune with Existence.

Masters are gratitude personified

When you watch masters, they appear to be so graceful, so miraculous and so divine. This is because they move in tune with Existence. But you don't understand their *state*; you see only their *status*. When you understand their state, you will understand that they have simply merged with Existence and that is why they appear so blissful all the time. *This* is the state that you have to try to achieve.

Instead, what do you say? 'Oh! He is a master; he is always in bliss. How will he know about my problems? I am struggling here for my bread and butter and he is asking me to be in gratitude all the time.'

You only see the rose petals at the master's feet; you only see his *status* and think that he knows nothing about your day-to-day matters. Remember that the respect he commands is to his *state*, not his *status*. You have no idea of the struggle that has gone behind achieving that state.

You talk of struggling for bread and butter. I tell you from my own experience that so many days of my wandering, I went without food. Of course, I never thought of it at that time as a shortcoming on the part of Existence. I was so fervently in search of the truth that everything became meditation, including going without food.

You know, barring a few charity houses, and in Northern India where *sannyasis* are given great respect, people always shun *sannyasis*. *Sannyasis* are always eyed with suspicion. People think that they have come to steal their property. I tell you, never shun them. Why don't you just give them a bowl of rice? That is enough for them. Never be miserly when it comes to giving to people. Remember: If you are not willing to be a *daani,* that is a man who gives a small portion of his wealth, you will be a *mahadaani,* one who leaves all his wealth and dies!

Anyhow, please understand that I am talking from my own experience. Even in the deepest of troubles and struggle, if you function with unwavering faith and gratitude, and use your inner intelligence in moving through them, you will see that you will emerge out of it successfully with only greater gratitude and intelligence!

Even if you lose something very precious, just feel grateful for having enjoyed it for awhile, that's all. When you become pure gratitude, you will not cry over anything lost. You will just enjoy it as long as it is there and then continue to feel grateful after it is gone also.

A small story:

A king used to go on rounds at night in disguise in his own kingdom.

Every night, he would see a master sitting under a tree in a blissful state when the rest of the city was asleep.

He felt deep respect for the master and requested him one night to stay with him in the palace.

The master said, 'Alright, I will come today because tomorrow is never sure.'

The king was taken aback at this rather abrupt acceptance of the invitation, but took him to the palace.

In the palace, he gave the master the best of rooms and the best of food.

The master enjoyed everything to the utmost.

The king was observing him as he enjoyed all the material comforts. He did not believe that a real master would enjoy things like this, so his respect for the master decreased day by day. He felt cheated.

Finally one day, the master said to him, 'Something seems to be troubling you. Why don't you come out with it?'

The king said, 'Yes, I can't understand the difference between you and me when I see you enjoying all these things like I do.'

The master smiled and said, 'Alright, let us go for a walk.'

The king agreed and they went for a walk. They walked in silence for a long time.

They came to a river that marked the end of the king's boundary.

The master said, 'Alright, my stay is over. I am going, leaving your kingdom. Are you coming?'

The king said, 'How can I? I have my kingdom and my people and so many things to solve!'

The master smiled and asked, 'Now have you got an answer to your question?'

The king was simply jolted at the master's words.

Masters know that everything belongs to Existence. That is why they live totally in the moment, enjoying it to the utmost. Every moment is lived with totality. They are not fearful of losing anything because *what is yours to lose?*

Always remember that everything belongs to Existence. You are a temporary possessor of it, that's all. Feel gratitude always whether or not you are in possession of many things. That is the way to a liberating life. You can enjoy tremendous freedom and contentment when you understand this one thing.

The beauty of contentment

To be discontented is like giving some food for the mind to chew. The mind will feed on it and keep itself busy. What happens when we feel too contented? The mind becomes starved. It doesn't know what to do. It starts searching for its food!

> A lady went to a shoe store.
> She asked for shoes to fit her feet and the salesman patiently showed her many pairs of shoes.
> She tried on one after another and felt that none of them fit her perfectly.
> Finally, the salesman showed her a pair and asked her to try them on.
> She tried them on and said, 'They fit too well. I wonder if this is the right size.'

When you are determined not to feel contented, then no one can help you. It is a state of mind which only *you* can help. Most of us feel a certain comfort zone in talking and feeling discontented, because there is always something to talk about; the mind is occupied all the time.

To feel contented always is like losing the mind. This is also why, although we claim that we want to feel contented always, we are not ready when it happens. Our mind plays cunningly because it needs something to chew on.

We feel secure when we run behind the horizon. The horizon is only an imaginary line, but we feel secure running behind it because there is something to run behind! The mind has been trained to run always!

When you are like this, you are actually fooling yourself, that's all. You are creating self-contradictory results for yourself. For example, you want to feel contented at the bottom of your heart, but you keep denying yourself contentment by constantly complaining and refusing to see what has been given to you! You *want* something but bring something *else* upon yourself. And you feel comfortable in continuing to try to achieve contentment as a lifelong process!

Understand that the moment you create self-contradictory results for yourself, your misery starts. Try to be clear on how you would like your life to be and direct *every* ounce of energy towards making it that way. When you function with this clarity, you will never delude yourself and you will see that you soon become what you want to be!

When you enter into a space where gratitude becomes your meditation, contentment automatically happens. The normal contentment that we all know always comes with a reason. It is related to something that has happened in the outer world that has temporarily put your busy mind to rest, that's all. When your mind is restful, you say you are contented. Real contentment is not this.

Real contentment is when you feel permanent gratitude towards the benevolence of Existence. Real contentment asks for nothing more. It simply enjoys everything without a reason; it needs no reason. When you reach this state, you will not know what discontentment is all about.

SWEET

A small story:

> A man once went to a doctor and complained of insomnia.
> The doctor asked him, 'So, you are unable to sleep at all at night?'
> The man replied, 'I sleep well at night, doctor.'
> The doctor asked, 'Then what is the problem?'
> The man said, 'I am unable to sleep in the afternoons and evenings.'

We are all asking for more and more without any scale of measure. Even if we have a scale, it is infinite; that is the problem. We are completely blinded by our attitude of asking for more. We don't even know where we stand, because of this. We haven't looked inwards in a long time.

Try to remember this joke whenever something is bothering you. Immediately try to connect with the joke and see with awareness what is bothering you. Go deep down and see whether you are

501

really having a problem or you are simply allowing your mind to play. You may just laugh at the end of it.

> A lady was traveling on a long-distance flight.
> The airhostess came serving food for everyone. She found one lady fast asleep and so she moved on to the next person.
> The lady woke up after a while and asked for her food.
> The airhostess brought her food for her.
> The lady touched the food and flared up, 'What sort of an airline are you running? The food is not warm. I have paid through my nose to take this flight and I can't even get warm food!'
> The airhostess apologized saying, 'Ma'am, please excuse us. The warmer is not working. The rest of the people also had their food this way.'
> The lady said, 'Is that so? Then it is alright.'

See, the food remained cold even then, but the lady was no more unhappy because she knew that everyone else also had their food that way! This is what I mean when I say that everything is a play of the mind; everything is an adjustment of the mind. The mind keeps switching its stance and playing on you, because you have allowed it to take over. You have not centered yourself on contentment and so you sway according to your mind.

So as I was saying, if you are not able to laugh at the end of the day, it means that you are still serious about the whole thing; you still feel that you are shouldering the whole world and that it is because of you the whole show is running.

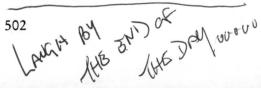

The beauty of Existence

You see, deep down, the truth is, we belong to Existence, which is the ultimate and all pervading energy which is controlling the whole show. Our inherent nature is also to find that connection back with Existence so that we flow without a problem. But somewhere, we miss this understanding and disconnect ourselves from Existence and start running behind material things thinking that that is what we are searching for.

If you have visited the zoo at least once in your lifetime, you might have noticed that the longest queues are in front of the cages of the lions and the tigers. Always, you will find people standing for a long time in front of the lions and tigers and admiring them with awe and respect.

We do this because, without even realizing it, we are strangely reassured by seeing things that are bigger or stronger than us. It gives us the comforting feeling that we are not the ultimate power. We know that we are not the ultimate power. Our being is actually searching for an encounter with any such grandeur that reminds us of our real role in this macrocosmic universe.

People go to the temples only for this assurance that they get when they see the idols. Those who don't find this kind of assurance in the temples find it elsewhere. But somehow, deep within we know that we are not the ultimate power. This feeling should become an experiential reality for us. Then we will know for sure.

If you go to the Himalayas, you will get a permanent and strong reminder of the profundity of Existence. From peak to peak, the mountains rise, the mountain becoming the valley and the valley rising into the mountain, with no perceivable beginning or end; and the river Ganges flowing continuously in the valley in different moods, in different colours and trails, chattering and laughing in the language of Existence. If there is a world not made by man, it is the Himalayas. The Himalayas prove that humans are not the ultimate kings.

When you see the Himalayas, you will see how, over hundreds of kilometers, ice mountains appear as just ice mountains and then become mountains and water and later just water. Such are the wonders of nature at its peak.

What books cannot teach you with words, the Himalayas can teach you through just the experience of seeing. Only you need to be ready to receive it. The Himalayas are a live energy body with penetrating silence. You just have to allow it to penetrate you. If you understand that you are but a speck of the splendor of Existence, you will accept it with grace and humility, with no questions asked.

When you open yourself to Existence, it fills you up. How much you open yourself out, that much it fills you up. You all think that you have to work hard to cling on to God. Not at all. Have you seen the way a young monkey clings to its mother? There is every possibility that it might let go and fall. Whereas with a cat, the mother clings on to its kitten; the kitten then is perfectly safe.

You don't have to cling to God. If you just allow yourself to do your duty leaving the rest to God, God will cling on to you. Falling for God is not a big deal. Making God fall for you is a big deal! This will happen when you have undaunted faith and live a life of love and service.

A beautiful small story: GREAT STORY

A man was very God-conscious and loving did a lot of good deeds in his life.

He came to know that there was a particular book with a person that had the names of people who loved God.

He was excited to find out if his name was there in the book and went to that person and asked if he could see the book.

He searched through all the pages several times but could not find his name in it.

He was very disappointed and went away.

A year later, he came back to see if his name had been added to the book.

Again, he could not find it anywhere.

As he was turning to leave, the man said, 'Sir, please wait. This book has the list of names of people who love God. I have another very small book that has a few names in it. It is the list of names of people whom God loves.'

He showed the man the book.

The man found his name in it.

It is very easy to fall for God. After all, he is so loving, so giving, so powerful and what not. You can continue to say that you love him and remain where you are. But when you start feeling God at the being level and the transformation happens in you, God will fall for you! You will find yourself being loved in many ways that you have never known before. Such is the compassionate love of God.

We have all along been taught to be wary of nature, of God, of Existence. We have been taught to wear slippers while walking so that the earth does not hurt us. We have been taught to stay away from rain. We have been taught to stay indoors when it is windy. We have been taught to stay away from animals and what not.

I tell you, Existence is your only friend on planet Earth. Do you know how wonderful it is to walk with a feel of the earth? I never used to wear slippers in my younger days except while in college because their rule demanded that I wore them. I just used to walk barefoot, whether it was at home or in school or during my days of wandering.

Even now in the ashram, I walk barefoot most of the time. Of course, the people around me insist that wear slippers saying that my feet will get hurt. I ask them how these feet that wandered the length and breadth of India *bare* can get hurt now!

You just completely disconnect yourself from nature by doing these things. So many people ask me, 'Swamiji, how is it that your feet are so smooth and flawless even after so many years of wandering in rugged terrain?' I tell you now: I have never felt alienated from Existence; that is why. That is the real reason. I always felt that I was a part of Existence.

I always felt that I belonged to nature. That is why I used to wander without a care, without being afraid of anything.

Just imagine if you had to be alone in the darkness of the jungle with wild animals, with no food and no idea of where your next meal would be and no place to sleep except under the cover of the sky? How would you feel? Totally terrified, would you not?

This is because you have never been taught that Existence is your unfailing friend. You have always looked to people for help because you believed that only people help. You fail to understand that Existence helps through people. Your faith has always been on people, never on Existence.

When you place your faith on Existence, you can live like a lord on planet Earth. I enjoyed my days of wandering. I used to simply walk where my feet led me, with no idea of my next destination. I used to get onto any train and get off at any station where the scenery attracted me. I did not know the Hindi language at that time and most of my wandering was in North India, in the Himalayas. I simply picked up Hindi words to find my way about.

Actually, to learn any language, the first difficulty is your thought that you don't know the language. You first alienate yourself from the language and then it seems difficult. Here again, you alienate yourself with your all-knowing nature.

Anyhow, most often, I wandered on my own and not with any group of wandering mendicants. Never did I feel that I was alone. I enjoyed being part of Existence. When you learn to relate with nature, you will feel the joy of Existence. I never had to beg for food. When I was hungry or even otherwise, food came through someone in some form. This is what I mean when I say, just believe and let go, and Existence will take care.

People ask me, 'Swamiji, you struggled so much in your life and then reached your goal. Should we also not suffer to reach our goal?' I tell them, 'I struggled because I was using 10,000 keys to try to open one lock. I experimented for years and finally found the right key. Now I have the right key with me. I am ready to give it to whomsoever wants it. It will take you only one moment to open with it! Of course, if you feel that you have to suffer, then that is your freedom; I will not interfere!'

SUFFER IS YOUR CHOICE

Q: How does meditation help in feeling contented?

When you continuously meditate, you become soft and vulnerable. You become porous, sensitive and aware. You will find that your consciousness is expanding every moment. Your consciousness determines your feelings and actions. That is why again and again, I ask you to meditate. It will purify your consciousness. Things will become clearer to you.

You will be able to feel your center shifting from your mind to your heart. When the distance between your mind and you increases, your whole being will start vibrating with a different feeling and this feeling is what is contentment, a deep fulfillment, a deep love without a reason towards the whole, a continued sense of joy and bliss.

508

Then, all the energy that you earlier spent on negative thinking and dissatisfaction is released, and you feel blissful and integrated and filled with energy. Gratitude then becomes your prayer and 'Thank You' becomes your *mantra*!

When you go to sleep, go to sleep with a feeling of gratitude for having spent one more day with Existence. When you wake up, wake up with the feeling of gratitude for having one more day with Existence! This is the simplest and most effective meditation you can do to make gratitude your very being.

I tell you, just by feeling and radiating gratitude from your being, you can change the face of planet Earth. All terrorism, wars, religious fanaticism, ill health, poverty etc. can be eradicated by just spreading awareness about the gratitude that needs to be brought out of each person.

When each one feels and radiates gratitude, there will be no love, no hate, no jealousy. All the possible roots for global negativity can be destroyed with just this one feeling, because the reasons for all negativity will simply dissolve with it. That is the beauty of gratitude!

Alright, now let us spend some time doing a beautiful meditation technique called the *Sahasrara Dhyana* – a meditation of gratitude.

Emotion: Gratitude

Chakra: Sahasrara chakra

Location: Top of the head.

In Sanskrit, *sahasrara* means 'thousand petalled' - from the mystical experience of a thousand-petalled lotus blooming on the crown, when this *chakra* is activated.

This *chakra* is closed by discontentment and the attitude of taking life for granted and it can be made to flower by overflowing gratitude and contentment!

Meditation Technique to flower in deep gratitude: Sahasrara Dhyana - a Sufi meditation technique.

The Sahasrara Dhyana

(Total duration: 1 hour)

Part of this meditation is the Nithya Dhyaan meditation

Why Nithya Dhyaan?

Emotions and thoughts give birth to our mental set up and attitude. Understanding the play of emotions and thoughts is the first and final step towards moving beyond it. Nithya Dhyaan is a 35-minute meditation designed by Nithyananda to un-clutch from the mind and move beyond it.

Man by his very nature is an *un-clutched* and blissful Being. What do we mean by the term *un-clutched*?

Every thought that arises in us is like a bubble that forms, rises and dies. Every thought independently rises and dies before the next thought comes up. For example, if you are sitting in a chair and suddenly get up, the moment you have decided to get up, *that* moment the thought of sitting has left you. If you are working on your computer and decide to shut down the machine, *that* moment, the thought that you want to *work* has died. So every thought is unconnected and happens in series, one after the other. One thought *has* to die before the next one comes up. This is our true nature.

Our true nature is to *renounce* thoughts every passing moment; to allow each thought to rise like a bubble and burst and allowing the next thought to rise. Our thoughts have only a vertical existence, like rising bubbles.

This process of allowing thoughts to rise and die without trying to connect them is what we mean by being *un-clutched*. As long as this natural process is allowed to happen, things are alright.

But what we do is, we start connecting these thoughts randomly and forming a shaft. By doing this, we convert the vertical and un-clutched process into a horizontal one with linear connectivity. Here starts the whole problem. As long as each thought is allowed to rise and die, we can take on any amount of load at the physical and mental planes and our consciousness will remain light and blissful. Once we start connecting the thoughts, our consciousness suffers and we start feeling burdened. It becomes damaging to our Being.

All emotions like worry, lust, discontentment, jealousy, fear, ego and attention-need are purely because we find a connection between independent incidents, between independent thoughts and create a concept for ourselves and start relating with that concept. We create an imaginary shaft with our thoughts and we suffer because of this.

It is these emotions that create all forms of violence be it religious wars, social conflicts or political unrest. The basis or the root of all forms of violence is our emotions and the basis of our emotions is our habit of creating imaginary shafts of our thoughts and empowering them to work on us.

The key thing we do while creating these shafts is, we choose the thoughts depending on whether we want pain or pleasure. We pick pleasant thoughts at random and connect them to form a shaft of pleasure or pick negative thoughts and connect them to form a shaft of pain. We create shafts of pain and pleasure alternately for ourselves and keep oscillating between these two emotions. To *un-clutch* from this shaft is the master key to a blissful life.

If you deeply analyse how we connect our thoughts instead of renouncing them, you will understand how we create suffering for ourselves. It is the mind that finds the connection. As such, there is no connection between our thoughts.

We have been trained to all the time feed on words and thoughts. That is why we create these shafts. We feed on words because we operate out of fear or greed all the time. Out of fear or greed, we create connectivity in our thoughts. We are afraid to let go of this process because if we let go, there is nothing else to hold on to. We have never experienced an *un-clutched* state of mind where there is no shaft, there are only bubble-like thoughts.

In the *un-clutched* state, there is no scope for fear or greed. You will simply BE, that's all. It is a dimension that we rarely experience because we are so used to clutching into the familiar shaft of thoughts.

A small story:

> An eye specialist was treating a blind man.
> He assured him, "Once I operate on your eye, you will have your vision back and you can throw your stick away."
> The blind man became afraid when he heard this. He asked the doctor, "I understand that I will get my vision, but how can I walk without my stick?"

The man was so used to walking with the stick that he could not understand that by getting his vision he can throw away the stick! In the same way, when the truth is that we can live in an *un-clutched* fashion blissfully, we wonder how we can be without clutching into the shaft of thoughts. We see it as something inevitable!

We fail to see how mythical the whole thing is. Our mind is a myth. We have empowered it and become a slave to it. It is nothing but mental slavery.

Just watch the thoughts rising in you. Clearly see how each thought rises and dies and the next thought comes up. Observe how you effortlessly connect these thoughts and create ideas and concepts. Watch the play of these concepts upon yourself; you will understand how you create the whole myth. Connecting thoughts is the original sin.

DON'T GET DRAWN INTO OTHER PEOPLE'S DRAMA

Living in an *un-clutched* fashion is the only way to a blissful living. Just decide that you will not connect any two thoughts, that you will not pass any judgment on any thought or any incident. The moment you find yourself connecting, simply *un-clutch* from it. Keep on *un-clutching* every time you remember this technique; your mental setup will automatically be transformed.

When you work in an *un-clutched* fashion, you will find your capacity expanding; you will take on a lot more responsibility without getting stressed; you will not experience mood swings between pain and pleasure; you will be blissful all the time. We are so used to happiness that comes in with a *reason*. This *reason* is again a shaft that we create with our thoughts. Once you stop creating these shafts, you will be blissful all the time.

The term *un-clutched,* does not mean that you should be aloof and cold to people and situations around you. Just don't connect your thoughts and start the process of creating shafts, that's all.

Remember that you are a beautiful and *un-clutched* being by nature; that is enough. You will stop creating misery for yourself and for others.

Nithya Dhyaan cleanses and energises the vital energy centers in your body which are responsible for the swaying emotions and stored negative memories. It brings intense awareness into your system to awaken the inner intelligence; causes to experience a growing explosion in consciousness that can steer you towards a life of totality. It expels deeply engraved and unwanted negative memories and suppressions.

Meditation as such purifies and lays the foundation to experience the true nature of your body, thoughts and emotions. It is the direct way to connect to the land of the beyond, of eternal bliss, free from the clutches of one's own mind.

Nithya Dhyaan is a technique that gives you what you need to balance your self and be in complete harmony with your body, mind and spirit; to harness the inner intelligence as a propelling force to excel in the inner and outer worlds.

It is a guided meditation technique comprising 5 steps. Please listen to the instructions carefully.

515

Instructions:

Step 1

Sit in *vajrasana* with hands on your hips. Sit on your mat on the floor with both your legs stretched out. Next fold both the legs, one after the other at the knees and rest your posterior on your heels with your toes turned outward. Let your hands rest on your lap. You can use a cushion or a rolled turkish towel under your ankles. Sit comfortably with your head,  neck and spine in a straight line. Now close your eyes and breathe chaotically for 7 minutes. Don't follow any rhythm in breathing. Just move your entire body and breathe aggressively and chaotically from the bottom of your stomach.

Step 2

Continue to sit in *vajrasana*. Form '*chin mudra*' with your fingers. This is how we form the chin mudra: Place your hands on your knees. Your hands with open palms should be facing upward. Let the tip of the index finger touch the tip of the thumb, as if forming a circle. The three other fingers, arms and the hands remain relaxed. You will now hum intensely for 7

minutes. The humming should be done with lips together with the sound coming from the navel center – as deeply as possible, as lengthily as possible and as loudly as possible. (This is actually the *mahamantra* humming).

Step 3

You may now sit cross-legged on the floor if you wish to or continue to sit in *vajrasana* and for 7 minutes you will take your awareness from the *muladhara chakra* to the *sahasrara chakra*.

Muladhara chakra – base of the spine

Swadhishthana chakra – 2 inches above the *muladhara*

Manipuraka chakra – at the navel center

Anahata chakra – at the heart center

Vishuddhi chakra – at the throat center

Ajna chakra – between the eyebrows

Sahasrara chakra – top of the head

Dwell on each *chakra* for a minute with the awareness that – the *chakra* is pure; the *chakra* is filled with energy and the *chakra* is radiating eternal bliss - *nithyananda*.

517

Step 4

For 7 minutes just be un-clutched in silence.

Guided meditation for offering gratitude

This guided meditation is taken from Sufism.

Sit straight, hold a few flowers as offering in your hands and close your eyes. Concentrate on your *sahasrara chakra*. Forget all other parts of your body. Concentrate only on your crown center and relax there. Wear a smile and relax.

With your whole Being, offer your gratitude to your mother for giving you this body. Remember and give your gratitude to her with all your Being.

Offer your gratitude to your father for giving you this life and providing for all your needs.

Offer your gratitude to all the doctors and nurses who received you when you came to planet earth.

Offer your gratitude to all the people who built the hospital or home where you were born.

Offer your gratitude to all the people who took care of you when you were an infant.

Offer your gratitude to all those who worked for your food, clothes and living when you were young.

518

Offer your gratitude to all the teachers who gave you primary education.

Offer your gratitude to all your young age friends who made your life happy and blissful, who shared their innocence and joy with you.

Offer your gratitude to your brothers and sisters and other relatives for nurturing you and caring for you. Seek their forgiveness for any hurt that you may have caused them intentionally or unintentionally, consciously or unconsciously.

Offer your gratitude to all the people who gave you professional education, who helped you stand in your profession, who gave you the courage to stand on your own feet.

Offer your gratitude to all the people who helped you financially, whenever you needed it.

Offer your gratitude to all the doctors and nurses who took care of your health, who gave you medical assistance whenever you needed it.

Offer your gratitude to your wife or husband for giving you love and security in your life. Forgive them for anything that they might have done to you that hurt you. Seek their forgiveness for anything that you might have done that hurt them with or without your knowledge.

Offer your gratitude to all the people who encouraged you and gave you inspiration in your spiritual life.

Offer your gratitude to all those who have served you in one way or another all through your life: the milk man who delivers milk, the grocer, the laundry man, the garbage collector, your servants, your driver, all these people who you take for granted. Seek each one's forgiveness for any hurt that you may have caused intentionally or unintentionally, consciously or unconsciously.

Offer your gratitude to your enemies and those who have hurt you, for making you strong and forgiving. Seek their forgiveness for any hurt that you may have caused them.

Offer your gratitude to all those who helped you physically, mentally, socially, economically and spiritually.

Remember each one of them and offer gratitude taking your own time.

Offer your gratitude to your body and all its parts one by one.

Offer your gratitude to your mind for its miraculous functioning.

Offer your gratitude to the Divine, to the Whole, to God, for making all these things possible in your life.

Step 5

For the last 7 minutes you may sit and chant the *Guru Puja Mantra* or just sway with the flow of the chant on the cassette and offer your gratitude to Existence and to the great lineage of enlightened masters. Offer your gratitude with your whole being.

You may now offer your flowers.

Appendix

ABOUT PARAMAHAMSA NITHYANANDA

Paramahamsa Nithyananda is an enlightened master living amidst us today. With a worldwide movement for meditation and inner bliss, Nithyananda offers solutions for situations as practical as every day stress to the quest for something as profound as enlightenment.

Nithyananda left home at a young age and traveled the length and breadth of India, visiting holy shrines, associating with several yogis and mystics during this period. He realized his intrinsic knowledge through the paths of meditation, yoga, knowledge, devotion, Tantra and other Eastern metaphysical sciences. With an enlightened insight into the core of human nature, Nithyananda has defined his mission for humanity at large.

Rooted in the *vedic* tradition and embracing all world religions as paths to the ultimate Truth, Nithyananda draws people from around the globe, crossing all societal, cultural, language, age and gender barriers.

Since its inception, **Nithyananda Dhyanapeetam** in Bidadi, Bengaluru, India has been a spiritual center for devotees from all over the world. The organization renders innumerable services and programs. **The** worldwide **ashrams and centers** offer programs in Quantum Spirituality, where material and spiritual worlds merge to create blissful living.

The services provided by the organization include ■ meditation ■ yoga ■ corporate leadership programs ■ free energy healing through the *Nithya Spiritual Healing system* ■ free education to youth ■ promoting art and culture ■ *satsangs* (spiritual gatherings)

■ free medical camps and eye surgeries ■ free meals at all ashrams worldwide ■ a holistic system of education for children through the ashram *gurukul* ■ a one-year residential spiritual training program in India and more. The **Life Bliss Foundation**, located in Los Angeles, USA spreads the powerful teachings and meditations cognized by Nithyananda to centers in North America, Europe and other parts of the world.

Nithyananda says, "Enlightenment flowers when individual consciousness disappears into Universal Consciousness. When you start living enlightenment, you automatically raise the human consciousness around you. Living enlightenment holds the key to global peace and inner bliss. Every individual should be a pioneer in the transition of human consciousness to Divine Consciousness."

PROGRAMS AND WORKSHOPS

Nithyananda Mission offers specialized meditation programs worldwide, to benefit millions of people at the levels of body, mind and spirit. A few of them are listed below:

Life Bliss Program Level 1 (LBP Level 1)
- Energize yourself

A *chakra* based meditation program that relaxes and energizes the seven major *chakras* or subtle energy centers in your system. It gives clear intellectual and experiential understanding of your various emotions such as greed, fear, worry, attention-need, stress, jealousy, ego, and discontentment. It is designed to create a spiritual effect at the physical level. It is a guaranteed life solution to experience the reality of your own bliss. When you are liberated from a particular emotion, you experience a new world, a new energy. It is a highly effective workshop, experienced by millions of people around the globe.

Life Bliss Program Level 2 (LBP Level 2)
- Death demystified!

A meditation program that unleashes the art of living by demystifying the process of dying. This program creates the space to detach from ingrained and unconscious emotions like guilt, pleasure and pain, all of which stem from the ultimate fear of death. It is a gateway to a new  life that is driven by natural intelligence and spontaneous enthusiasm

Life Bliss Program Level 3 - Atma Spurana Program (LBP Level 3 - ATSP)
- Connect with your Self!

An indepth program that analyzes clearly the workings of the mind and shows you experientially how to be the master of the mind rather than be dictated by it. It imparts tremendous intellectual understanding coupled with powerful meditations to produce instant clarity and integration.

Life Bliss Program Level 3 - Bhakti Spurana Program (LBP Level 3 - BSP)
- Integrate your Devotion

A program that reveals the different dimensions of relating with others and with your deeper self. It clearly defines relationship as that which kindles and reveals your own unknown dimensions to you. It allows you to experience the real depth and joy of any relationship in your life.

Life Bliss Technology (LBT)
- A free residential life sciences program

Life Bliss Technology (LBT) is a residential program for youth between 18 and 30 years of age. With its roots in the Eastern system of *vedic* education, this program is designed to empower modern youth with good physical, mental and emotional health and practical life skills. By nurturing

creative intelligence and spontaneity, and imparting life skills, it creates economically self-sufficient and spiritually fulfilled youth. Above all, it offers a lifetime opportunity to live and learn under the tutelage of an enlightened master.

Inner Awakening

An enlightenment intensive program for sincere seekers offering yoga, powerful teachings, meditation, initiation and more. This program is an intense experience to prepare the body-mind system to hold and radiate the experience of 'living enlightenment'.

Nithyanandam

An advanced meditation program for seekers where the presence of the Master and the intense energy field lead one to the state of *nithya ananda* – eternal bliss. It offers a range of techniques from meditation to service to sitting in the powerful presence of the master.

Kalpataru

An experiential meditation program sowing in you the seed of:

Shakti, the Energy to understand and change whatever you need to change in life,

Buddhi, the Intelligence to understand and accept whatever you don't need to change in life,

Yukti, the Clarity to understand and realize that however much you change, whatever you see as reality is itself a continuously changing dream,

Bhakti, the Devotion, the feeling of deep connection to That which is unchanging, eternal and Ultimate, and

Mukti, the Ultimate Liberation into Living Enlightenment when all these four are integrated.

This program empowers you with the energy to align your actions with your intentions so you move with success and inner bliss.

NITHYANANDA MISSION HIGHLIGHTS

- **Meditation and de-addiction camps worldwide:** Over 2 million people impacted to date

- **Nithya Spiritual Healing:** A system of cosmic energy healing administered free through 5000 ordained healers, through our worldwide ashrams and centers, touching 20,000 people globally every day – healing both mind and body

- ***Anna Daan*: free food program:** 10,000 nutritious meals distributed every week through all the ashram *anna mandirs* for visitors, devotees and disciples thus improving health standards

- **The Nithyananda Order and its training:** Spiritual aspirants ordained as *Sannyasis, Brahmacharis*

and Brahmacharinis: who undergo years of intensive training in yoga, meditation, deep spiritual practice, Sanskrit, *vedic* chanting, life skills, and who run the 100% volunteer based ashrams of Nithyananda Mission worldwide, working in all Mission activities

- **Nithya Yoga**: A revolutionary system of yoga in the lines of sage Patanjali's original teachings, taught worldwide.

- **Nithyananda Vedic Temples and Ashrams**: Over 30 Vedic temples and ashrams worldwide.

- **Meditation Programs in prisons**: Conducted in prisons and juvenile camps to reform extremist attitudes – resulting in amazing transformation among the inmates.

- **Medical Camps**: Free treatment and therapies in allopathy, homeopathy, ayurveda, acupuncture, eye check-ups, eye surgeries, artificial limb donation camps, gynecology and more

- **Support to children in rural areas**: School buildings, school uniforms and educational materials provided free to rural schools.

- **Life Bliss Technology**: A free two year / three month program for youth teaching Life Engineering and the science of enlightenment

- **Nithyananda Gurukul**: A modern scientific approach to education combined with the *vedic* system of learning – protecting and developing the innate intelligence of the child who flowers without repression, fear or peer pressure

- **Corporate Meditation Programs**: Specially designed and conducted in corporate firms worldwide including Microsoft, AT&T, Qualcomm, JP Morgan, Petrobras, Pepsi, Oracle, American Association of Physicians of Indian Origin (AAPI) – with focus on intuitive management, leadership skills and team work.

- **Nithyananda Institute of Teachers' Training:** Over 300 teachers trained to teach: transformational meditation programs, Quantum Memory Program, Nithya Yoga, Health and Healing Programs, Spiritual Practice Programs and more

- **Media**: Articles in national and international newspapers and magazines, carrying transforming messages from Nithyananda

- **Nithyananda Publishers:** Over 4700 hours of Paramahamsa Nithyananda's discourses transcribed, edited and published in-house and made available in stores through books, DVDs and CDs

- **Life Bliss Gallerias:** Worldwide stores and mobile shops retailing recordings and books of Nithyananda's discourses and Nithya Kirtan recordings in 23 languages

- **Nithyananda Meditation & Healing Centers:** Worldwide, offering meditation and healing services

- **Nithyananda Sangeeth Academy:** Music, dance and other forms of art taught and encouraged in youth and elderly alike - live and through internet

- **Free Discourses on YouTube:** Over 500 free discourses on www.youtube.com – wisdom from the Master, easily accessible. Ranked top in viewership

- **Support to scientists and researchers:** Continually bridging gaps between science and spirituality through researches on spiritual energy and healing.

- **Nithyananda Youth Foundation**: A collection of inspired youth, building a divine and dynamic society with a common ideology of peace and enlightenment

- **Nithya Dheera Seva Sena:** Through transformation of self, this volunteer force of *Ananda Sevaks* trains and functions in the service of humanity, also serving as relief wing working towards disaster recovery management.

CONTACT US

Listed below are some of the main centers of Nithyananda Mission.

USA:

Los Angeles
Nithyananda Vedic Temple
9720 Central Avenue, Montclair, CA 91763
USA
Ph.: +1 909 625 1400
Email: programs@lifebliss.org, shop@lifebliss.org
URL: www.lifeblissfoundation.org

MALAYSIA:

Kuala Lumpur
14, Jalan Desa Gombak 5, Taman Desa Gombak
53000 KL, MALAYSIA
Ph.: +601 78861644 / +601 22350567
Email: murthi.kasavan@gmail.com, manirantaraananda@gmail.com
URL: www.mynithyananda.com

INDIA:

Bengaluru, Karnataka
(Spiritual headquarters and Nithyananda Vedic Temple)

Nithyananda Dhyanapeetam,
Nithyanandapuri, Off Mysore Road,
Bidadi, Bengaluru - 562 109
Karnataka, INDIA
Ph.: +91 +80 27202801 / +91 92430
48957
Email: mail@nithyananda.org
URL:www.nithyananda.org

Sacred Banyan tree at the ashram in Bangalore

Varanasi, Uttar Pradesh
Nithyananda Dhyanapeetam
Leelaghar Bldg, Manikarnika ghat
Varanasi, INDIA
Ph.: +91 +99184 01718

Hyderabad, Andhra Pradesh
Sri Anandeshwari Temple, Nithyananda Giri,
Pashambanda Sathamrai Village, Shamshabad Mandal
Rangareddy District - 501 218
Andhra Pradesh, INDIA
Ph.: +91 +84132 60044 / +91 98665 00350

Salem, Tamil Nadu
Nithyanandapuri, 102, Azhagapurampudur
(Behind Sharada College), Salem – 636 016
Tamilnadu, INDIA
Ph.: +91 +427 2449711

Tiruvannamalai, Tamil Nadu
(1008 Lingangal ulla Ananda Linga Kshetram)
Nithyanandapuri, Girivala path
Tiruvannamalai – 606 604
Tamilnadu, INDIA
Ph.: 04175 237666 / 94449 91089 / 94450 56262 /
94874 52555
E-mail: anandalingam1008@nithyananda.org

Rajapalayam, Tamilnadu
Nithyanandapuri, Kothainachiarpuram,
Sankaran Coil Road,
Rajapalayam, Virudhunagar District
Tamilnadu, INDIA
Ph.: +91 +4563 230001 / +91 +98421 30008

Pondicherry
Nithyanandapuri,
Embalam to Villianoor Main Road,
Embalam Post, Pondicherry - 605 106
INDIA
Ph.: +91 94420 36037 / + 91 97876 67604

For further information visit www.nithyananda.org

NITHYANANDA GALLERIA

A wide range of products for blissful living:

- Nithyananda's insightful messages on video, audio tapes, CDs and books in over 26 languages.

- Enlivening music and chants for meditation and inner healing.

- Meditation and yoga books, kits and CDs for rejuvenating body, mind and spirit.

- Energized rosaries, bracelets, photographs, clothing and gift items for a stimulating life style.

- Ethnic energy bead jewelry for men and women for tranquility and continued high energy.

Visit www.nithyanandagalleria.com or www.lifeblissgalleria.org for more information. E-mail: nithyanandagalleria@gmail.com & shop@lifebliss.org

SUGGESTED FOR FURTHER READING

- Living Enlightenment (Gospel of Paramahamsa Nithyananda)
- Guaranteed Solutions
- Don't Worry Be Happy
- Nithyananda Vol. 1
- Instant Tools for Blissful Living
- You Can Heal
- Follow Me In!
- The Door to Enlightenment
- Songs of Eternity (A coffee table book with Nithyananda's messages and pictures)
- You are No Sinner
- So You Want to Know The Truth?
- Uncommon answers to Common Questions

Over 500 FREE discourses of Nithyananda available at http://www.youtube.com/lifeblissfoundation